Praise for
THE NEW MARKET...

'John Grant is one of the sharpest and most creative minds I have come across in my encounters with the advertising business. His insight and clarity makes this book compelling reading for every executive involved in marketing.'
ANDERS DAHLVIG
CEO, IKEA Retail Europe

'John Grant has a stunning mind and inspired insights into how to grow a business. His ideas about communication as a way to drive volume reflect the new economy.'
NICH HAHN
Director, New Brands & Strategic Marketing, Coca-Cola

'We're all in marketing now. We all need to think about brands and people. Intangible values makes up most of a company's value. This book stimulates new thinking in these areas.'
STEPHEN HAILEY
Managing Partner, Business Consulting Europe, Arthur Andersen

'This book is full of original thinking which well anticipates the future.'
TIM PARKER
Chief Executive, C&J Clark Limited

The New Marketing Manifesto

The 12 Rules for Building Successful
Brands in the 21st Century

John Grant

TEXERE

LONDON · NEW YORK

Copyright © 1999, 2000 John Grant

The right of John Grant to be identified as the author of this work
has been asserted by him in accordance with the Copyright, Designs
and Patents Act 1988

First published in Great Britain in 1999 by Orion Business

This edition published by

TEXERE Publishing Limited
71–77 Leadenhall Street
London
EC3A 3DE

Tel: +44 (0)20 7204 3644
Fax: +44 (0)20 7208 6701
www.texerepublishing.com

A subsidiary of

TEXERE LLC
55 East 52nd Street
New York, NY 10055

Tel: +1 (212) 317 5106
Fax: +1 (212) 317 5178

A CIP catalogue record for this book is available from the British Library

ISBN 1-58799-024-5

Set in Monotype Sabon
Designed by Staziker Jones
Printed and bound in Great Britain by
Cox & Wyman Limited, Reading, Berkshire

This book is dedicated to Yong Ja
('Uncountable')

CONTENTS

PART FOUR

ACKNOWLEDGEMENTS

I'd like to thank all the people who have made this book possible.

I'd like to thank all my mentors over the years. In particular my old boss Nigel Jones who taught me that strategy is like chess (and who always beat me at chess into the bargain).

I'd like to thank all the shareholders at St. Luke's. Especially the planners – Phil, Mari, Cathy, Saipele, Freddie, Jonathon, Debbie, Andrew and Ken – who sat through long discussions of some of the ideas in this book. They helped me get my thoughts straight. And added quite a few of their own.

I'd like to thank all the other marketing people and businesses I've learned from. This book is the product of thousands of conversations. I'd particularly like to thank Nick Hahn at Coca-Cola, Christie, Stephen, Terry, Joel and Richard at Arthur Andersen, Matti and Ingallil at IKEA and Steve Hewlett at Carlton TV for having the foresight to buy into my New Marketing consultancy! And for being such formative influences on the book. Special thanks to Anders Dahlvig at IKEA who became St. Luke's first new client at a time when everyone else thought we were a silly company with a silly name.

I'd like to thank Martin Liu, my publisher. For seeing something in this project when it was a messy ramble and helping me to get it in some sort of order. And thanks to Clare and Liz and all at Orion for their work and support.

I'd like to thank Naresh Ramchandani, my creative alter ego and the talented one in the partnership. If one person got me to think outside the box it was Naresh. I hope we'll be hatching devious New Marketing schemes together for years to come. And also thanks to Naresh for reading this book over a busy family Christmas. And for being my best man so diligently, that he even reminded me in the middle of all of this that my anniversary was coming up!

Finally, I'd like to thank my wonderful wife Yong Ja. For persuading me to get off my backside and write 'that book' I'd been talking about for ages. And for supporting me in writing it. And for putting up with all the disruption. And for reminding me that 'it's only a book'. I'm always very proud of Yong Ja in all she does and if this book makes her just a little bit proud of me then it will have achieved its main purpose.

FOREWORD

For many years I have had an interest in marketing. This has become an increasing fascination over the last ten years, both in my management role and as consultant and adviser to many companies. What is the most effective way to market goods and services? What importance should you place on advertising? If intangible (brand) values are the only real values of the future for businesses, how do you build brand value? This book has helped me to bring these thoughts and many others on marketing together. It helps to put marketing in the broader business context. Most of all, John Grant has made me think and challenge many existing views.

Business thinking is often driven by very impersonal words such as strategy, structure and systems. My experience has shown that success is much more about people and what they set out to do with others. Powerful businesses are based on strong individuals who build strong teams around ideas that matter to them. Marketing has often seemed to ignore this aspect of business and has been based on vigorous, impersonal analysis, treating people as mass markets to be exploited and to some extent duped. As the world around us changes and change becomes the only constant, then we need to rethink our 'conventional' approaches to problems.

John describes a shift away from the conventional view towards achieving results through people, in an economy increasingly driven by knowledge and ideas. He describes a 'third age of branding' where brands take on a life of their own, where brands become 'popular ideas that people live by'. The popularity is one that covers not just consumers but all the people whose lives they touch. John's rules are often about personal things, 'getting up close and personal', making a closer connection with everyday life, 'tap basic human needs', 'cultivating authenticity' where there is a real involvement with people and the need to 'build communities of interest'.

THE NEW MARKETING MANIFESTO

New Marketing also links into increasing business trends, giving importance to innovation and creativity, seeing suppliers and customers as partners rather than the opposition. Perhaps most importantly John sees marketing as moving from 'shining a torch at people's feet', to 'shining it at the path ahead'.

In a crowded consulting market place, differentiation becomes a real key to effective marketing. John's emphasis is on tangibility and trust, about brands being built around personal references and the domino effect of word of mouth rather than clever marketing to mass audiences. Companies that are true to themselves, where the inside and the outside look and feel the same, are companies (people) that we can all trust. Together we will deliver, not enduring, unchanging goods and services, but what is right for the here and now, experiences which connect with people now.

John takes the world of business gurus such as Handy, Peters, Hamel and Ghoshal and brings marketing into the new world. He has helped me to see new ways of approaching my market and can challenge the conventional marketing wisdom for many others as well. Increasingly we understand that the most important ways of building brand value and shareholder value is dealing with the intangible values. In a fast changing world we need new marketing ideas to complement this new business thinking.

Stephen Hailey
Arthur Andersen
(Managing Partner, Business Consulting Europe)
May 1999

INTRODUCTION
WHAT IS NEW MARKETING AND
WHY DOES IT HAVE RULES?

What is New Marketing?

It is a more creative style of marketing.
It treats brands as living ideas that can transform people.
(Not as boring bland essences.)
It is entrepreneurial in spirit.
It favours constant change over conservatism.
It is more humanist, less 'scientific'.
It is driven by insight not analysis.
It is part of a new consumer culture.
It is exciting to be part of.
It is offering more cost-effective solutions.
It is not an invention for the purposes of this book. It is a living
reality. As hundreds of current case examples will show, New
Marketing is happening right now. And it is bringing dramatic results.

It may be that you need to read the whole book to grasp these
points. New Marketing is something I've been doing for the last five
years and still I think I've only just started to grasp it as an entirety.

I've tried to make this book very modular. It's full of bite-sized
chunks, that you can pull out and use; trends to spot, ruses to try,
examples to quote. I want people to use the book rather than just
read it and forget it. I want New Marketing to thrive and spread.
Because it's a force for good in our industry.

Why Write Rules for a Discipline that's about Ideas?

There are no rules to follow that can help you to have an idea.

Or are there?

Surely ideas are a product of a certain way of thinking? The product of a certain set of assumptions and mental models. Isn't that why most artists go to art college?

Even if you have an idea by accident or random association, what makes you think it is a good idea? Isn't it your implicit set of rules or assumptions that you judge it against? Isn't it usually the case that you were already looking for just such an idea?

The big breakthroughs in the history of ideas have been caused by a shift in these fundamental assumptions. Like the shift Darwin made when he included man in the animal kingdom. Or the shift Copernicus made when he took the view that the earth orbited the sun. What tends to follow these shifts is an avalanche of new ideas. This move to a new set of rules is called a paradigm shift. Paradigm shifts are often as much about sub-cultures forming around the new assumptions as any abstract 'truth'. New rules are often first greeted as heresy. If they survive they later become orthodoxy.

New Marketing is about exactly this sort of shift to new rules and assumptions. To have great New Marketing ideas, you need to think about brands and customers in a radically new way. The rules in this book are there to make this new way of thinking explicit. Of course marketing does not rank with the great academic subjects of human enquiry but it does have assumptions and rules. And it does rely partly on creative innovations.

Three Disclaimers

① I am aware that this is quite an extreme book. It is about a New Marketing which is the opposite of old marketing. I am ready to accept that the truth lies somewhere inbetween. That there is still a place for some of the older ideas and techniques of marketing and that some established brands will continue to thrive. (Although they will be complacent at their peril.)

It was important, I think, to state what is new in New Marketing very starkly at the beginning of this chapter. Not to simply merge it with the old marketing. Marketing, as a whole, may settle into some happy medium in the long term but meanwhile, a lot of the breakthrough ideas will come from the new rules not the old certainties.

After all, Darwin was partly wrong. As well as continuity, there is a discontinuity between people and animals. We are intelligent in a way animals are not. Copernicus was partly wrong too. The earth and sun rotate around each other. It's just that the sun is so much heavier that it moves much less. The important thing was that they took human thinking to some new extreme. Human sociology favours allegiance to the assumptions behind our ideas. Which means that progress is bound to be a "slalom" not a "downhill".

② I am also aware that this is perhaps a rather clumsy book. Because I am drawing out 'rules' or consistencies that are new. Things only tend to get articulate when they are widely accepted: They get polished by being worn in many hands.

③ I've found that the tricky thing about writing this book is knowing how to position myself, relative to the subject matter and the reader.

This is my first book. And New Marketing is something I passionately believe in. So although the temptation has been to be didactic, I've tried to be a little more even-handed, open and enquiring than that.

I know that what is important is what the reader takes out of this book. Often when I read this sort of book myself, I cherry-pick ideas rather than buying into the whole argument. So I've tried to write the kind of book which is stuffed with useful examples and perspectives rather than just hollow assertion. In positioning this book in my own mind, I found the introduction to another book very inspiring.

For myself, I have never supposed that my mind was in any way out of the ordinary; indeed I have often wished I could think as quickly and easily, have the same capacity for forming sharp and clear images, or a memory as ready to command as some.

But I shall not hesitate to say that I consider myself very lucky to have found myself, from my early youth, on certain paths which have led me to considerations and maxims.

However, I may be wrong, and perhaps I am now mistaking a little copper and glass for gold and diamonds. I know how easily we can be mistaken in matters that concern us closely.

So my intention here is not to teach the method which everyone must follow if he is to conduct his reason correctly, but only to demonstrate how I have tried to conduct my own.

That book was *Discourse on Method* by René Descartes.

I do not believe that my book is a great work of philosophy. (I wish!) It is a practical book on some trends in marketing. But I do hope this book will change the way a few people think.

Why has a New Marketing emerged? Why here and now?

New Marketing is not just *new media* marketing.

I believe that New Marketing will thrive in future on the desperate need to construct new ways to reach people and build brands. Things tend to change most when they have to. For me, sitting in an advertising agency, this is a survival issue. New Marketing is our Noah's Ark.

But advertising has not died yet. In fact, contrary to all doom stories, it continues to grow. Even now, with worries of recession all around us, advertising expenditure is growing. A 1998 survey by Zenith media found that total advertising spend grew in European and American markets during that year, and based on a survey of client plans for the next year, it is forecast to grow in 1999 too.

New Marketing is as much about using conventional advertising spaces in new ways as it is about using other media. As we'll see, New Marketing is about big brand ideas that transcend media. It is 'media neutral'. So New Marketing is not driven by the death of mass advertising. Not yet.

To answer 'why?' we need to see marketing in some other context of change. If the rules have changed then the context in which marketing operates must also have changed. I believe that changes in four different contexts have led us to this New Marketing with its new set of rules:

① The 'New Marketing' title is a deliberate echo of 'New Britain'. It is here, in Britain, that New Marketing is to be found in its most developed form. It is from Britain that many of the examples come. Britain has been through a creative renaissance over the last five years; in politics, art, music, film, fashion, design and, I am going to argue, in marketing. The same questions apply to other countries but British marketers seem to have found some novel answers. A notable example is Richard Branson and Virgin.

② 'New Marketing' is the mindset of a new generation of marketers. If, like me, you are somewhere between your mid twenties and early forties, you may be aware that you are part of a new generation. In America they call us Generation X. I like the connotations of the 'X'. In mathematics 'X' is unknown. We are a generation that isn't sure of much and are inclined to question and reinvent. We are also a generation that refused to grow up – hedonistic, iconoclastic, informal – a bunch of 'half adults' as the *Baby Boomer* author, Robert Bly, called us. This mindset is an important part of New Marketing as a creative project.

③ New Marketing and corporate culture.
New Marketing would not have got far if it was just the creative mindset of a bunch of 'half adults' who do the marketing. It must also have found favour with the people approving their work.

Previously, in a more rationalist, corporatist, conformist business culture, New Marketing ideas fell on very stony ground. They were for mavericks like Virgin and The Body Shop and Apple and for youth brands like Diesel and Levi's, but not for 'proper' business. It was for Davids not Goliaths.

But the culture of the boardroom has changed too. The new mantra in business is dramatic reinvention and transformation. Even former bastions of conservatism like Procter & Gamble have leapt onto this creed. Most senior business people now believe in thinking outside the box. In this context New Marketing is suddenly all the rage. Some examples in this book come from blue-chip companies like British Telecom, which is Britain's biggest company and biggest advertiser.

④ A New Marketing for a New Society.
Even if it is in tune with management theory, New Marketing would have been short-lived if it didn't work. The new rules in this book are woven through current success stories. They reflect a change in the way brands work, which in turn reflects a shift in society in general.

It seems we have entered a 'third age of branding'. Societies are becoming more inner directed, as we enter a 'post-traditional society'. In this context brands have taken on a new role. They act as surrogate traditions or ideas to live by.

Having covered the background theory that ties it all together, we'll then dive into the twelve rules. These chapters are practical and laden with examples and ideas. I think it could work to use this book as a resource just to dip into, provided you get the twelve rules straight in your mind. So I've put a one-minute summary at the start of every chapter to help those who are chronically short of time.

We then go on to the rules applied in combination. I have taken twelve major case studies and looked in detail at how all the rules apply.

Finally, I have set out a vision for the future. This short sci-fi fable recounts what marketing might look and feel like at some point in the future.

PART ONE

THE FOUR CORNERSTONES
OF NEW MARKETING

1. New Marketing and New Britain

There is a practical reason why many of my examples are from the UK. As the advice to authors goes, 'write what you know'. And for the last twelve years I have been working in UK ad agencies on mostly UK-only marketing campaigns. I have also been influenced most by the UK marketing activity and marketing people around me. But that is not the whole story. For the last two years I have been mostly working on international marketing projects. For instance, one of my clients has been the Director of New Strategy and New Brands at Coca-Cola's headquarters in Atlanta.

Why, you might ask, would someone come all that way for marketing ideas? Well largely because there have been some exciting things going on in London and I don't mean just in marketing. London's stock as a creative and cultural centre of excellence has risen dramatically. New Marketing is, in my view, part and parcel of that cultural renaissance which the American media describe as 'Cool Britannia'.

The link between Cool Britannia and New Marketing was showcased in an exhibition of Britain's creative industries called 'Powerhouse UK'. It displayed the best of British design and computer software and recent inventions. Cool Britannia was not just a fashion and music phenomenon, it embraced the whole culture industry. It is just as well represented by world-beating advertising and graphic design.

New Britain is at heart a political programme. The hope is that, in the New Economy, Britain could become a powerful player again – a 'European Tiger'. Charles Handy described this as the potential for

London to become the 'New Athens'. Because the New Economy is about ideas. And its natural resources are creative mavericks – something which Britain, with its culture of individualism bordering on eccentricity has a fair supply of. Britain does not have the infrastructure to be a leading player in areas like e-commerce. But in ideas-led areas like fashion, music, art, film-making and marketing Britain has shown it can be a world leader. Examples like Alexander McQueen, Oasis, Damien Hirst, *The Full Monty* and The Body Shop leap to mind.

This renaissance spirit relates to a general mood swing in Britain. Tony Blair's New Labour party was swept into power with a huge majority under the banner of 'New Labour, New Britain'. The national character itself seems to have shifted. We have been through something of a second sixties with huge raves, World Cup fever and a more passionate Latin sexuality (and cuisine!).

Cool Britannia is an atmosphere which has favoured new ideas. An atmosphere in which people have responded to innovation with a general enthusiasm. It is a culture tuned into the zeitgeist, which keeps asking 'what now?' And so it has become a test-bed for a lot of breakthrough marketing ideas. A lot of the 'Cool Britannia' cultural phenomena were themselves great examples of New Marketing in action; the marketing of New Labour, the Spice Girls and *The Full Monty*.

Cool Britannia itself was the ultimate new marketing exercise. It took 'Britain' as a brand somewhere new.

Even the most upstream part of Cool Britannia – New British Art – relied on New Marketing ideas. Many new British artists came out of one fine arts course at Goldsmith's college. It was run by a professor who believed that for art to survive it had to get out there and sell itself. The most famous graduate of that course, Damien Hirst, ranks with Richard Branson as a marketing genius. Both have the central principle of causing a sensation. It is no accident, perhaps, that New British Art was first recognised and promoted by one of Britain's great ad folk, Charles Saatchi.

There is another way of looking at the Cool Britannia phenomenon. It is a generation thing. As Tony Blair set out in a 1995 Conference Speech:

'I want us to be a young country again.'

A new generation has taken over the reins, earlier than in other more mature countries and industries. New Marketing dynamos are often just plain young in their jobs. Five years ago when we set out on the adventure that was to become St. Luke's, we were, with one exception, a management team in our twenties. Many of our clients, including some CEOs, have been in their thirties or early forties. With so many Peter Pans running British marketing it's no wonder it took a new turn.

2. New Marketing and Generation X

Generation X by Douglas Coupland was a defining book. I'm sure many readers of this book have read it. And if they haven't they must have seen hundreds of presentations and reports that refer to it.

Generation X was a discovery. A bit like the discovery in the 1950s of 'the teenager'. Like the teenager it is the story of a generation gap. But it was about the next age-group up – people in their twenties (in the late 1980s). They had very different values from their parents (the 1960s generation which in America is called the 'Baby Boomers').

All of this is just as true of Britain as it is of the United States. But the trajectory of the UK's Generation X has been very different. I did a conference presentation last year about 'adultescence'. This is the story of Generation X in Britain, nearly ten years on. The talk was based on social attitude data which I had analysed into age breaks – looking at 25 – 35 year olds and the age-group either side of them. I found the results a bit like looking in a mirror.

Compared with both older and younger groups, we in this middle band were less sure of any values, motivated by short term projects of achievement, hedonistic, very into self-reliance and self-advancement, into anything new and anti any conventions; from traditional ones like marriage, to new ones like political correctness and vegetarianism. We were very likely to have a lot of credit cards and little in the way of pensions and savings. We were, and probably still are, a live-fast, die-young bubble of workaholic idealists without a cause. As someone said to me recently, 'we're a generation that's got to learn to get some sleep'.

This is a very different Generation X from Douglas Coupland's. Our American cousins arrived in early adulthood and found themselves shut out from the prosperity of their parents' generation by a 'ring of barbed wire'. We arrived in early adulthood and found careers in the full – helter skelter – sense of the word.

It seems now, if publications like *Fast Company* are anything to go by, that the American X-ers are also making their mark. But so many of the American business heroes still seem to be in the older Baby Boomer camp. The Steve Jobs' and John Gage's of this world. They seem to have a benign grip on corporate America, a bit like that of the post-war 'founding fathers' in Japan.

In Britain we seem to have had a bit more room for manoeuvre. Like Tony and Cherie Blair for example. Like my friend Stephen Carter, who joined Britain's second largest ad agency in 1987, and by his late twenties was running it. New Marketing is partly a result of this trend to young hot-bloods getting their hands on budgets and tasks:

It has a strong anti-establishment, or new establishment ethos.

It values energy and ideas over dry research and analysis.

It is emotionally inclined not just to consider but to favour innovation.

It works on Tom Peters' principle that 'If it ain't broke, you haven't looked hard enough, fix it anyway!'

It looks for exciting things we could bring to market this year, rather than some five-year plan.

It distrusts conservatism as timidity.

And it is very flexible, rather than having some sense of grounded certainty about what is good or how things should be done.

This may be a temporary phenomena. Research studies, such as the Industrial Society's excellent 2020 *Vision* report, show that the new generation coming along behind us are a much quieter – some would say boring – bunch. 'Neurotic neo-realists' as their art movement is called. This isn't going to matter too much for the time being. Like the American Baby Boomers we are going to keep blazing our trails for a while yet. Quite a few may keep rising and spreading our ideas further into the heart of the establishment. And if the generation after us favour a more balanced and quiet approach to work and life, that might be a nice world to retire in!

All of this may explain why New Marketing has emerged in Britain at this time. But it doesn't explain why it is no longer the preserve of mavericks and youth brands. To understand how New Marketing found approval in the boardrooms of mainstream business, we have to look at a broader context of changes in management theory over the last ten years.

3. New Marketing and Competing for the Future

Hats off to Procter & Gamble. They have not just discovered their own forms of New Marketing. For instance they say that 80 per cent of their marketing budget in future will go into electronic media. But they have used it to transform their company culture. And the central idea for this company transformation is their new mantra, 'Breakthrough'.

'Breakthrough' is an exciting expression of a consensus that is emerging in business theory. It's a consensus that explains why a Generation X-er like me has found himself working with another company who, five years ago, you wouldn't have expected to be part of this movement – Arthur Andersen.

The sea-change has in my view been best captured by the seminal business book *Competing for the Future* by Gary Hamel and C.K. Prahalad. Their argument, in case you haven't read it, goes something like this: The future belongs to companies that can come up with a clear and compelling vision of their market and their place in it in five years time and then transform themselves to get there first. This reminds me of Kennedy setting America the task of putting the first man on the moon. It's exciting and it's all about radical innovation rather than what the authors call 'incrementalism'.

If that is how business leaders now think, then marketing was bound to change. Rather than creating long term, unchanging brands, marketing has to set its sights on dramatic change. Marketing is no longer the peace time army, going through manoeuvres to present the appearance of stability and order. Marketing is becoming dynamic, a central part of these great transformations. Marketing has gone to war.

One implication of this is a thread that runs through the book (see especially Rule 12 – Vision and Values). Marketing is now part of much bigger changes and issues within companies. It can no longer be a separate department that puts the icing on the cake. It is part of the cake. And, because marketing is the creative, expressive, cultural side of business, it can play a strong role in bringing the future vision to life, in making it engaging and inspiring.

As well as the impetus to breakthrough innovation, several other big pieces of new business theory have let New Marketing loose.

One is the breaking down of the business as institution. We now live in the time of the 'Individualised Corporation' – a paradigm shift according to the authors of a business book by that name (Ghoshal & Bartlett).

This book describes a shift away from conformist bureaucracy towards achieving results through people. In an economy driven by knowledge and ideas, the company as production line and hierarchy had to go. Individuals needed more freedom to be entrepreneurs and imagineers.

As more businesses moved to entrepreneurial and people-based models of management, New Marketing ideas had a chance to take hold, whereas in the previous, hyper-hierarchical era of management new ideas about building brands had fallen on stony ground. This was a time when it seemed all of marketing was heading to a junk mail and price promotion hell. The darkest hour comes before dawn!

Another change in business favouring New Marketing is a subtle one. Marketing has become more valued within companies. We have seen more marketing people moving into the board room. There are New Marketing – friendly CEOs who have come up through the traditional Finance ranks, of course. (Such as Doug Ivester of Coca-Cola who preaches ideas like 'Viral Marketing'). Most Information Age executives are marketing-aware and customer-led. But there's still, in my experience, nothing like having a born marketer on the senior client team. If you want approval from someone like Richard Branson, or Sergio Zyman, or Anita Roddick you need to excite them.

But for all of this New Marketing would ultimately have consisted of some very short-lived experiments if it didn't work. Not only did it need to work, it needed to bring dramatic results compared with established methods that had shown their worth over the last century.

This book is full of dramatic success stories. Businesses that had been blocked or even threatened finding new leases of life – like IKEA, BT and French Connection – some even going onto Alexander the Great-style conquests like Virgin, New Labour, Gap (and also, perhaps surprisingly, Coca-Cola).

4. New Marketing and the Culturequake

I want to pinpoint how New Marketing chimes with changes in modern society. I'm going to introduce the idea of a big transition in society. A transition I call the Culturequake.

I believe that what we've seen of this Culturequake so far are the warning tremors, and that the full Culturequake will coincide with the passing of the Millennium. Because this will be a time of re-evaluation, when we discard many old habits and ideas (and brands) that no longer fit. There was a kind of rehearsal for this in 1990. When many countries swung from a materialist – aspiring 1980s to a softer, eco-concerned and more inner directed 1990s.

But I don't want to lapse into futurology. I am going to stick to what we know. To big changes unfolding in the present. After all, anything could happen in the year 2000. Some of the more apocalyptic futurologists have suggested, for instance that the Millennium Bug could put societies back 50 years!

This survey of society in transition gets a bit complicated, as you'd expect. So now seems a good time to define my terms. One that causes a lot of confusion in marketing discussions – because it means different things to different people – is the idea of the **brand**. In the first part of this section I am going to look at the history of the brand in order to make one simple point. New Marketing is about creating a new type of brand. A brand of the third kind to be precise.

The Three Ages of Branding

The first age of branding was the age of the Trademark.

Imagine the USA at the turn of the century. Actually it's quite hard to do. We can imagine the Hollywood version, but the reality was much nastier and dirtier. In most measures of hygiene, health, education etc. America was then, roughly where Sub Saharan Africa is now. Trading standards were virtually non-existent. People could sell any old rubbish and they often did.

Into this world was born the trademark. A sign of guaranteed quality, reliability and safety. Trademarks like Coca-Cola literally painted the town red. By early this century Coca-Cola had 29 million square miles of signs in the USA. The trademark brand was a name you were familiar with. Out of this familiarity came trust – a guaranteed consistent experience. A basic brand.

The second age of branding was the age of Aspiration.

This was already emerging in the 1930s. The trademark brands hired Hollywood stars to appear in their posters, and soap companies ran beauty contests. But it really came into its own in the 1950s with the advent of television.

The idea was that people aspired to social ideals – like being a screen idol or an aristocrat or a perfect mother. If these ideals were linked to brands then these brands would become more valuable. This was the time when terms like 'brand image' were invented for brands chosen to reflect the buyer's station in life and aspirations; the right car, newspaper, beer. When people in marketing say 'added value' what they often mean is 'added aspiration values'.

Now we're into the third age of branding and it goes something like this....

Aspiration has become quite an uncertain concept to base brands on. People don't seem to aspire to external ideals in the same way – in the 1960s you were keeping up with the Joneses next door – in the 1990s it's very unlikely you even know them and even if you do you don't really give a stuff what they think of you. (In the Rule 2 chapter we'll look in detail at this breakdown of aspiration and the social institutions like class that supported them.)

In this third age brands seem to have taken on a life of their own. They have become quite free-standing ideas that take hold and spread. So that Virgin can span many markets, and Viagra can become a potent icon, even in markets where it is not yet available.

The dividing line between brands and other parts of culture seems to have become rather faint too. So Princess Diana is a brand – and *The Full Monty* and the Tamagochi and Career Woman and Delia Smith Cookery and Ecstasy and *The Little Book of Calm*. And strong brands and associated ideas play on this same media-celebrity stage, like the National Lottery, IKEA ('Chuck Out Your Chintz'), BT ('It's Good to Talk'), ('Beware the Power of') Playstation, FCUK and The Body Shop.

To appreciate what these brands have substituted for slivers of social aspiration, we are going to have to explore how society has changed and to become more inner directed and less tradition bound.

But I hope it is fairly clear from these brand lists that;
1. these are some of the more luminous brands of our time
2. they are not obviously working through social aspirations
3. they are ideas that are quite free-standing and which have engaged people

These examples (along with hundreds of others) justify talking about a new third age of brands – the age of more inward ideas. That is all we need to know to justify exploring New Marketing as the art of creating and managing these new brands.

But to grasp something as fundamental as **New Rules** we need to know more. We need to understand how the new brands work. Which brings us on to the social theory.

The Three Ages of Society

There is a branch of social research which neatly explains why brands have changed – passing through these three phases. The theory is backed up by big surveys over the last thirty or more years in many markets. (Conducted, for instance, by Synergy in the UK, and the Noetic Institute in the USA.)

The theory stems from a book called *The Lonely Crowd*, (David Riesman, 1950). According to this theory there are three types of people depending on how they deal with the social world around them. You can think of this as three different mindsets; other (or outer)-directed, tradition-directed and inner-directed. This theory has a practical research application. Any person tends to fall into one of these camps. You can find out which mindset any one person has by asking them a whole load of social attitude questions.

The three typologies are characterised as:

Sustenance/Traditional. People who focus on day to day concerns (like survival) and have traditional values and outlooks. They tend to be bound by ideas of community, duty and family.

Outer-Directed. People whose main concern is what others think of them – their appearance, image etc. They tend to favour progress over tradition and be conspicuous consumers of icons of their own progress and status.

Inner-Directed. People who look inside (rather than defer to the group consensus like the other two) and 'do their own thing'. This is often presented as the most advanced or 'self-actualised' mindset. People in this group are self-reliant but also have collective tendencies – such as eco-concerns.

What research tracking these three mindsets over the last thirty-five years or so tells us is that there has been a big shift, from tradition-directed, through outer-directed, into inner-directed. In some European countries inner-directed is now the biggest group. (Whereas in the States it's still only 25 per cent.)

I think we can see this trend in our own lifetimes; from the 1970s when things still were a lot more traditional – for instance in ideas about families – through the conspicuous consuming 1980s – to the caring sharing 90s. But compared with a hundred years ago, perhaps this is just the late stages of a bigger glacial shift in society.

I don't think it's too fanciful to view this transition right across the century. From a hundred years ago when communities really were more traditional and bound by a strong social fabric, to the 1950s and on, when post-war affluence and consumer society brought in social aspiration and mobility. And now at the end of the century going into a new phase – the post-consumer society. (The only type of society where ideas like 'down-shifting' and 'shaker furniture' would seem exciting!)

Every country may have followed the same path from a different starting point at a different pace. America, for instance, started more modern, yet has perhaps changed more slowly. While Europe has old churches, they are empty now. In America the majority are still God-fearing folk. But the relative pace of change doesn't matter as much as the direction. And global studies, such as Manuel Castells' *The Network Society*, point to similar changes occurring across the globe.

The inner-directed society would explain the turn away from Aspiration brands. (Aspiration taps into the outer-directed mindset.) And it explains a shift towards cultural ideas that are about transforming ourselves from within, like learning to cook, or talk, or be Calm. Or towards brands which offer more intense and personal experiences, like Haagen Dazs, Viagra and Ecstasy.

But then we hit a bigger question still. Why is society becoming more inner-directed? If you can't answer that, then it's quite conceivable that these changes are exactly like tides of fashion that rise and fall: interesting for this year's ad campaign but you wouldn't build a whole new theory on it.

For there to be a new marketing that we can expect to grow and develop, we ought to have some confidence that this is more than some New Labour – related fashion cycle in values. And there is just such a big theory of lasting change. It comes from the head of the London School of Economics, Tony Giddens, and it's called the post-traditional society. I say theory, but it is backed up by an abundance of evidence that is easy to grasp and hard to argue with.

The Dawning of a New Society

The idea is that:

① In previous human epochs people had their lives pretty well plotted out for them – born into living out a similar life to their parents. Of course there were some rags to riches stories, but these were exceptions that proved the rule. Of course there was progress of a sort, but everyday life was rooted in the traditional ways of community, the rule of church and law, the fitting behaviour for age, gender, trade, education and so on.

② And now it is not. We have less traditions to live by, or which we believe in, which is like losing the instructions for something very complicated. It doesn't get much more complicated than everyday life. Some scientists think that's why we developed intelligence – just to manage our relationships.

I think the best way to grasp this is to recognise it personally in our own lives and experiences; that in our own lifetime the ground has shifted under us. Things didn't turn out as we were led to expect....

Remember when...

Men were men, and women were going to be housewives after a stint as a hairdresser, nurse or stewardess?

People went through clear lifestages and were never 'mutton dressed as lamb'?

Jobs and marriages were for life?

We all ate local food, and believed in local history?

People knew their place in life and even criminals 'came quietly' when they had their 'collar's felt'?

The voice on the television was the official voice of the establishment.

Sexual and other liberation movements were on the "fringes"?

And when everyone was happy. At least in America, where surveys show that the happiest time in recent history was the mid 1950s.

In our lifetimes we have lost much of this certainty of tradition. It's not just that the ground has moved. It's more like it's disappeared. (I've noticed people often get a kind of vertigo when I talk about these sorts of changes.) Elements of this include the disappearance of:

– **Trust.** We no longer trust and follow authorities and institutions; from church to politicians to science to policemen to bank managers to....

– **Parochialism**. We have a new breadth of experience – of foreign travel, of global media, of career- and relationship- and home-mobility.

– **Certainty**. With this comes an unavoidable awareness of plural traditions and there being no one right way to live and think.

– **Some of our fundamental ideas**. Having children, marriages, jobs and other relationships for life, which means we have had to accept some new, less defined ones like sexual equality, ethics (e.g. medical ethics), spirituality....

– **Repression**. New found freedoms, leading to a general informality of lifestyles and a regression to play at all ages (these days it's only the young who are serious).

– **Simple things**. We have more technology than ever to do more things for us than ever. Raising all sorts of questions like 'what happened to nature?'

– **and we're miserable, stressed, stretched, lost, anxious** – all the things that people who lose some of their certainties and routines become. We feel lost the way that people feel lost when they leave the army or prison!

These aren't just stylistic changes in individual patterns of life and thought. It's a structural change. Looked at on a macro level it's a story of a society losing its solidity or grid-like structure:

- Demographics like age, gender, class, religion etc. matter less and less. People are becoming more and more similar.
- People are more alike in their ideas and activities; a kind of mass middle class devoted to quality of life and leisure.
- And in response our culture is more focused on individuals – closer to everyday life, more realistic, more informal etc.

Rather than a fragmenting society where the centre cannot hold, all the evidence shows that people across the world are getting more similar. There really is such a thing as the global teenager and they've got far more in common with each other than with their (tradition-age) grandparents.

There are counter-trends within all this too. This low grid society has compensated by becoming quite high group, with a tendency to form voluntary 'we' communities; Neighbourhood Watch and NIMBY protests, internet communities, style tribes and football fans. At the same time, the traditions have tended to resurface in extreme forms: retro fashions, Promise Keepers, the Cultural Chernobyl protests and Countryside Alliance.

These counter-trends are seen by most commentators as last stands rather than genuine revivals. But for the moment it's a complicated and dynamic general picture. However, one central fact drives all of it – tradition loss. Leaving us as individuals with a tradition hunger – needing ideas to live by.

Tradition-Loss Leads Us to How the New Brands Work.

Culture and media's main role has become meeting this hunger for meaning and order. Rather than simply elaborating as in past ages, culture is now needed to fill great gaps of meaning in our lives, which is ironic because it was modern media which undermined traditional ideas as much as any shift in patterns of living and working. This double action perhaps explains why television has such an extraordinary grip on modern people's lives. Anyone arriving from another age would be astounded to find a society where people are so hooked to a medium – literally spending nearly all their waking, non-working hours staring at a light box.

A good example of the media plugging gaps left by tradition is the identities that we latch onto. In the past we would have a set largely chosen for us; Roman Catholic, man, white collar etc. Now identity is something we can choose and change. Examples supplied by the media include; new man, new lad, career woman, girl power etc.

Other media ideas taking on the role of traditions include Delia Smith's recipe's, 'don't drink and drive', 'brown is the new black'. Along with countless other ideas from the media that have become part of our everyday lives. In a way, the media have become surrogate tribal elders.

This shift has fundamental implications for creating powerful brands. Here is a definition of the brand in this new marketing age:

A brand is a popular idea or set of ideas that people live by.

I think it's arguable whether 'popular' implies 'being liked'. I mean it in the sense of 'well known' and also 'of the people'. 'Don't drink and drive' was a powerful brand/idea created over recent decades. It's not necessarily liked by everyone who is tempted to have one for the road, but it seems to have had an effect on attitudes and behaviour.

The list of third age brands mentioned earlier have become new traditions. They shape and give meaning to everyday lives. This means they have established or reinforced new patterns of belief and behaviour. Have another look at that list and check that this seems true;

Princess Diana
The Full Monty
Tamagochi
Career Woman
Delia Smith Cookery
Ecstasy
Viagra
The Little Book of Calm
The National Lottery
IKEA (Chuck Out Your Chintz)
BT (It's Good to Talk)
(Beware the Power of) Playstation
FCUK
The Body Shop

Defining brands as popular ideas makes a simple extra point. Brands only exist as ideas in people's minds. They have representations outside people – like packaging and adverts – but these are ways of spreading these ideas (that only exist in people's minds). All the rules can be related to (if not quite derived from) the role that brands now play – being surrogate traditions.

The idea that brands are popular ideas is a radical one. It detaches the ideas from the trademarked objects. As I mentioned earlier, it starts to explain why an idea like Virgin can span so many markets. Why an idea like Viagra can be such a powerful brand in countries where it is barely available yet. It also implies that other ideas than packaged goods can be brands.

To Summarise – The guiding theory of this book is that:

In our society nowadays brands increasingly play the role that tradition used to play (by giving people ideas to live by).

Or to give this a more snappy expression:

Brands are the new traditions

This is why branding is such a powerful force in modern societies. Brands, achieving popular acceptance shape people's lives in ways that brands never used to. Brands used to be ornamental. They reflected traditional and slowly-changing cultural ideas. People bought the right brands for their station in life – the right car, the right newspaper etc. Now the brands, as ideas that we 'buy into', are a much freer force of transformation. They are instrumental.

That sounds like brands as propaganda but it is actually a step in the opposite direction. The age of branding as brain-washing device was the social aspiration era. That was the time of the book *The Hidden Persuaders* by Vance Packard, which covered the New York ad agencies that hired psychoanalysts and supposedly went in for subliminal advertising. Now branding is voluntary. It can only work through ideas that people want to catch, that they need to live, that excite them.

The ethics as well as the economics of new marketing stack heavily in its favour, because it is asking to be adopted by people not just remembered. I'll return to ethics and New Marketing later in the book.

That's enough great sweeps of history for the time being. We've covered the context – the 'why?' Lets now dive into these 12 so-called 'Rules' of this so-called 'New Marketing'.

PART TWO

RULE 1

GET UP CLOSE AND PERSONAL

The One-Minute Summary

This rule is about marketing having a closer connection with everyday life.

It is in marked contrast to the distant ideals projected by aspirational brands, and with the stereotyped ways people were understood as target audiences. It is time for marketers to get off their pedestals and get closer to the real world. You can think of it as a kind of marketing informality, a bit like Casual Friday.

For the more theory-inclined reader, what this amounts to is a subjective (rather than objective) thought process in marketing. For the practical reader it means that walking the market and having discussions with real customers can be worth more than whole volumes of consumer research. But what really counts in either case is the result: marketing activities that make a closer connection.

Give Me an Example

The recent shift in Nike marketing:
1. To advertising which is closer to real life, like the World Cup spots, with stars like Ronaldo having a kick-about on the beach or the 'I'm Tiger Woods' spots featuring child golf players.
2. To event marketing that is closer to people and closer to the action, like their assault-course-like 'have a go' urban running road show, their publishing of local running guides and their staging of sports events, like soccer tournaments.

Get Up Close and Personal

If there was only one rule in the book this would be it.

What this rule does is put marketing in a different territory. All the other eleven rules then do is elaborate on the rules of operating in this new territory. If you grasp this rule completely there is probably very little else I could tell you about how to think like a New Marketer.

But there is a catch.

It is the hardest rule to explain, because it involves a different way of thinking about the world. And trying to convey a different way of thinking is very difficult, some would say impossible.

Buckminster Fuller apparently once said that you cannot teach people new ways of thinking, you can only give them the tools that they would use if they thought that way. (Quoted in *The 5th Discipline Workbook* by Peter Senge). My tools in this book are examples. And what I am going to do in this chapter is quote a very wide range of examples of the same basic shift – such a wide range of examples that hopefully every reader who doesn't already think this way will at some point go, 'oh I get it!'

What all the examples have in common is that they are **subjective marketing**, reflecting a shift from an objective (tradition and institution bound) culture to a subjective (inner-directed and 'doing your own thing' culture). I told you it wasn't that easy to grasp in theory!

I don't know if it will be helpful, but I think it is possible to express what all the examples have in common through a diagram. The expression 'up close and personal' is suggestive of some sort of shift in marketing geometry. I think it looks something like this:

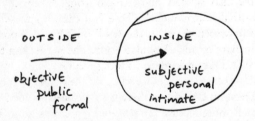

The phrase I really like – from the title of a photography exhibition – for this circle which New Marketing is stepping into is 'the sphere of intimacy'. The INSIDE in this diagram is 'inside customers'

everyday thoughts and activities'. Another way of conceptualising this same shift – something all the examples do – is removing the barrier between people and the company/product/brand. Or equally you can see them as building a bridge of connection.

It might be helpful to see it in human terms – as similar to the shift from being a stranger to having some connection. I've found this a useful way to evaluate marketing when you're in the process of creating some. I ask myself: What's the relationship between a single person and this piece of marketing? What close connection does it make with them? What examples do I know of things that have made a similar personal connection with me?

I'm hoping that these models may make sense as a kind of pattern to recognise. So it may help to bear them in mind as I go through the examples.

Here are thirty examples of brands or similar things that have become much more engaging and successful by being more up close and personal (more than they had been before, or more than alternatives). Nearly all of these crop up elsewhere in the book as examples of something else. Here I have just outlined how they got more 'up close and personal':

① **Nike.** Was beginning to look like 'Mc.Sport', because its advertising and other marketing activities were all about distant superstars. So they shifted to find ways the audience could connect with those stars as people. Like the 'I'm Tiger Woods' spots, which shows a succession of child golfers saying 'I'm Tiger Woods'. Or the World Cup spots which show Ronaldo kicking a football around on the beach as if it were filmed when they were off duty.

② **Nike.** Has also started marketing through events. Not only things like football tournaments where you can go and stand close to their stars or watch them 'in the wild' on TV (as opposed to in the staged captivity of ads). But also events the public can take part in like their assault course urban running road show.

③ **British Telecom.** Was the archetypal 'institution' everyone loved to hate. Distant, bureaucratic and only after our money. Tried for years to do 'friendly' personal advertising, for example the Maureen Lipman 'Beattie' campaign which featured a fictional Jewish grandmother who berated her family for never phoning. The ads were very popular but people still hated BT.

Then they came one step closer to our lives – they started to teach us how to use the phone to have better relationships. In a self help campaign with the slogan 'It's good to talk', they offered advice like 'try to talk to your dad before he hands you over to your mum'. Now BT has quite a friendly intimate profile as a brand (although not everyone liked the ads).

④ **Pizza Express.** Took down the barrier between people and food preparation by putting the kitchen in the restaurant – you could see the pizzas were handmade. Still the only UK food chain that feels intimate and special in my view.

⑤ **The BBC.** Has gone through a similar transformation to BT as a brand. Ten years ago it seemed increasingly stuffy, irrelevant and institutional. Since then it has become the strongest brand in television and radio. Not (as in its old heyday) because it is a public service and non-commercial, but because they leveraged that to develop a special relationship with the talent and so became identified through those strong relationships with a series of popular faces of British culture. From Jeremy Paxman to Harry Enfield to Jill Dando to Delia Smith. The BBC summarised this brand positioning as a friend and home to people we love – with the film and pop video and song *Perfect Day,* featuring just about every big name in popular music from Bowie to Pavarotti.

⑥ **Oddbins.** Has turned intimate scruffiness into an art form. Sawdust and wooden crates, serving staff in jeans, hand-written signs and recommendations, ink-blotched Gerald Scarfe cartoons. All part of the 'wine club' mentality that makes it one of the UKs most successful retail brands.

⑦ **Soap documentaries.** The hit phenomenon of recent TV schedules, the soap documentary is closer to real life because it shows real life people and situations. The trick is to get these to tell entertaining stories, so they pick dramatic situations where human tensions are played out – often in work situations like the staff on a cruise ship or in the Royal Opera House. They've even made one set in my own company, St. Luke's.

⑧ **Diaries.** Another trend in creative media. From *Fever Pitch* (the only slightly fictional account of a football fanatic) to *Bridget Jones' Diary* (ditto for a neurotic career woman) to the recent hit novel – soon to be a Spielberg film – *Memoirs of a Geisha.* First person accounts take us inside a story, and they seem to appeal greatly if the best-seller lists are anything to go by!

⑨   **Lexus.** How do you design a luxury car that fits into the yuppie high life better than a Mercedes? By getting closer to that lifestyle in all the design details. Like an impressive heavy key fob for handing over to valets. Or a door like Fort Knox's that clunks into place beside the passenger you are whisking home. How did Toyota get this sort of up close insight? By sending the Japanese design team to live like yuppies in California of course.

⑩   **IKEA.** An up close and personal company in so many different ways. It's a self-service, self-delivery, self-assembly concept. The store experience is so different that people describe it as like a parallel universe – like Disneyland. One of the reasons for the store being so customer-centric is the way Ingvar Kamprad, the founder, fine-tunes stores during arduous eight-hour visits. What he does on the visits is play a game. He pretends that he is a fictitious customer shopping with his (imaginary) wife (Ingvar plays both parts). At every roomset and display and corner he checks these imaginary shoppers have everything they need. This is subjective retailing as an art form.

⑪   **Tango and milk.** Two UK soft drinks commercials aimed at children in the late 1980s worked in exactly the same way. They gave children something to copy. Tango gave kids the slap around the ears as administered in their advertising by a big fat man painted orange who represented the 'hit of real oranges'. Milk gave kids the phrase 'Accrington Stanley – who are they?' as spoken by a little boy telling his friend why he drinks his milk (because he wants to play soccer for Liverpool). This became the playground catch phrase of the year. The result – both drinks boomed and all other soft drink marketing instantly looked plastic, naff and unreal. Because these two drinks and their ads were part of the gang, and everything else was left in the 'grown up' world of marketing.

⑫   **Billie.** A pop star sensation just turned sixteen, who had three number one singles in her first four months. At St. Lukes we did some work for the record company in thinking about how to launch Billie Piper. Billie has a great voice, looks good and can dance. But the market for girl bands two years after the Spice Girls could not have been more crowded. Billie's point of difference is her age, which makes her closer to her audience. We knew she would be a hit when girls in focus groups said they could really connect with her because she was one of them – 'she could be me'.

⑬ **Rock the Vote.** How do you get more young people to vote? The reason they don't vote isn't apathy. They are passionate about causes they can connect with, it's just that voting and political parties seem so distant and institutional. The idea we developed with the music industry to try and change this took a different tack. The strategy was to show voting as making your mark – a bit like a signature or graffiti. In the States they took a bigger but similar stance, making the whole election about one issue which was pro-freedom of speech and anti-censorship. Both approaches used pop stars that young people can identify with to deliver the message.

⑭ **Boots No 7.** The TV campaign we produced for the Boots No 7 cosmetics range was very up close and personal. Instead of showing models using the product, it featured abstract, swirling colourscapes – with the inner voice of a woman talking about why she chose that colour to match her mood and the effect she wanted to create. One commercial featured a woman who chose cold steely blue because she is about to sack someone. We hear her practising the wording, 'What I'm asking you to do is to leave the company.'

⑮ **'Chuck Out Your Chintz'.** While we're going through my favourite St. Luke's projects lets look at IKEA's TV commercials. They don't look intimate in the way No 7 does. It's the message that made the commercials get closer to people. The ads questioned British people's taste in décor. They criticised fussy old-fashioned 'Chintz'. The first reaction, from people in my focus groups, was to mentally look around their own home and see if they had any offending items (like doilies and flowery pelmets). Or as they say in Goodfella's, 'Are you calling me funny?'!

⑯ **The Millennium Dome Kid.** New Labour is a brand founded on bringing politics into closer connection with the people, and this is one of my favourite examples. They appointed a single eight year old boy to vet all the creative proposals for the Millennium Dome. To give the whole experience what Tony Blair called the 'Euen factor' (Euen being Tony Blair's son). This was a turning point in the coverage of the Dome in the tabloid press. Up until then the press had been highly critical of something being created so on high, without considering what the people would want. Since then, the coverage has been far more expectant and excited about what we can look forward to.

⑰ **Autobiographical companies.** Companies are institutions so of course it's quite hard to have a relationship with them because they are so big and complex and anonymous. One answer is the company personified by a leader, like Virgin, Apple, Microsoft, The Body Shop, Ben & Jerry's... Companies with any sort of 'human'-face have this sort of close quality – it doesn't have to be the leader, it could be something like Disney's animated characters. There is a big difference between your face (integral to you) and a mask, which is what happens when you hire someone famous to represent you.

⑱ **Getting on TV.** Television programmes do all sorts of things to get viewers more closely involved in shows. In one extreme form of this the viewers are the show. Like the ubiquitous video clip shows capturing moments of real life slapstick. Or the shows like Channel 4's *Right to Reply* where the viewer gets a chance to voice their comments and appear in the medium.

⑲ **The National Lottery.** Gambling, so long a dwindling working class dinosaur, was the fastest growing area of consumer spending last year. The reason was the National Lottery. The National Lottery centres around the drawing of the numbers on primetime TV – a kind of bingo game with millions of players. The television show is a linchpin – it gave everyone an accessible point of connection. Then there is the message of the marketing campaign for the lottery – a great hand in the sky points and a voice booms 'It could be you!'. And to reinforce this, there are all the brilliant tabloid lottery winner stories.

⑳ **Clinton's mid-term elections.** How did the President on the brink of impeachment, who lied on national television, sweep to the biggest mid-term victory of the century? The best explanation I've heard is what all those ordinary Americans said on the news, when stopped in the street for vox pop interviews – all the scandal made Clinton seem human and real. It made him someone you can relate to, as opposed to some powerful stranger up on Capitol Hill. He's only human and so he's made a few mistakes... with 27 women allegedly.

◈ **Gap.** Is making rapid progress from an American fashion brand to a global clothing brand. I think their advertising is helping. The Gap advertising is generally good – engaging, original, distinctive, but the ads that seem to have really struck a chord are those ones for Khaki's, where the communication is not through words and famous people, but through the exuberance of music, movement and dance. Managing to convey how something would feel if you skateboarded or jived in it – basically talking directly to people's bodies. This is a very intimate idea.

◈ **First Direct.** Is banking brought up close and personal. The world's first 24-hour telephone bank – it fits into your life rather than vice versa. It's a kind of 'Walkman' idea applied to the stuffy and distant institution that used to be British high street banks.

◈ **The Automobile Association.** Also went in for Walkman marketing with their idea that 'you're the member, not the car', so that if you're a passenger in someone else's car that breaks down you can still call for vehicle rescue. And there are some really up close and personal commercials for insurance where real people talk naturally about how they got a better deal.

◈ **The Personal Computer.** From mainframe to my frame. Probably the biggest and most inspiring example of all.

◈ **e-mail.** The real success story in new media is e-mail, not the web.

◈ **Lara Croft, Kyoko Date, Tamagochi.** Lara is the character in the hit Playstation game *Tomb Raider*. Kyoko is a virtual Japanese pop star that only existed in her website. The Tamagochi is the computer pet that millions nurtured. All of them brokered more intimate relationships with technology.

◈ **Questions.** Questions are more intimate and involving in marketing than answers. Like Microsoft's 'Where do you want to go today?' And our press ad for the Midland Bank's mortgages, 'Is Now a Good Time to Buy a House?'

◈ **Diesel.** I went to a talk once by Renzo Rossi, founder of the ultra hip Italian fashion label. They have a very effective strategy for being in close rapport with their young, trendy audience. They hire them. The average employee age at Diesel is under twenty-five. And then there are their ultra ironic and iconic marketing communications all themed under the idea of Better Living.

◈ **Virgin Atlantic.** Onboard cinema was a smart piece of old airline marketing. It answered the question how can people comfortably adapt to sitting in this kind of arrangement? Virgin went one better with the personal entertainment system. Virgin flights are strangely quiet as everyone gets lost in their own little media world.

I also wish they had done what was originally proposed for the names of the different classes. They went ahead with Upper Class, but dropped Riff Raff. I saw a great example of this kind of 'my language' branding recently – a minibus with the brand 'The School Run Company' stencilled on the side. I now know everything I need to about their service and I also trust them in a strange kind of way. Because they talk my language, they are part of my world.

◈ **MTV Unplugged.** MTV was running into serious competition from rival music television stations, who showed all the same promo videos. 'Unplugged' took the brand and its audience closer to the performers. It worked for the same reason as (apparently) big concerts are now starting to struggle to sell tickets. It was intimate and took down barriers (whereas real concerts now seem very distant).

I hope this collection of thirty examples gave you a fix on what I mean by getting 'up close and personal'. It's a big shift in creative marketing. And it also has big implications for the way we work and in particular the way we talk about marketing. The conversations which marketing people have need to be more authentic and human. Objectifying things is an easy defence mechanism. Having a conversation about the subjective aspects of your market takes a bit more courage.

A surprising ally in this often comes from senior management. I've found board meetings are often more convinced by human insights into what makes their customers tick – and ideas to get closer to them. Perhaps they don't really like all that marketing jargon and research they are fed as justification. What I have found is more often a problem is the hierarchy in the middle. Given that what I've already shown is thirty case histories of astounding breakthrough success by tackling brands and media in this way... could it just be that it's the way many companies manage marketing that is wrong?

What are we left with at the end of this chapter? I think it's a kind of vision or challenge. You are about to embark on some marketing. And while you have no idea at this stage what exactly it is going to turn out like, the one thing you now desire is a closer connection with customers, so it will somehow feel a bit like some of the examples I've quoted.

If you accept that it makes sense to aim for that sort of territory (because you buy the idea that that is the way the world has headed) then what you will want to know next is 'how?'. This is the subject of the next 11 rules.

RULE 2

TAP BASIC HUMAN NEEDS

The One-Minute Summary

This rule seems obvious but it runs against every (learned) instinct in the classical marketer's body. 'It's too big'. 'We can't own that'. 'We need our own positioning'. The old marketing was nuance marketing, with comparative brands based on distinctions. The new marketing is superlative and taps into universal needs.

This makes life simpler. It gets a lot of now irrelevant detail out of the way. There is a 500-page book from the 1960s called *The Handbook of Consumer Motivations* by Ernest Dichter. It covers thousands of little psychological nuances associated with different markets. Now all you need to know is that there are fifteen fundamental human drives and any strong brand taps straight into one of them.

The question of owning these drives doesn't arise. All you need to own is your unique expression of them. The existence of Playboy or Wonderbra – based on the sex drive – did nothing to rule out the appeal of *The Full Monty*.

Give Me an Example

I think I just have. Another would be Gucci. Once languishing as a niche brand of luxury goods for rich old ladies, now a broadly appealing brand, based on designer Tom Ford's unique vision of GLAMOUR.

Tap Basic Human Needs

This rule is another big shift in thinking about marketing.

When thinking about what makes people tick, the old marketing reference point was the hierarchy of needs: people's aspirations and needs were conditioned by their place in society. We'll see that this no longer holds.

The New Marketing equivalent is a non-hierarchy of universal human needs. It turns out that there are fifteen of these needs or drives. We will explore each one by looking at some of the luminous brands that have tapped into each. Then we will look at several case studies where moving from niche distinctions to universal needs has catapulted a brand to success. Finally I will cover a great untapped need that could build some of tomorrow's most powerful brands: education.

The Structured Society and Maslow's Hierarchy of Needs

Our story starts with the demise of the great social classifications.

The class system was a defining part of consumer markets. In Britain it was so finely graded and rigidly defined as to be almost a caste system. This mattered to marketers. People bought the brands that reflected their station in life. Our ideas of class were historically fairly new. The mass middle classes were a product of the wealth and work created by the industrial revolution. But the idea of knowing your station in life is a very old one.

This was a very stable system of tradition. It was embedded in people's unconscious ideas of themselves and it was reinforced by peer pressure. People who got 'above' themselves (or married 'beneath' themselves) suffered rejection and exclusion. And the great success and irony of this system was that people – wherever in society they stood – felt superior to wherever anybody else stood. The system was self-supporting.

'Strata' as a metaphor for the class society makes it sound like there were layers of equal size. This is a convenient fiction, perhaps put about by those nearer the top. A more accurate metaphor is the pyramid, with fewer people at the peak and bigger and bigger wedges of people down in the lower levels.

Economically, society is no more equal nowadays. Britain and America in particular have moved in the opposite direction. The economic historian John Gray recently pointed out (in *False Dawn*) that our distribution of wealth is more similar to Brazil than to other European countries. Social exclusion is the gnawing question of our times. And it is the kind of problem that tends to resolve itself in moments like the French Revolution or LA Riots if it is left unanswered.

The growing economic inequality is a matter for politicians. What is important for marketers is that people's culture – their tastes and ideas, their identity and activities – is no longer predicated on a clear sense of their 'station in life'. It is a fact that they have a less sure sense of where they are in society (other than in the middle) and that wherever they are they share many of the same influences.

Economic social class categories never adequately described where people were in the great scheme of things. They tended to take snapshots rather than showing the movie. So that a future MD would be classed as clerical or skilled manual. And with the unemployed, retired and students all lumped in one rather confusing bundle of 'E'. What has always mattered more is people's own sense of who they were and where they were headed. But these ideas were grounded in some hierarchical grid of society.

A better description of how needs were conditioned by place in society was contained in something which I am sure is quite familiar to most readers – Maslow's hierarchy of needs. This is our pyramid, redrawn to reflect people as individuals at each level.

It was a pretty good model. If this system no longer applies, if people at any level of society tend to have similar needs, then a central pillar of old marketing has toppled. This will lead us to new ways of understanding what switches people on to brands.

How did this hierarchy of needs work?

The hierarchy of needs was formulated by Abraham Maslow in the 1960s. It is, at the lower levels, a hierarchy of worries. The argument starts with the common sense idea that if you are on the bottom rung of society your main concern is physiological needs like getting fed. If fed and housed you would next worry about keeping safe and other anxiety needs. As life's basic worries are got out of the way, the individual moves up to 'nice problems to have', progressing to learning, the arts, self improvement.

The progression up the ladder is linked implicitly with material wealth. The more developed and wealthy countries have more people closer to the top. The full hierarchy of needs looks like this.

(reproduced from The Henley Centre; *Planning for Social Change*, 1998).

It is ironic that this hierarchy was used by market researchers to put people into boxes, because Maslow was challenging the de-humanising view of people in psychology – a science of statistics and laboratory rats. He was one of the founding 'Humanist' or 'Existential' psychologists.

It is easy to look at modern society and conclude that this hierarchy still fits. You can point to partial examples. Hollywood 'Shirley Maclaine' types with their New Age tendencies are aiming for self-actualisation. Contrast this with the underclass of our societies, who media stereotypes portray as addicted to television, cigarettes, lager and crisps; people who tend the needs of their physiology and little more.

But resorting to stereotypes is misleading. This is a model which held when societies were more stratified and traditional. But now it is wrong. Not just a bit inaccurate but completely untrue.

Here are five current cultural examples of how the hierarchy doesn't fit;

① People at the bottom of the rung have other needs than survival. We did some research groups on a very poor housing estate in Buckinghamshire where we asked the long term unemployed about the television they watched as we were researching how daytime television could be improved and this was one of the core audiences.

The one programme that stood out for all of them was a children's art programme. Quite a few of them joined in the exercises – making things themselves. It was something fulfilling to do with their time. Aesthetic needs exercised by the underclass – surely not?

② You'd assume, wouldn't you, that the self-education revolution was fairly upmarket? The preserve of the 'Guardian reader'?

In fact, recent data from the Henley Centre (*Planning for Social Change*, 1998) shows that the 'lower' classes are more inclined to self-education. Even allowing for the fact that the 'E' class includes students, this chart suggests that people like factory workers self-educate more than people in professional occupations.

Percentage of people who are 'Studying on my own using books or other materials'

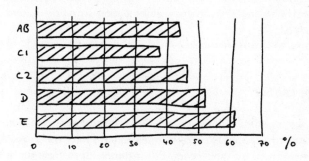

(reproduced from The Henley Centre; *Planning for Social Change*, 1998).

③ The major malaise of modern society is stress.
Stress is broadly a middle class disease, like flu. Not that stresses of poverty aren't great. Just that people who are poor call it being poor, miserable etc. not 'stressed out'. Stress is largely time-stress. This puts 'anxiety needs' high up the social spectrum.

④ Self-actualisation is supposed to be a luxury few can afford.
So how can we explain the self-help books market with its heartland appeal among mid- to down-market women? Or the most 'new age' group of all, the new age travellers, living out of squats and caravans? When the bottom rung can be a lifestyle choice, the whole hierarchy gets scrambled.

⑤ Hunger is a bottom rung concern, though. Surely?
That doesn't square with a world in which 60 per cent of women are on a diet.

Self-imposed hunger is part of a world in which the hierarchy of needs is secondary to our own ideas about our identities – or in this case our weight.

I could go on. But that's not really the purpose of this section. What I have shown is five counter-examples that say people anywhere in society can have needs at any level of the hierarchy. If the hierarchy was true to social realities there wouldn't be so many exceptions.

Marketing examples make the same point even more convincingly. Brands of gourmet food, wine or designer clothing, for instance, now have quite a broad mass market rather than appealing to the top echelons of society. Similarly art galleries and museums with their 10 million UK visitors a year seem to have found a broader audience than Maslow might have expected. Conversely football has found a strong constituency among men formerly known as middle class!

Welcome to the mass society.

The Age Ladder

A lot of what people did in more traditional societies was also down to their age or lifestage. People were expected to act their age. And this was enforced by their peers. For instance, until recently in the UK, women were only supposed to dress sexily until somewhere in their mid twenties. Doing so 'too old' would be ridiculed as mutton dressed as lamb.

I am not suggesting that people no longer hit different stages in life. But rather that this is their own journey through their own calendar at their own pace. And they have more flexibility and choice. I can act like a teenager (at least at weekends) if I like, in my thirties. I can decide fundamental things too, like when and if ever to have children. And hopefully when and if ever to retire!

New markets have flourished around people exercising these new choices. One example is loose fit, classic jeanswear for older people (Gap).

The Gender Divide

Another fixed distinction which has become more of a continuum is gender. We'll look later at identities like 'new man', 'himbo' and 'career woman' on this new spectrum. Factually, you can now choose your gender surgically. But the bigger issue for most people is *what kind* of man or woman to be. This was very much not up for grabs in the very recent past.

What we've seen so far is that who you think you are – and what your needs are – is much more up to the individual and much less down to 'demographic destinies'. This is all part of moving from an objective to a subjective culture. Objects are defined by others. Subjects are self-defining. (You'll remember for instance this is the difference between the object and subject of a sentence.) Which is also a way of saying the world is becoming more inner-directed.

Fixed distinctions and layers in society have crumbled in the Culturequake:

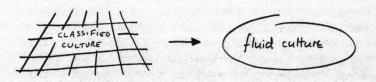

In the new fluid culture, people are much freer to be people. And their needs tend to be more of the fundamental human drives and less of the acquired tastes that fit their idea of who they are supposed to be.

Whether or not you view this as progress depends on your values. The Victorians saw sublimation and distance from our human desires as the epitome of civilisation. Since the 1960s (and perhaps ever since Freud) we have been more inclined to see getting in touch with your inner urges as more advanced.

Similar swings can actually be seen throughout human history. In *Thought Styles*, anthropologist Mary Douglas shows how ancient Chinese ceramics went through swings between excessive refined glazing and the kind of bare earthenware now sold in Habitat.

What may be new about this Culturequake is that it is taking us beyond tradition as a force that shapes human life. Perhaps. We aren't the only age which has believed itself to be at the end of history. Maybe the religious and political fundamentalism of regions other than the 'decadent' West is the way forward. It seems likely, judging by the other past swings observed in human history, that it will take several centuries to find out.

The Fifteen Fundamental Human Drives

Rather conveniently, a survey was published in 1998 by a team of American psychologists which listed fifteen fundamental human drives. One interesting finding was that twelve of them are instincts shared by much of the animal kingdom. And that only three were unique to human societies.

I don't think it's a perfect list. For instance it makes no mention of the human drive to religious ideas. This has been a constant theme of all human societies. A study in brain science found that most of us actually have an area in our brains which glows when we think religious thoughts. The all-pervasive spirituality – New Age sects, magical symbolism in computer games, alien abductions – must have something to do with this drive. Spirituality is religion when it is not bound by the structure of organised religion.

But I think it is still a very good list. I've found it a very useful checklist for thinking about brands. Lets go through the fifteen needs identified by the survey. For each, I'll point to some luminous brands and media ideas that have attached themselves to that drive.

Sex
If there is one human drive that has most characterised 1990s culture it is sex. This will undoubtedly be seen at some point in the future as another 'naughty nineties' like the 1890's of the Follies Bergeres etc. Some commentators say this is the 'post-AIDS' culture – all for show. I'm not so sure. I think it is simply the further dismantling of Victorian repression.

Luminous brands and media ideas that have tapped into the sex drive include Haagen Dazs, *The Full Monty*, the internet, zippergate and the tabloid newspapers who like medieval monks seem to see sin everywhere.

Hunger
Hunger has already been mentioned in connection with dieting. In psychoanalysis they say there are two ways to 'get off' on a drive. One is to feed it. And the other is to deny it. The theory of

anorexia and other eating disorders is that of a gluttony drive taken to its logical antithesis.

On a more benign level foodie and gourmet markets, cookery and exotic spices, delicatessens and organic vegetables have all been vibrant. And on a more basic level (than all this M&S foodhall provender) is Nissin 'Cup a Noodles' in Japan whose marketing slogan is 'Hungry?'

Physicality

We live in a physical, tactile, experiential culture. One of the later rules will deal with this and the importance now of tangible brand experiences. This is a reversal of the Victorian straight-laced society, which distanced people from their bodies and bodily functions.

The 1990s has been something of a second 1960s in this respect. With physical brands like Ecstasy having instant dazzle – along with The Body Shop, dance music, Nike, the gym, mountain bikes, massage, body piercing and so on.

Avoiding Distress

According to many commentators, the number one global trend is stress. This is a kind of brand idea in its own right. I don't remember it being a big feature of culture twenty years ago (any more than flu). It is the cultural label that is important, not just the lived experience. You can be cowed by stress or alternatively a 'stress junkie'.

Brands that tackle stress have boomed. The *Little Book of Calm* is one of my favourite brands of the last year or so. And Prozac is another of those brands that has burned itself into the public consciousness.

There are also quite a few brands around the slightly perverse area of seeking distress. Perhaps they are cathartic. Or perhaps it's us getting off against our need for security. Brands like bungee jumping and dangerous sports of all kinds, crime TV shows and dark console games like *Resident Evil*, not to mention the revival of the horror films like *Scream*.

Curiosity

This is the learn and play drive. Adults nowadays are learning and playing a lot and I'm going to cover education in detail later. If you are not looking into education – as a medium, as well as a drive – then it's about time you did.

Microsoft has grounded their brand in curiosity and exploration.

They even called their internet package 'Explorer'. And there's that slogan 'Where do you want to go today?'

Honour
There's a great analysis in Francis Fukyama's *The End of History* of the ancient Greek concept of Thymos and its role in modern society. Thymos roughly translates as righteous indignation, or ruffled honour.

We can see many brands/ideas surrounding the drive to honour; the *Jerry Springer Show*, NIMBY (Not In My Back Yard) protests, the World Cup, 'New Britain' and other nationalisms, The Countryside Alliance, The 'Promise Keepers' (US religious rights protesters), Political Correctness etc.

Order
The desire for order is constantly frustrated by our chaotic, less structured and less certain world.

One culture brand that strikes me as particularly concerned with tidying up our fractured lives a bit is down-shifting or voluntary simplicity. And the latest thing in luxury is harmonious, minimal 'stealth wealth'.

Brands/ideas that have focused on order as their drive include Psion Organisers, the booming market for history books – especially those dealing with the history of science like *Longitude* – Feng Shui, yoga and tea.

Vengeance
This is another drive like 'honour'. Vengeance is very much at play in the media, take for instance the fascination with celebrity divorces and court cases.

There aren't many consumer brands that leap to mind, admittedly, as agents of vengeance – unless you are prepared to stretch to the self defence markets, from kung fu to burglar alarms.

But perhaps there should be, as benign versions like practical jokes are booming. Whole TV shows delight in slapstick – Tango is one brand which taps this delight in comeuppance, and what a brand!

Social Contact
One idea, which I will explore later in the book, is that this is an increasingly lonely, solitary society. Getting, having and maintaining relationships is far more of a struggle than it would be on a more 'village community' traditional model. (Although village relationships presumably had their own problems.)

Brands that have tapped this drive include BT (and many of the mobile phone brands like One 2 One), *Friends* (and other friendship based sitcoms), soap operas like *Neighbours*, e-mail and dateline services.

Family

The drive to have a family is also finding many surrogates in culture as fewer of us find ourselves following this instinct in reality. The many great 'family drive' brands (real and surrogate) include Disney and Tamagochi. The nesting instinct is fuelling another wave of décor enthusiasm, and this may also connect with cookery, and with the idea that staying in is the new going out. Conversely there is a mass market for both broodiness and childishness in all sorts of adult markets where cute is the thing – even the fashion. There are reports in American high fashion magazines that babies are the new accessory as in for instance Madonna and her child.

Prestige

Prestige is a basic drive but how we satisfy it depends on our orientation. Outer-directed people seek symbols of prestige and approbation. The inner-directed rely more on measures of self-respect. We can probably see this in our own ideas of career.

Rule 11 will deal with the idea of fame or celebrity as a kind of brand prestige. Other (non-social-climbing) outlets for prestige include glamour and education and then there's 'underground' rarity for instance in music and clothes. Conversely the whole supermodel, supergroup etc. pop culture phenomena reflects the new kind of prestige. The way it seems to work is a bit like the law of increasing returns – if a lot of people like it then it must be good!

A great attempt at a prestige brand based on beauty was that of Martini's UK relaunch. Public castings were held for stars of the commercial allowing the customer to get in on the act.

Power

The drive or will to power is a big theme of modern-ish philosophy. It also has made for some great brands.

Power no longer equates with social position in traditional terms. Prince Charles appears powerless. Princess Diana, after their divorce, grew in stature and influence.

The melting of the old social order that shared out power has let loose lots of new expressions and brands. One obvious example is Girl Power. And New Lad was very much a male mirror image of this. Knowledge is power and so is money. These combine to make fascinating brands – like Bill Gates and the smash hit Carlton TV quiz show *Who wants to be a millionaire?*

Citizenship

The urge to participate in the civic is another drive that has been set loose by the thawing of the old social superstructures. Examples include the strong 'cause' brands; Gay Pride and Greenpeace, the new communities on the internet, local self-help schemes like LETS (Local Economics Trading Schemes), which are a growing feature of the new economy. New Labour is a citizen brand. As is Neighbourhood Watch.

Later on we'll cover brands of belonging under 'communities of interest'. Clubs, hobbies, venues etc. also tap this drive.

Independence

This is an age of independence. Brands built on this include mobile phones (notably Motorola), the self-reliance and self-help books, and *Ally McBeal* the hit TV show. Self-reliance boosting products like pensions and evening classes seem a hot area too.

Social Acceptance

Excessive reliance on social acceptance is other-directed. I believe this is receding (like prestige in the old sense). But it is obviously human to value fitting in, even if we are not governed by it. One hot area for a time after the certainty of tradition – even if we take or leave the answers – is 'what are the rules and conventions?'

The answer to this question comes from all sorts of corners, from magazines like *Cosmopolitan*, from books like *The Rules*, from IKEA (Chuck Out Your Chintz), from Gap clothing, and from internet etiquette to name a few.

Our relationship with these edicts is ambivalent. I think a good analogue is horoscopes. I read the horoscopes. Sometimes I even adjust my behaviour as a result. Perhaps something they have said strikes a chord, like needing to apologise to someone. But I don't *believe* in them.

Some Advice on Handling These Fifteen 'Hot Buttons'

When you tap into a fundamental human drive – and many of these are quite primal and instinctive – the brand glows with a certain

luminosity compared with all the brands that satisfy an acquired taste or social standing, or the brands that just do functional things for people like unblock the drains.

This is good news for brands. It gives them a more universal human currency. At this deeper level of human motivation, many of the problems with global marketing and brands evaporate. Why else would Hollywood movies cross so many borders?

How you tap effectively and credibly into these fifteen primal needs is a matter for the other rules in the book. An example is Rule 4, which is about mythologizing new social trends. Brands are made out of deep permanent human drives, crossed with new life situations and values. So pornography is back – provided it is for women. It's the age of 'Full Monty Marketing'.

The brands that used to glow brightest were those that take you up the ladder. This was the social aspiration stage of marketing. Aspiration was what underpinned the idea of brand image – coffees ('Richer, smoother...'), cars, beers, after-dinner chocolates, designer clothes and interiors, lifestyle magazines... What these brands offered was a bit of social advancement.

This approach nowadays looks quaint. Ferrero Rocher had a hit advertising campaign on its hands because its 'Ambassador's Reception' ads were so over the top in offering access to the lifestyles of the rich and famous, that people thought they must be joking! The equivalents now are 'inner aspirations'. Products like gourmet coffees, cars based on needs such as safety or space for a family, authentic real beers such as Belgian beers, comfortable clothes, sports clothes etc. interiors with benefits – like Feng Shui and magazines based on interest not image.

If you are responsible for a brand that relies on social aspirations it is time to have a good, long, hard think about your next move!

The Gucci Story

Remember when Gucci was synonymous with luxury goods and haute couture fashion? Synonymous, in turn, with a very small select group of oldish ladies. (The image I have in mind is something like Miami High Society.) The need which Gucci then tapped into was exclusive luxury.

Exclusivity used to be something that fashion houses guarded fiercely. There's a great case study in old marketing ingenuity from America, when Chanel found its perfume was becoming too mass market and losing its cachet. In response they produced advertising which was so avant garde and discordant to mass tastes that they halted this slide into the everyday. And it worked. And they stayed a special and exclusive luxury.

That was then and this is now. Gucci it seems was getting locked into a disappearing and ageing niche. Sure, there were more rich old ladies than ever. But even they were starting not to want to look like rich old ladies. And while Gucci was a rich old ladies brand, there was no ready market for the diffusion range that fed most fashion houses with easy profits. (Diffusion ranges offer affordable 'foothills'. If well done, they don't damage the exclusivity of the 'mountain', but they open the brand out to a much broader audience. Paul Smith jeans is a tasteful example. But to have foothills you need a mountain that appeals to the mainstream. This was something that Gucci lacked.)

What Gucci did next was change their brand fundamentally. They depositioned themselves. They did this by hiring the ultra-trendy designer Tom Ford, who created an acid-colour, satin, hipster look reminiscent of the disco glamour days, which quickly became all the rage with trendy and beautiful young things. (No point in even thinking about these clothes if you were over a size ten!) The broad mass need that Gucci tapped into was GLAMOUR. Not everyone wants to look rich but everyone wants to be glamorous.

This positioning did no harm to their luxury goods sales. Presumably being all the rage in *Vogue* was more valuable than a few ads with bags in them.

Depositioning is a Key Concept of New Marketing.

The standard big marketing manoeuvre used to be repositioning. This was a bit like the Biblical Exodus. Things had got tough in Egypt, so you headed to the promised land. But brand positionings were partly based on the old finely divided social order. They had to be exclusive to one type of person, one station in life. Now this order is crumbling into a mass society, where people have similar fundamental needs and are happy to buy into correspondingly mass brands with the right qualities.

In this situation depositioning has replaced repositioning. Like Virgin which refuses to acknowledge boundaries. Like Gucci in leaving its 'rich ghetto'.

Gourmet Food Gets Depositioned

Another great example of getting out of the rich niche is the various markets for gourmet products.

Take gourmet ice-cream. Ten or so years ago gourmet ice-cream was such a luxurious, upmarket, niche product that one of its main outlets was West End theatre intervals! Then along came Haagen Dazs. Drawing on its Scandinavian sounding name, Haagen Dazs tapped a much bigger truth about luxurious indulgent creamy products. For many people they are surrogate sex. (As in 'chocolate is more pleasurable than sex'.) And sex is the most fundamental of all human needs – at least if you believe Freud.

The easy part of New Marketing is figuring out which of the fifteen needs you are tapping into. The difficult part is expressing that need in a way that works.

One of the things about our fundamental human needs is that we tend to have hang-ups about them. In the case of eating fatty foods as a pleasurable – almost sexual – experience there is a major block. No-one wants to be a sad, fatty comfort eater. The Haagen Dazs campaign featured nearly naked couples using the ice-cream for foreplay. It would be interesting to know how many couples actually did this! My guess is that the majority of the Haagen Dazs sold did end up in people's mouths. But what this idea did do is establish a completely new occasion for ice-cream – the romantic night in – perhaps with a video and a bottle of wine.

This is what all powerful brand-building must do – channel fundamental needs met by the product into attractive, acceptable and original expressions.

This is a key point about tapping fundamental human drives. People in marketing used to say things like 'we can't own that need – it's generic' or 'it belongs to so and so'. This is a fallacy. The old marketing was comparative. Ideas like positioning implicitly assume that you can't take up the same position. Which is rubbish.

What if all the fashion houses decided that, 'oh well, Gucci now owns glamour. So we can't do glamour. We'll have to do something else'? Obviously what each fashion house must do is own their own vision of glamour in their own style and expression. Gucci's vision is something like 1970s Disco meets Lolita. Versace's vision is more last days of the Roman Empire. Alexander McQueen's fashion has everything to do with glamour – but in the gothic and romantic traditions, with a very avant garde punk streak.

Just because someone else taps into a need it doesn't mean that they "own" it. Human drives are by definition inexhaustible.

A lot of recent new marketing and media ideas have tapped into sexuality, for instance, but every new expression for a different brand has its own independent life. Soft porn web sites do not detract from Cosmopolitan magazine's 'how to' guides do not detract from *The Full Monty* and other titillating films do not detract from sexy advertising like Haagen Dazs or Wonderbra do not detract...

It's the expression of the drive that should be unique not the drive itself. You don't own 'my needs' as a customer, you arouse them.

Loosen Up Marketing!

One of my favourite depictions of marketing is in the film *Crazy People*. The story so far, in case you haven't seen it, is that Dudley Moore was admitted to a lunatic asylum by jealous colleagues in his ad agency. Here he enlists the help of his fellow inmates in writing ads. They come up with insanely truthful ads. Like those for Volvo – 'They're boxy but they're safe'. Or for a laxative – 'Take this or you could get bowel cancer and die'. The film is a melodrama and needless to say these ads are a great hit with the public.

The scene I have in mind takes place back in Dudley's old agency. His colleagues are trying to get the hang of this 'honesty thing'. The managing director is haranguing the staff in a summit meeting for their shampoo pitch...

   MD: 'Say something truthful.'

   Copywriter: 'I like small boys.'

   MD: 'About the product, you idiot!'

A problem some marketing people have with tapping big human truths is that business culture is very uptight. Business conversations are not conducive to tapping into human needs. The language tends to be stilted and formal. How can you produce marketing – like Haagen Dazs featuring foreplay – in a company that only takes its tie off on Friday?

This, one line of argument goes, is why advertisers need agencies. Because ad agencies give people the creative and social freedom to say things which the public will respond to. I'm not sure this has ever been that true. A lot of ad agencies are woefully out of touch. While their clients live and work in the real world (Slough), the ad industry luvvies all too often live and work in a trendy and glitzy bubble (Soho). But we're coming to a time when creativity has to be an intrinsic part of marketing and not the icing on the cake that ad agencies used to provide. Hiving off liberated creativity in this context is clearly the wrong answer.

If marketing ideas are to plumb the same deep well as the movies and other creative media, then marketing conversations have to allow human and subjective feelings into play. Which means having less guarded sessions. People have to be able to say how ideas make them feel as human beings. They have to be able to recount their own inner hopes and fears. To tell stories that illustrate their experiences and motivations.

We have pockets of this conversation now. The best thing about market research is that it can allow real human responses to ideas into the conversation. But all too often this response is muted and objectified by reporting for a business audience. Sanitised ideas are repressed ideas.

We also have sessions like brainstorming that should help business loosen up; where people are supposed to put aside their self-censorship. But all too often these descend into point scoring competitive exercises, rather than reaching up to a more authentic conversation.

My guiding principle on this important issue is that good New Marketing conversations – those that get to the heart of brands and find out what makes people tick – have one special quality. That quality is the gift of inarticulacy.

People in marketing – as with any human, creative endeavour – must be allowed to say stupid, or difficult, or felt but only half-expressed things. These sessions are hard to build and fragile to maintain. To get this kind of conversation going in a company takes an unusual culture. It involves the absence of hierarchy, which makes people want to impress rather than improve. It involves mutual respect and support. It involves a willingness to build on people's ideas rather than cut them down.

If you don't have these sorts of sessions you should try them. You could call them truth sessions. You might even show that *Crazy People* clip to break the ice. Contrary to the film portrayal, these sorts of meetings have a liberating, exhilarating quality. And they are hyper-productive.

Getting Blunt

There's another feature of big need brands you may have noticed from the list. They are often very simple to the point of being blunt. Like Girl Power. Like Wonderbra posters. Like Nissan's 'Hungry?'

I think this blunt-ness starts with clarity – the one word brand planning approach. Try to get what your brand offers into one word (or at most a phrase). If that word on its own is powerfully evocative then you are probably on the right track. Here are a few more examples of great one word brands:

- The Kodak <u>Fun</u> camera.
- Coca-Cola – an anchor of tradition in our own times – or <u>Always</u>.

All too often companies spend ages working on their brand essence and come back with crafted phrases like 'Gateways to Autonomy'. Which is about as vivid as cold porridge. Anyone who thinks that is the essence of a powerful brand has missed the whole point about brands. One word evocations of brands are exceptionally stimulating and evocative. Especially if they are strong words that tap human needs. It's not poetry. It's just honesty. For instance the brief I wrote for the ailing Express newspaper was: **Success!** The justification being that the paper was under dynamic new management.

Here are some of my favourite one-word briefs from St. Luke's planners over the last few years:

Calm	(Eurostar)
Torture	(Vault – a drink)
Feminism	(IKEA)
Adult Playground	(Clarks)
Totalitarian	(The Comedy Channel)
Harmony	(First Direct)
Sensuality	(Boots No7)
Reality	(Radio 1)
Fetishism	(No7 Sale Offer)
Money	(Midland)

Education is It

If I had to focus all the marketing I did in future on one area what would it be? My answer would be 'Education'. We're heading into a world where the nearest thing to social class that may emerge is the knowledge have's and have-not's.

A journalist once asked me to complete the series 'Designer Eighties, Caring Sharing Nineties...'. My answer was 'The Knowledge Noughties'. I believe that education on an unprecedented scale will be a key feature of the decade to come. Partly for the very simple economic reason that in the service and knowledge industries (i.e. 70 per cent of all jobs) you need to learn in order to survive. Here are a few glimpses of this drive to learn starting to work on consumer culture and brands:

- As the earlier graph showed, a very large number of people are 'studying on my own using books or other materials' (46 per cent of adults).
- The books market is one of the key growth media along with cinema. And not just any old book. The best-seller lists are full of brain-stretchers like *A Brief History of Time* by Stephen Hawking, *Emotional Intelligence* by Daniel Coleman, *Sophie's World* by Justin Gaarder and *Longitude*.
- We are seeing the rise of the cinema film with a bit of added knowledge. I call these films the 'doc-busters'. They happen to be among the most successful of recent years: *Jurassic Park* (Genetics), *Titanic* (History) *Romeo and Juliet* (Literature).
- Galleries and museums were another beneficiary of our desire to improve our knowledge as proven by their 10 million UK visitors last year.
- In general, brands which offer increased knowledge are doing very well: Waterstones, personal computers, specialist magazines.
- Not to mention that admissions into further education have doubled since the 1970s and now stand at over a third of all young adults.
- These drives to knowledge are starting to be reflected in our ideas of social values and priorities.
- A survey I commissioned earlier this year found that 79 per cent of adults in the UK agreed with the statement 'I'd rather be more clever than more good looking'.

People used not to want to be seen as brainy. In the Anglo Saxon cultures at least. (In France being intellectual was one of the main class distinctions.) Think back to your own school days. No-one wanted to be teacher's pet did they? Now everyone wants to be brainy and the nerd or geek is a bit of a hero. It's a great time to be a Bill Gates.

And as the reading graph showed earlier, this is not a class-based thing. Knowledge used to be a niche upmarket need and value. Some people felt because of their station in life that they ought to be educated. Now it has a mass appeal and value. Education – particularly continuing self-education in adulthood – sits near the top of the old marketing's hierarchy of needs. It is part of what Maslow called 'Cognitive' needs. Now it is just, in my view, THE NEED.

I also think it is a great cause and potential leveller of social inequality. A human drive where good business can be good business.

RULE 3

AUTHOR INNOVATION

The One-Minute Summary

This is another rule which is a total contrast to old marketing.

The very idea of the brand in classical old marketing was that of unchanging essences. Hence repetitive activity to reinforce these essences. Brands could be expressed in contemporary ways, but this was like painting a fence post to keep it white, so branding as a metaphor (livestock tattooing) was quite a good one.

Now the brands which become great and stay great demonstrate an astounding dynamism and mutability, and they thrive most when they change. This being so, branding is a disastrous metaphor. Anything indelibly branded can become a real liability.

The idea of the brand in this rule is that of an author – a constant presence behind new ideas, not a fixed image as an end in itself.

Give Me an Example

Of the value of innovation: the round tea bag. One change toppled a 35 year brand leader.

Of the brand as author: Red Bull. Author of successive ideas such as Wipeout 2097 – marketing within a computer game – and the Stolly Bully a new cocktail. Ideas which have added up to this being the night-club drink.

Author Innovation

This chapter is about two things: the need for constant innovation; and the need for the brand to be flexible rather than fixed.

The best analogy I've found for this is that *the brand should be like an author – a constant background presence across a series of new works*. Whereas the old idea of the brand was more like a mask – maintaining appearances and disguising change.

Schematically, the old idea of a brand was that of building more and more concentric layers of similar meaning. Whereas the new idea of the brand is something that flows, being the sum of its recent innovations.

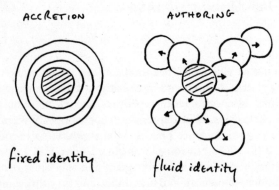

Innovate or Die

Lets start with innovation. Why do we need brands now that don't stand still?

'Innovate or die' was the motto on one of the Chiat/Day t-shirts I was given when I first joined the London office of that ultra-cool and radical Californian agency. Along with another which said 'Good enough is not enough'.

Chiat/Day was the agency which had launched the Apple Mac in the States and was voted Ad Age's 'Agency of the Decade' in the 1980s. It was the parent company of St. Luke's and Jay Chiat, their founder, gave us much more than t-shirts to set us on our way.

My move to Chiat/Day was quite a culture shock after seven years at the two London advertising agencies which jointly invented 'Account Planning' in the 1960s – JWT and BMP. And working in this innovate or die culture was probably what led me to a realisation that the key things I had been brought up to believe about brands was no longer valid. The whole idea of a brand that I was taught at my previous companies was that of something whose value was precisely that it *didn't* change.

This rule says firstly that brands should be innovative and dynamic, not static. Like a shark, they move or they die. Which, on the classical theory of brands, is probably the biggest heresy in the book. The classical theory of brands is about enduring value and relevance. It was the answer to the big problem in consumer markets of the product life cycle. With a strong and unchanging set of brand values, the theory said you could keep introducing more modern products to keep pace, while sticking to the same core appeal to the same loyal consumers.

The clothes detergent 'Tide' has been through thirty product formulations in the last thirty years. These improvements allowed them to keep up with more and more demanding consumers, without the bother of starting all over again with a new trademark. The brand was a mask hiding the fact that the product behind it kept changing.

In this view of brands, the core essence of the brand should be defined and fiercely guarded. They could be re-expressed to reflect the values of the day. So Persil which was 'mothers care for clothes'- would gradually change in line with popular ideas of being a good mother. Just as the packaging and design elements of the brand might get the occasional update, to keep them fresh and modern. But the core essence of the brand would never change.

The advertising which emerged from this theory of brands was the long running brand campaign; the same creative idea, again and again, in new forms. The brand campaigns that my first two agencies both produced were classics of this – warm, popular and memorable. And the brands which they advertised seemed unassailable, even in the late 1980s, as household names. Brands like Dulux, Oxo, KitKat, Persil, Kellogg's and PG Tips.

The problem with this sort of brand is that society now favours innovation over stability, and brands of this sort are in increasing danger. Nike was held to be one of the strongest brands in the world, so I was shocked to hear last year from a friend that works with Reebok, that Nike were suddenly on the ropes in the USA. Not just over the child labour scandal, but because people got bored with wearing Nike. And as he said to me, 'it goes to show there's no such thing as consumer loyalty'.

Consumer lifestyles are more volatile now. When people's lives change can you expect brand loyalty? With 'job for life' and 'relationship for life' and 'fixed station in life' has gone brand for life. And what's even more important – the culture is positively foaming with change.

Unchanging Brands Can't Cope with a World that Skips Breakfast

Consumer markets have speeded up. Not only in cycles of innovation within those markets, but also in the definition of the markets and who the competitors are.

As an insurance business you suddenly find yourself competing with everyone from banks to supermarkets.

As a maker of breakfast cereals you find yourself competing with fruit and with diets, with breakfast at work and with 'no time for breakfast'.

To keep pace with these changes, brands themselves need to move fast. Brands are ideas (linked with the product) that people live by. These ideas increasingly are intervening in new situations, not following old situations, for instance cereal bars and eating on the run.

The brand that comes out with a new idea about how to have breakfast is redefining the market – as the cereal bar has. Or as the introduction of American style 'coffee and muffin' cafés in train stations has. Or the real butter croissant and gourmet coffee Sunday-with-the-papers breakfast. And the brand that used to define breakfast – Kellogg's – looks suddenly out of date. Although I like their defence: they tackle the new competitors by claiming that they are the healthy option. ('Serving the Nation's Health'.)

On the other side of the coin is habits. People used to say that old habits die hard. Now the opposite is true. Old habits simply die. We have grown used to change and nothing in life has turned out quite as we expected. The picture of the world that was painted for us when we played with dolls houses and Action Man thirty years ago has turned out to be false. Compared with our parents at the same age, we are dealing with unprecedented issues and situations. If traditions were a map we were given at birth, we have gone off the edge and are constantly redrawing it to suit ourselves. Not only is life not what we expected, but it keeps surprising us. Changes of lifestyle, relationships, work, social and physical mobility...

That is why in the introduction to this book I suggested that now strong brands are strong because they are giving people ideas to live by. They are dealing with the world that skips breakfast.

The Economy of New Ideas

This might be a good time to clarify what I mean by idea. This will explain why I prefer the word innovation to creativity.

Ideas are surprising combinations of previously unconnected things.

These things can be tangible – like the Sol and the lime – or they can be purely conceptual – like Haagen Dazs and foreplay.

Ideas are 'symmetrical' as they say in Semiotics. What this means is that, just as when someone invents an idea they go 'Aha!', the same thing happens when someone encounters someone else's great idea – the two things fit together and they go 'Aha!' I see this 'Aha!' moment as a time when energy is released – each bit of the idea had some energy stored up in it and getting them together causes some sort of chemical reaction.

That releases energy.

That engages and fascinates.

That moment of energy release is when brands get re-evaluated. Things that were stale and lifeless can suddenly become luminous. These energy surges can have amazing economic effects. I'm convinced that economists have never got to grips with brand value – or its offshoot, company market value – because they cannot conceive of something whose value is *so* subjective and variable. It is literally irrational.

A good example of this in our culture now is retro. Take a fashion or music style that has some tug from the past but is now completely out. Then remix it with something current. And it's a hit again. Flares came back this way, in new colours and fabrics and with new 'ironic attitudes' e.g. the Diesel 'trash aesthetic'. Last year Hip Hop was back – with a house music beat. So for that matter, rather appropriately, was the yo-yo.

This is a clear signal that we are in a time when things work in a new way. It is the main example quoted by post-modernists. But I prefer our red thread, that this is a post-traditional time. These ideas-brands are ideas we live by. We have a storehouse of ideas from the past with some energy but not a lot of relevance. And we recycle them to face new situations.

Here's a trend prediction. The person that works out how to do a remixing retro job on any major studio's back catalogue of TV shows is going to be the first trillionaire of the next century. Given that we are going to be content poor and channel rich, it would be like working out how to drill oil. My money is on someone using the video reserves for computer gaming footage. With enough fast storage you could do away with most of the expensive animation and mix up 'real life' instead. So there are big markets for old ideas given a new spin. But the other side of the coin is a massive disloyalty and boredom when those ideas don't move.

This boredom factor can shatter marketing people's illusions of consumer loyalty. Loyalty was always a questionable concept applied to consumer markets. What was in it for the consumers? Loyalty is supposed to be loyalty to some cause, or idea, or powerful person or regime who you serve with devotion. The idea of being loyal to a brand is in retrospect a bit ridiculous although it is obvious why marketing people liked the idea! This adds up to an economy of new ideas. Meaning that, like trumps in a card game, a new idea has far greater value than an established and familiar one.

A Case in Point – the Round Tea Bag

Here's a case history of the shattered illusion of loyalty and the value of innovation.

Some years ago I worked on the brand leader in the tea market, PG Tips. This popular brand had an advertising campaign based on a chimpanzee's tea party (something they actually used to do at zoos when the campaign was launched in the 1950s). The chimps had human voices and actions and lived in everyday human settings. They mirrored the conventions of everyday British family life. Despite the questions we raised about the changing climate of opinion about circuses and performing animals, this was still one of the British public's favourite advertising campaigns.

The number two brand, Tetley's Tea, had a similarly long-standing and old-fashioned advertising campaign featuring the cartoon 'Tetley tea folk' – Northern working class types who always looked forward to a good cuppa.

Tea had been under threat from coffee in the 1980s but was still a huge market – about £600 million in sales. PG Tips had been the brand leader since the 1950s. And the campaign was held up as a prime example of the value of long running, unchanging brand advertising. PG Tips looked like the brand with no life cycle. A testament to the power of long-term repetitive advertising campaigns. Until what happened next.

Tetley launched a seemingly small innovation – the round tea bag.

They used this small change to galvanise all their marketing, from trial promotions to advertising in modern animation styles where their tea folk had become pop stars singing classic tunes such as the launch commercial's *I get around.*

Every conventional wisdom about marketing would say that this kind of innovation wouldn't work. It would be dismissed as a gimmick by loyal followers of PG Tips, who were hooked to the brand's slightly sharper taste and its consistent place in their (and often their parents) lives. It might even put off some of Tetley's older, more traditional following. Or at best what it would do was restage the brand. To suggest that it was keeping up with the times and also gain a fraction of a share point from disloyal people at the margins who tend to buy whatever is top of their mind.

What actually happened was that Tetley took brand leadership, within a year.

Why?

To paraphrase Marshall McLuhan – the change was the message. In a market which had become dull, quaint and boring, somebody did something new and dynamic. I don't believe for a minute that round tea-bags are preferred for some subtle psychological reason. (Any more than the lime in the neck of a bottle of Sol was part of the foodie movement.) The brand changed and it thrived.

In the light of the round tea bag, we could see that people had become bored with tea and tea brands. It was there, taken for granted, bought out of habit, but very recessive. And ripe for innovation.

This is my favourite example to make brand Pharisees stop and think. One change was all it took to topple thirty-five years of what they would call loyalty or goodwill. Constant innovation is the first lesson of marketing in post-traditional times. But there is also the question of the nature of brands and branding.

The Narcissus Trap – as Learned by British Airways

Narcissism, in the ancient Greek myth is what happens when you stare at your own image; you get transfixed. The problem is creating brands as if that were an end in its own right. Brands are planned, expressed, measured, even put on the balance sheet as if they had enduring value. Which is about as smart as earning some money then putting it under your mattress. Changing consumer culture is the "inflation" in brand marketing.

British Airways was a modern classic in the theory of branding.

The story started in the mid 1980s when British Airways decided to become customer-led. They introduced a massive culture transformation programme. Every member of staff went on a customer service programme and learned to make everything revolve around the individual customer and their mindset. To deal with problems quickly and in a reassuring manner. To make fragmented experiences, like transfers, flexible and smooth. And so on.

I'm sure that all this learning is still valid. That airline service needed to get more up close and personal. It needed to revolve around the experiences and needs of the passenger. So far, so good.

The advertising that was aired at the time emphasised the super-human efforts which staff would make for customers. It used 'superhero' characters doing 'superman' good deeds behind the scenes to smooth the way for passengers. It was a campaign largely aimed at the staff, to reinforce the training message. It was slightly clumsy by today's advertising standards, but it did the job.

Then British Airways did something which at the time looked great and now looks fatal. They fixed the identity of the brand to the creative theme of 'British Empire'. The advertising campaign was changed to 'The World's Favourite Airline'. Expensive, expansive, almost stately commercials were produced showing British Airways bringing people together (in formations that became their logo). It looked like the opening ceremony of the Olympics – and at the time it looked great. In the Margaret Thatcher and Merchant Ivory Britain of the 1980s, a British Airways that was presented in this way was perfectly in tune with the prevailing culture. It offered the promise of oak-panelled service and classic sophistication.

Now, in the more internationalist and softer-edged 1990s this 'Best of Britain' image is a millstone around British Airways' neck. It makes them look like William Hague's Tory party. It could not be more out of tune.

BA are now engaged in what the business author Tom Grundy (in *Breakthrough Strategies for Growth*) wittily calls a 'detergent' strategy, i.e. cleaning up the mistakes of the past. They have taken the Union Jack flag designs off the tail fins and replaced them with more internationally attuned modern art. In an echo of our recent IKEA advertising, an article in *The Sun* newspaper revealed that they have even gone as far as to tell the cabin staff to 'stop being so British'.

British Airways' revival was born out of a new dynamism and flexibility. But they were seduced later by the 'baked beans' strategy of building a fixed enduring brand. They fell prey to Narcissism. This is such an easy trap to fall into, because it *is* an act of narcissism. Nine times out of ten, fixed brands are born out of success. You have a hit piece of branding one year that everyone loves and your only mistake is to repeat it for ten years, not noticing that the times have changed.

The Brand as Author

The alternative model of branding which I want to put forward is that of authoring.

The authors of books are more flexible as brands. They are known by their latest works. They do have consistency – a constant presence and temperament, but they can also develop and reinvent themselves, and most importantly grow and improve. And fundamentally the author is something you deduce from the work, rather than being the work.

A great example of a brand as author is Marks & Spencer. This is the strongest brand in UK retailing. But it is not fixed to one statue-esque identity for one audience. It has managed to vary what it sells from cheap knickers for the masses, to luxury pre-prepared foods for the cash-rich and time-poor modern couple. If it has any sense it is now preparing another massive step-change. As the supermarkets have caught up with the deli-like foodhall, it is time for M&S to enter pastures new. Maybe education?

Marks & Spencer is the author of innovation across all they do. They have consistent values. They would say quality, value and service. I would say middle class, middle England – the BBC1 of the high street.

You could say that M&S branding is the product of a very strong heritage and relationship with customers. So this stance is fine for old brands but could you create a brand this way? Surely you need that public fireworks display at the outset to say 'here I am and here's who I am'? But there are just as many new brands built on authoring innovation. The example I've chosen is Red Bull – the energy drink.

Red Bull is a potent mix of caffeine, taurine and sugar. It packs a punch of about two hundred calories a can. Consider that the soft drinks market is probably the toughest market in the world into which to launch a new brand. That there was already a strong 'energy brand' in the UK called Lucozade with a long heritage. That every health trend says 'do not even rub this stuff on your body let alone drink it'. This was a launch that shouldn't have worked.

The standard approach would be to become a 'hey big spender!'. The Oasis soft drink was one example of a brand that tried to break into the market in this way. TV adverts from day one. Big distribution pushes. You get the picture. Oasis is still on sale in my local deli, so they are clearly here for the long-haul too, but I don't think anyone would claim that this was the brand launch of the century. It's hardly the new brand name on everybody's lips, is it?

That's the standard approach. And judging by the number of soft drinks that don't make it to year three, it can't be that effective.

What Red Bull did instead was take its product in gleaming jeeps painted in their silver and blue brand livery (designed like the football shirts which were then the height of clubbing style) to the exits of clubs and festivals across the country. Here glamorous women handed the drink, like angels of mercy, free to tired revellers. Crude maybe but very effective. It was a perfect bit of Walkman marketing – fitting the brand into the customer's life and immediate context and needs. Knackered? Drink this!

Another inspired piece of marketing of Red Bull was the high speed rocket race game *Wipeout 2097*. *Wipeout* is a Playstation game targeted at the dance music generation. As well as home play, you should bear in mind that at the time many night-clubs had Playstation consoles lying about in the chill-out room. Given that about 3 million young people have Playstations and a great proportion also go clubbing at the weekend this is actually quite a big medium. Especially after the game had taken off and they were selling twenty to thirty thousand copies a week, and given just how many times us *Otakii* (Japanese for 'people who play computer games too much and should get out more') will spend playing that game.

Wipeout has a soundtrack mixed by famous club musicians like the Chemical Brothers. In the game you race along a variety of sci-fi tracks and along those tracks in the game are posters telling you that Red Bull improves concentration and reaction times. Which in the clubs with Playstation terminals and people drinking Red Bull is like having somebody along from the marketing department helping you to notice what effects the product is having.

The development which has sealed Red Bull's success as an integral part of the club scene is the invention of a new cocktail – perhaps the first widely successful new cocktail to be invented since the 1950s – the 'Stolly Bully' (Stolicknoya vodka and Red Bull). This has become a staple drink in night clubs for the post-ecstasy generation. It is the epitome of function and culture fused. It is perhaps the only drink (apart maybe from Hoopers Hooch in its very early days) that has managed to compete in the market created by illegal drugs for mood and body enhancers.

Then and only then was a consumer advertising campaign launched to catalyse Red Bull's spread into broader use and acceptability. I'm not sure this was necessary, incidentally, but it was probably done to secure broader grocery distribution.

I don't know whether the marketing team at Red Bull had a hand in creating the Stolly Bully. Perhaps at some point they featured this drink in venue promotions. Whoever came up with the idea, it quickly became owned by the audience. It is an idea attached to the original brand idea that transformed it from just another energy drink, to an iconic part of club culture.

If anyone thinks that Red Bull was a fluke, they should bear in mind that the marketer behind it all was the same one that eight years earlier had managed Sol into hyper-growth in the supposedly impenetrable beer market. His name is Harry Durneck and he clearly knows how to author brands that run circles around the big old brand leaders. This is something that may be a lesson for marketing departments in the future. Brands which act like strong authors often actually have strong authors at the helm. And not just for eighteen months which is the average employment life expectancy of a marketing director!

Working with the Brand as Author

The 'brand as author' model says that what you need to focus on is your next great work. The brand is a succession of good ideas associated with your good name.

The Spice Girls as a brand had a number of good ideas:

- Launching a girl band modelled on playground friendship groups.
- Giving each girl a very different identity, so the group became a 'cast of characters' and hence an ongoing drama, not one fixed aggregate 'brand'.
- The idea of 'girl power' as a rallying cry.
- The idea of working through different media like the *Spice World* film.

Looked at this way the departure of Geri Halliwell should have been an opportunity to move forward – to add a new idea, like a new band member or two. Imagine if they'd conscripted a boy into the gang for instance.

The same pattern of successive innovation from the one author can be seen in many of the great brands in this book:

- Virgin's innovations are brand stretching into disparate markets.
- Tango has launched flavour variants and all sorts of odd add-ons like the Tango Orange Voodoo Doll.
- Playstation has developed a constant stream of great games, developed innovations such as the analogue controller that rumbles when you crash, and they've even toyed with the programmable Playstation.

It takes great courage to continually develop new ideas. It's not that hard when you are in a corner going nowhere to come up with the first innovation, but there is a 'second novel crisis' that follows this. It is very hard to junk something that worked, and it is very easy to fall into the trap that BA did of becoming fixed and statue-esque.

In the 1960s there was a seminal paper about *marketing myopia* (by Philip Kotler) which described the tendency of success to make business forget why it succeeded, to become complacent. This is a key lesson for the 1990s too – don't forget that your brand shot to success because you changed something. And if you don't innovate again, you are going to see that success fade just as fast.

That's why, after the most successful brand campaign I've ever worked on – 'Chuck Out Your Chintz' for IKEA, we introduced a totally different campaign the following year. That's why in fact, my company, St. Luke's has never produced a long running brand campaign. By the time the next year comes around there is always something sharper to do than repeat yourself.

And of course advertising is only the visible tip of what I'm talking about. Many brands would do well to consider if they are even in the right market from year to year.

Where do you get the ideas for your next 'novel'?

In the next section we are going to cover 'new life situations' which in my view are the key opportunity for brands. This is nearly always the place that new ideas – ones that people will seize and live by – will come from. It is common sense if you think about it. People only need new traditions for areas where they are a bit lost.

But there is another place the innovation can come from. That is from new business definitions. Or new business models as my consultancy friends call them. These can redefine how you do business. Or more powerfully for many consumer brands – what market you are in.

A prime example of this was Boddingtons. This is the beer that looks and tastes halfway between traditional English bitter and continental lager. The marketing all grew out of this combination: the stylish and ironic look (lager) at traditional northern working class culture (bitter) in the 'Cream of Manchester' television advertising. Or the original posters which combine surreal art (lager) with a down to earth wit (beer).

Boddingtons reflected a new reality in the beer market. Beer drinkers used to divide into two opposed camps: lager drinkers and bitter drinkers. By the time Boddingtons was launched the market was more experimental and most people tended to drink both in a repertoire.

A great starting point for inventing new brands for apparently lock-tight markets is to ask: what distinctions used to divide the market but no longer apply as powerfully? And what credible hybrid could emerge in the middle? People talk about looking for gaps. But the biggest gaps are usually those that lie between assumptions made by your market research when it categorises the market.

To Summarise

In this chapter I have explained why brands should emerge as the by-products of innovation – the brand being consistent, in a fluid way, as the author of these successive ideas. Previous rules showed that the brand should tap into broad, fundamental human needs, not niche distinctions. And that the brand should be up close and personal, not distant and abstract. These are all challenges to the classic theory of brands. In a sense they are slightly negative rules – corrections to past ways of marketing that don't fit today's markets and social realities.

Now we are going to look more positively at the exciting opportunities for brands. Starting with the most natural source of these – the new situations and challenges people face in the post-traditional society.

RULE 4

MYTHOLOGIZE THE NEW

The One-Minute Summary

This rule is about applying the kind of information that good marketing people have always had at their fingertips, in new ways.

There's nothing new, per se, in keeping up with social trends that might impact on your market. The classical marketing approach was to reflect social trends – for instance in advertising – to make brands appear modern and in touch. Marketing people of a certain persuasion called this the 'key consumer insight'. As in 'always open your advertising with a key consumer insight'. Such as 'mothers today never seem to have enough time to get things done'.

The new marketing approach is to offer brand ideas as a way of negotiating with new life situations. It means acting as the new traditions – not simply an addendum to the old ones. That is why I call it 'mythologizing'. It sounds a subtle distinction but I think it is quite a big shift to a more constructive role for marketing in society. From shining a torch at people's feet to shining it at the path ahead. This can mean, for instance, projecting new types of behaviour (like jogging), or validating ones which are emerging but not quite recognised in culture yet (like male grooming and 'new man').

Give Me an Example

The Clarks Shoes relaunch, 'Act Your Shoe Size Not Your Age', which legitimised a new idea about being middle-aged. Not a sad decline into middle-age spread as portrayed by numerous sitcoms, but a vibrant and active 'new playground years'.

Mythologize the New

In the introduction I defined a brand in the new social context as:

An idea (or set of ideas) that people live by.

If there was a *Mastermind* quiz for marketing people the general knowledge quiz would have to be on social trends. How could you work in the food market without a fix on vegetarianism, gourmet authenticity, time pressure, dieting and health, cooking as a hobby, and so on?

Marketing has often been good at using these trends to develop products, but when it came to brands – because these were supposed to be fixed – the majority just paid lip service. All too often it is just for show – a part of the styling of the brand – so it appears relevant for the way you live today. This chapter is about a more powerful way that a brand can connect with these trends in everyday living. Which is to mythologize new ways of life.

'Myths' as defined in the dictionary, are purely fictional accounts. But they also have some relationship to natural or historical phenomena – they explain, illuminate and invest with imagination. Myths are the stories that carry traditions. In modern social theory (for instance, Roland Barthes' *Mythologies*) the idea of myth has been extended to new traditions.

I am using the term here to describe how new ways of life become invested with human imagination. For instance, the way that a term like 'new man' becomes associated with fictional characters and roles like *Three Men and a Baby*, or the UK advertising for Miller Lite.

If the new ways of life are skeletal, factual choices then myths are the clothes that make them attractive, living possibilities.

When brands do this they become instrumental in people's lives, expressing the choices they are making and supporting them. This is the most powerful thing a brand can do because it is the most valuable. One of the best gifts brands can offer to people in our post traditional time is validity. Validity as in 'it's OK to live this way' or 'this is how things are done'. Validity for actions but also validation for ourselves and our identities. Brands now are here to say 'It's OK! You're OK!'

This can mean brands working in a self-help way, as in the BT campaign which tells us how to have better phone conversations, but it can also be more celebratory and imaginative. As a few examples will illustrate.

Brand New Identities

One way to mythologize everyday living is to create a new identity. Identity is a composite picture for most people. We choose it in the way we choose clothes – by shopping around for things that fit. The components are off the shelf, but the outfits are our own.

In some areas of life it can be quite hard to find the identity ideas we need because there aren't any old ones that deal with our new situation. Here are some examples of what I mean by 'new identities'. You'll notice incidentally that these fit the definition of 'an idea' in a particular way – each is a combination of an old cultural idea with a new social reality:

- The career woman ('male' ideas of career power + woman working).
- The sloane ranger (country aristocracy + living in the city).
- Girl power (teenage girls with adult sexuality and assertiveness).
- New man (soft, caring, feminine).
- Middle youth (still living a teenage lifestyle + nearing middle age).
- Muscle mary (the he-men on the gay scene).

These may be a bit make-shift. Perhaps they are only adopted for a while. They certainly aren't as deep and permanent as the old identity traditions. But they are the same sort of answer to the same question, 'who am I for other people?'

Calvin Klein Swings Both Ways

A good example of a brand with an identity idea was CK One – the unisex scent from Calvin Klein.

CK One celebrated androgyny and in the process broke every other rule of perfume marketing; it wasn't French and seductive, or sporty and macho, it was about groups of people together not individuals, it was casual not formal.

CK One was a great idea because men were going in for more and more 'feminine' grooming. Only twenty years ago, men who wore aftershave ran the risk of being teased. Now men spend nearly as much on toiletries (excluding cosmetics) as women. And conversely women are going in for more and more 'masculinity'. Twenty years earlier women in big boots who drank pints of beer sent similarly mixed signals.

Androgyny was a big fashion theme in the mid 1990s. And not just in niche fashion magazines, but right on centre stage of the culture. Madonna was androgynous and so was Prince. Androgyny was hip, and Calvin Klein bottled it. And it was an outstanding global success.

The follow up brand CK Be seemed to me to be less innovative; casual, inner-directed, a bit like Gap Perfume but not creating any dramatically new crossed currents in the culture. If I were Calvin Klein I'd have tackled the young-old divide next.

CK One is an example of what I earlier called depositioning. At the most basic level it ignored some fundamental category distinction in its market (between men and women's scents) and created a hybrid.

Clarks' Shoes Hits Middle Age

A more subtle approach than badge identities (which tend to be boldly branded, like girl power) is to mythologize a new lifestyle or attitude. A good example is the relaunch I worked on in 1997 for Clarks' shoes. This case history makes several further points – how to listen to customers, and how brands as ideas can 'legitimise' behaviour.

Clarks had a big problem with their adult shoes. They were seen as very old-fashioned and for old people. The majority of their adult customers were over sixty. Not only were they missing out on the vital 'middle' of the market, who spent more on shoes, more often. But their position was gradually worsening, because old people were getting younger in outlook, and didn't want to wear 'old shoes'.

Clarks overhauled their range to appeal to the vital thirty-or forty-something customer. These people were already visiting Clarks' shops in many cases to buy shoes for their children, so what the marketing had to do was to get them to consider Clarks for themselves. The new range would help. But somehow, because of that strange powerful thing called branding, a shoe with a Clarks logo on looked strangely old fashioned and dowdy, whatever its style. We look at branded products through 'branded spectacles'.

Our story starts in some research groups near Bristol.

A simple open-ended question was put to some people in their thirties and forties where each member of the group was left to answer in their own way and their own time:

Tell me where you have got to in your lives at the moment.

What they told us about their lives became the whole focus of the relaunch.

The media idea of people turning forty is that of the middle-age crisis. The slightly silly, resigned image of settling down for a long decline into old age. Or perhaps a foolish last fling or other clutch at lost youth.

But what people told us was a very different story. They were having the time of their life. Gone were the sleepless nights and stressed days of being at the bottom of the career ladder, of raising young children, of coming to terms with yourself. When they were in their late twenties they had felt 'no-one ever told us life was going to be this hard'. Now the tide had turned and 'no-one ever told us it was going to be so much fun'.

The life they lived in their shoes was a playing-with-kids-at-the-park, dancing-at-the-seventies-night-at-the-pub, hiking-home-across-the-field romp. Not only were they having an exuberant great time, but it had everything to do with Clarks' shoes. It was a 'new playground years'. The last time they had felt and behaved like this many of them had been wearing Clarks' shoes to school.

Our advertising under the slogan 'Act your shoe size not your age!' was full of the kinds of scenes they were describing. Not just to reflect their lives, but to say 'It's great, go ahead, enjoy yourself'. Judging by a recent issue of *The Guardian*, the advertising has done more than we could have hoped. Not only was there a big fashion article about how Clarks are now 'in', but the next article in the same paper was about how life really does begin at forty.

When brands tap into new ways of living they change the rules of their marketplace. Clarks redefined adult shoes as things to romp around in. When this is your criteria, then Clarks is the natural answer.

We've looked at some cases of mythologizing in practise. Lets stand back and look at changes in people's lives in general.

The General Knowledge Round

I said earlier that if there was a *Mastermind* quiz for marketing, then the general knowledge section would be about trends.

Someone who approached me after a recent conference talk wouldn't get past the eliminators. 'It's all very well talking about brands being based on big new ideas', he said 'But surely there aren't enough of them to go around'. I think this is someone in marketing that needs to get out more, or at least to read a newspaper. If you have your eyes open, then you see nothing but constant change in everyday living and opportunities for brands.

I'm sure most readers will be pretty well up on social trends. If you're not there's no excuse because there are enough research reports and books on future trends out at the moment to fill a small library. But just in case, and because I want to demonstrate their application to brands, here are nearly forty new situations in people's everyday lives and some brands that have mythologized them.

New Stuff in Life to Deal With and Brand Mythologizers

① Age and lifestage

As discussed in rule 2, age is now a much more flexible concept.

The Clarks relaunch celebrated the freedom, in your forties, to act your shoe size. The original Gap concept was a brand of casual classic clothing aimed at this generation gap of forty-something's who still wanted to wear jeans.

Many fashion brands and magazines tap into the market one decade younger to act like a teenager in your thirties. Although none has quite defined this age group since the American TV series *Thirty Something*, the nearest would be another US sitcom, *Friends*.

There are loads of un-mined identity questions in this area. The young-old or 'grey panthers' as they call them in America are one. These people are the main market for adventurous long-haul holidays and also for new cars. Another ill-defined group is the teenager. Today's teenager is far more grown up, deals with adult emotional questions early in life, and is also focused on self-reliance, studying hard and building a career. Far from being rebellious they get on almost too well with their parents. Half of all young men aged 18-25 still live at home. I call this group the Getset.

And what about the idea of flexi-age? My identity age varies from late thirties for big client meetings to late teens at the weekend, and all points between.

② Gender
This is the big identity question of our age.

CK One is one of many brands that have staked out a new gender identity for people to pick up and wear. Others include *Loaded*, *The Marchessa* (a self-help book for using femininity at work) and *Red* (the latest 'modern woman' magazine).

There are still many opportunities for new identities to be explored and valorised in this changing gender-scape. One example could be the changing split in housework (currently still 70:30, women:men but falling fast). Plus the growing number of men living alone. I'd call this something like the 'housebloke'– think trendy cookbooks and Black & Decker drills. What about masculine approaches to housework e.g. blitzing.

③ Friends
One of the most successful TV brands of recent years was *Friends*. At its height this was the top-rating TV show in the world.

Our reliance on friends as surrogate family is a key modern social phenomena. It's the same idea as underpinned The Spice Girls and other 'pal pop groups'. Why then is it that we have so many hundreds of greeting cards and rituals for family and so few for these friends? There is also loads of potential for us to have a whole emotional register of different sorts of friends just as varied as those of the extended families. Platonic couples seem quite big at the moment, for instance.

④ Meeting and mating
The long running *Blind Date* is one of the most successful primetime shows in the UK. The reality of many people's lives is that they find themselves in the whole dating game rather more often than they would have expected.

One potential powerful role in culture is that of the matchmaker. In Japan they have the 'sex hunter' (an agent who will proposition people on your behalf). Here we have a more standard range of dating agencies, single bars etc. A great brand idea was that of *Cosmo* and *Esquire* magazines getting together to run a joint dating service.

A cultural opportunity is the dating of older singles, for which we have few positive archetypes in Anglo Saxon culture. Look forward to brands that celebrate this identity – along the lines of *Sleepless in Seattle*.

⑤ Not having children

According to a 1997 UK Government estimate, a third of women of child-bearing age now will never have children. And those that do have children are having fewer, later. In my view, this explains two major currents of society now.

One is the new broodiness. Evident in all sorts of adult culture – from the baby aesthetic in women's fashions to the Tamagochi to the waves of programmes about cute and sick animals. And the tendency of the media to act like a crowd of aunts every time a new celebrity has a baby.

The second is the baby/cute aesthetic. Like the LA 'Candy Ravers'– boys in huge bell-bottom jeans, caps and other Gap Kids style clothes and girls styled after Betty Boop and Pippa Long Stocking, all with an obligatory lollipop.

But where is the strong positive image of the childless woman in her forties?

⑥ Class mobility and fusion

Trustafarians (trust fund heiresses in Notting Hill), ex-council homes with Georgian panelled doors, the cutting edge fashion for looking like a geography teacher, open collar Microsoft millionaires. Class identities and signals have got scrambled.

Class is no longer the rubric under which we all live. But there are great needs for brands brokering upward and downward mobility, for instance. The yuppie was an identity idea that caught millions of 'City Strivers' (many of whom were actually estate agents, not Wall Street brokers!). This identity was tapped into by brands from DKNY to BMW.

More current now perhaps is the idea of 'stealth wealth' which Audi among others are pursuing. And downshifting is the clearest idea that has emerged for those opting down.

⑦ Risk and chance

How do we cope with a more roller coaster and dynamic life, career, relationships and numerous new risks to health and welfare?

One response is a more risk- and chance-embracing culture.

Taking in brands from dangerous sports to the National Lottery. Rolling Rock picked up the idea of the 'dice man' for their advertising and I think 'fortune cookie' branding is worth a look. On a darker level 'bareback riding' (unprotected sex) is reported to be a hedonistic trend in the USA and small illegalities such as drug use and non-payment of fines and local taxes are lifestyle accessories for adultescents.

⑧ New communities of interest

The forming of new communities of interest is the subject of a whole rule later. Community brands are very powerful now – from turnkey TV programmes like *South Park*, to Playstation, to Oddbins and car boot sales and local causes. This trend encompasses football fever, communitarianism and much besides. It was spotted by the Henley Centre as a swing towards the idea that 'it's better to look after the community's interest than your own'.

Many brands have sensed or followed this swing – including St. Luke's campaign for Foxes Biscuits 'Don't be a stranger' using advertising, but also local community activities, to bring people together for tea and biscuits.

⑨ Self-improvement

With inner-directedness has come the urge to develop and reinvent yourself. Self improvement is the new DIY and areas like the gym, dieting, self-education and self-help are booming. Hobbies have taken on a kind of vocation status as sustained projects of self-improvement, displacing the central place of work in some people's lives. Among the many brands covered elsewhere in the book that tap this broad current are BT, IKEA, Delia Smith, Nike and Microsoft.

⑩ Homes from home

Modern sociologists say that man is essentially a homeless being. The lifelong geographical origin from which we come and to which we return is being lost, leaving us adrift. And the modern home is increasingly a boarding house rather than home.

One response is the creation of 'homes from home': From the new architecture projects (pedestrianised and personalised), to homely book shops, cafés and offices. A novel adaptation of a public space is the café trams in Berlin. And a big story in the car market has been 'the home on wheels', for instance the Renault *Espace*.

⑪ The end of fashion?

What are you supposed to wear in an age when according to most research 'what is cool is to do your own thing'?

Apart from the dictates of high fashion that filter down into mainstream media, one of the big influences seems to be feature films. *Boogie Nights, Jackie Brown* and others seem for instance to have sparked a global craze for disco music and clothes.

What to wear is a key question in an age that is losing its uniforms. Casual Friday has posed this question of many office workers and brands such as Rockport shoes have rushed to be the answer.

⟨12⟩ Partnership and responsibility

With the decline of institutions that tower over us, has gone the expectation that there is a paternal state there to take care of us.

In politics we see growing use of the concept of partnership between state, private sector and individuals. And in individual attitudes, a growing recognition of the need to take personal responsibility for your destiny.

'New Deal' was a brand of government employment scheme that brought these ideas into focus.

⟨13⟩ Globalisation

As the Sociologist Tony Giddens points out in his latest book, *The Third Way*, Globalisation is a word that was barely in use ten years ago, even in journalistic and academic writings.

There is a growing sense of being a citizen of the world and being connected to many more country cultures and events than your own.

Brands that have tapped into this include Guinness, The World Cup, Benetton, Diesel, fusion cookery and the New Orientalism (e.g. *Memoirs of a Geisha*).

⟨14⟩ Lifelong learning

This trend and some of the brands tuned into it was covered under rule 2. From doc-busters to Microsoft. One interesting development would be that of an identity for adult night class students. 'Eveners'?

⟨15⟩ Genetic and other medical advances

Over the next ten years or so, medicine is likely to become what IT has been for the last twenty-five years. Products that delay the signs and effects of ageing – ceramide creams, Viagra – are probably the tip of the iceberg.

We have some identity ideas for those who have plastic surgery (e.g. *Hollywood Women*) but what about absorbing genetic and prosthetic medicine into our culture? We have to do better than Frankenstein and Dolly the Sheep!

This is currently an obsession of avant gardists like Damien Hirst and David Cronenberg, but it must nearly be time for a perfume called 'Clone'! Meanwhile the inventor of the CD is now working on pharmacology products from brain candy to the orgasm intensifier. So we can expect a lot of self-medication brands to emerge too.

⑯ Losing our religion

The demise in one human lifetime of many organised religions across the world is the most astonishing shift of our times. And the spiritualised New Age from alternative medicine to Feng Shui and rave culture is a profound trend.

You might think this has nothing to do with marketing, but that may be because you are thinking of another scientific age. *The X-Files*, Playstation and Tango are brands that glow with this energy and there will be many more to come.

⑰ The rules

Instructions are a feature of a time when we are losing our traditions. From fashion's 'brown is the new black' to the best-seller *The Rules* to countless instructive daytime shows on cookery and infidelity.

Expect quite a few more bossy brands to come. Bossier even than 'Chuck Out Your Chintz' and 'Don't Drink and Drive'!

⑱ Post-scientific era

Another part of the holistic New Age is losing our faith in science. Alternative medical practitioners have overtaken GP's in the States. Nothing is as guaranteed to make us panic as a scientific expert on the news saying there is no cause for alarm!

The counterpart of science in human cultures is nature. And the most powerful brands in technology have evaded alienation through 'natural' brands: graphical personal computing, organic bodily techno music and gadgets.

⑲ End of patriarchy

A very interesting question for society is the position of the father, figure of authority. In business culture this is already being superseded by the steward or enabler. Will we see new counterparts of identity and role in other social relationships? What about the family for instance?

Many brands aimed at children have acknowledged a shift in the balance of purchasing and power across the generations. What interests me more is ideas of non-hierarchical family equivalence – such as Baby Gap and the supermarkets which now provide child trolleys. And the 'man's movement' of 'Iron John' is bound to hit the mainstream in more forms than 'New Man'.

⟨20⟩ Experience-led

Rule 5 covers the big shift in our culture from the visual to the sensual and the related concept of 'Doubting Thomas' consumers.

Brands with strong experiential components are thriving, from Guinness to The Body Shop to dance music. And the big question for intangible products is how can the brand create compensatory tangibles?

⟨21⟩ Looseness and informality

A simple shift. Perhaps one hundred years ago you would generally be known by your surname. And now you are generally known by your first name. You would mostly shake hands and now you increasingly hug. You would have an official vocabulary and accent for most situations outside the family. And now you converse with complete strangers in loose idioms and slang.

Too many brands are stuck in the stiff formality of the surnames era. Brands look uptight relative to most media. And those that don't, like Microsoft and Oddbins, glow with the warmth of familiarity. Increasing informality is still a big opportunity. Anything with a high degree of inherent formality – like banks, newspapers and public transport – would do well to develop its brand in these directions.

⟨22⟩ Gentleness

I owe this trend spot to the anthropologist Mary Douglas.

'Gentleness' is an idea that collects everything from vegetarianism to fear of crime under one general trend to meekness.

There is a related idea that all previous human societies were predicated upon readiness for war. That the factory and the family and even the welfare state were part of this general martial ethos. And that since the 1960s the driving ethos in societies has been pacifism which is the root cause of all the resistance to establishments values. Are we children of flower power and Vietnam? Maybe. And the meek brands shall inherit...

㉓ Going green

Not a new trend, but given its roots in some of the main public concerns like pollution, not one that is likely to be swept under the carpet.

Unleaded petrol and recycled packaging were some early answers, but the long-term deeper shift is to sustainable lifestyles – taking on our conscience and drive to citizenship, to personal responsibility and restraint. For any brand that hasn't done an audit into its green credentials, now would be a good time.

And what will be the power brands of a post-consumer mindset? They might look a lot like IKEA or the (Japanese) Muji or 'No Brand'?

I think downshifting mentioned earlier is a serious contender for the keynote theme of our culture and many futurists agree, predicting home farming, shared housing communities and a shift to local business loyalties.

㉔ Crime and chaos

As they sing in the film, *The Italian Job*, 'This is the self-preservation society'. There is a booming market for self-defence courses, true crime TV programmes, home and car security systems. It is all partly a factual adjustment to higher crime.

But there is also a growing cultural value in self-protection. For instance, the Volkswagen Polo that is advertised as a protective car that makes you feel safe. One commercial even features a martial arts class.

㉕ Quality of life and leisure

Have you noticed what has happened to Sunday supplement magazines? In place of many of the old profiles and pictures of lifestyles of the rich and famous are huge lush close-up photographs of foods or beauty treatments, holiday panoramas, lifestyle photography and features, country walks and new fabrics and places to eat and visit. These are the lifestyle pages turned inwards from aspiration to quality of life.

We went through the same shift for No7 cosmetics, with our lush, sensual and inward advertising for a brand that was once the 'poor woman's Chanel'.

㉖ New technology

New technology-culture is the main imaginative thrust of modernity. Think back to classic works of science fiction like *Metropolis* or the novels of HG Wells. Modern, more friendly myths include techno and other electronic music, mobile phones and other prosthetic technologies and so forth.

The big new technology to hit our lives recently is digital television. We already have zapping and surfing, but what this medium badly lacks is a more human interface and story than the text based channel guides. The satellite medium took off as a brand (as well as something valuable) through Soccer on Sky Sports. Minitel, the French phone-based version of the internet took off when it became a dating medium. My guess is that Sony will do the myth-making when they launch the Media Station.

Great technology myths in advertising have included Audi's 'Vorsprung Durch Technic' and other equations of technology and Germanic culture.

✷ Body consciousness

As we have become more inward looking, the body has become a cultural fascination. Body art (like tattooing and scarring) and art about the body (like Damien Hirst's *pharmacy*) are the avant garde extremes. More mainstream myth making surrounds drugs like Ecstasy, Viagra and Prozac, as well as aspects of physique (e.g. the *six-pack* stomach), digestion (e.g. *live* yoghurt) and so forth.

Body brands include The Body Shop, currently running campaigns about body shape, Lycra and BUPA (medical insurance linked to the body as 'miracle').

✷ Beyond good and evil

How do we decide what is right and wrong? Morality is another big cultural theme, which runs across daytime chat shows and company ethics reports.

Morality is now a more subjective, personal choice than at any time in the past, but it is still tied with belonging to communities. We share moral codes with those we commune with, whether we are politically correct liberals or white supremacists.

Brands can be exemplars of different moral codes – from the hedonistic promiscuity of Club 18–30 holidays to the aggressive political correctness of Benetton. There are also off-the-shelf moral codes like the 'Celestine Prophesies'.

✷ Fame

The pursuit of celebrity and celebrities is a kind of super-myth of our time. Celebrity is a kind of Mount Olympus, on which the gods of many other myths reside.

Brands that have connected with this quest include *Hello* magazine, Ritz Carlton Hotels (every guest treated like a celebrity), theme cafe's belonging to famous people, Martini and the 'beautiful people' and daytime soaps like *The Bold and the Beautiful*.

◈ Polymorphous perversions
Freud's phrase. He said that without the external strictures of society we are all sexually omnivorous.

In a time when the grip of the social grid on our lives is loosening, more and more sexual choices are out in the open. There is almost a carnival culture around fetishes – they've become a popular fashion and nightclub theme. On American campuses the more experimental and fashionable become 'BUG' (Bi-sexual Until Graduation).

Because it is near to taboos and hence authentic, sexy, modern brands flirt constantly with what the Victorians would class as perversions. Tango, Guinness, Levi's, Diesel, Haagen Dazs. More interesting and genuinely dangerous are the brands which question genuine taboos, such as fashion advertising playing with paedophilia, and films about incest.

◈ Causes and crusades
The cause is dead – long live the cause.

The old causes like socialism have floundered. Labour Party and Trades Union membership is at an all time low, but new causes proliferate around new political issues like ecology – such as protecting trees from road building and releasing laboratory animals and protesting against genetic crops and reclaiming the roads...

Causes are learning the skills of branding, such as the AIDS ribbon, the fashion industry 'target' for breast cancer, Glasgow 'Smiles Better'. And what's more, brands are learning that causes are a great way of getting people together – like the *Independent* newspaper's campaign to legalise drugs, or Tesco's 'Computers for schools' promotion.

◈ Virtuality
Many brands have been on hand to mythologize our transition to a new economy of virtuality: *Wired* magazine, Nasdaq, IBM's e-business, the i-MAC, along with identity/role ideas like telecommuting and the virtual office.

◈ The end of authenticity/copyrights
This has gone from art movement to pop culture, with sampled music and retro. Post-modernism made an academic movement out

of the lack of authentic traditions (if only anyone could understand it). More interesting new myths include identity theft and fraud (as portrayed in the film '*Single White Female*').

Brands founded on the lack of authentic 'gold standards' in culture include Seconda watches ('Beware of expensive imitations'), FCUK (styled after bootleg brand t-shirts) and Labbatt's 'Brand X'.

A great advertising stunt from my good friends Naresh and Dave was the 'bootleg endorsement' campaign for Molson in the UK. It featured photographs of famous people, juxtaposed cheekily with interviews with quite separate ordinary people. Unfortunately the ad featuring Bill Clinton was blocked by the White House, but Norman Tebbit still ran.

Customisation

An 'up close and personal' trend is the growth of customised products and services – designed around individuals.

Brands have caught this trend. Like 'Egg' the new bank account. And the new Levi's made-to-measure jeans vending machine. And Dulux's marketing of their almost infinitely variable paint colour range to match things that inspire you, like the colour of a leaf.

Time pressure

We live in an age of what some call 'hurry sickness'. Especially for women torn between longer working hours, child care, more demanding relationships and 'me time' – the space to relax or reinvent yourself. So brands and media are called upon to offer 'value for time'.

Great time stress brands include *The Little Book of Calm*, Psion and other personal organisers, 'voluntary simplicity' and media that edit choice and information like the Sunday print and TV news digests.

On a slightly more mythic level; ideas about the new time pressure include *Stressed Eric* the cartoon, and the Guinness 'fast-forward' commercial.

The end of privacy

A widespread trend is taking down the barriers between public and private. This is evident in new exhibitionism, like Jenny, the teenage girl who has her bedroom relayed live by video onto the internet and the autobiographical art of Tracy Emin. More subtle trends include open plan office space, shared changing rooms in clothes stores and the trend to big, clear windows – from trendy restaurants to Norman Foster apartment blocks.

Media ideas that mythologize the death of privacy include hidden camera TV shows (like the Japanese show that follows a naked actor who is locked in a flat and who survives only through magazine competitions via the post!), the film *The Truman Show*, and TV shows such as *Changing Rooms* and *Through the Keyhole* that take us into people's private spaces.

Brands tapping the same new condition include commercially available lie detectors, the truth or dare board game *Scruples*, and the recurring fashion for see-through and revealing clothes.

One publicity stunt in our first IKEA campaign was building 'living rooms', with glass walls which were home to actors for a week in the concourse at Liverpool Street station.

❧ Videophones and other new intimacies

The culture is increasingly 'close to our faces' and I think videophones are a natural medium of communication that will sky-rocket when some info-com companies break ranks and actively promote them. Currently you can get a basic videophone package from Intel at $150.

'In your face' brands mythologizing this closeness include our own original close-up photography for Boots No7 (fingernails piercing peaches, teeth biting into sugary doughnuts etc.), live nude teleconference services in Germany, the 'Patchiclub' photo booths in Japan that merge your face with a famous cartoon character, the recent film *Face Off* and the Gameboy face photo and animation add on.

We increasingly only relate to people close up and face on. Jean Baudrillaird tells a story to illustrate this: in the 1992 Olympics, the tenor singing at the opening ceremony was a distant small figure, so many in the crowd turned to the big screen. Seeing this he turned to look at the screen himself, which put his face in profile. So the crowd turned back to look directly at him. And so on.

❧ The weather

Freak weather conditions and growing predictions of global warming for the next century make this more than the traditional English non-conversation. Weather disaster movies like *Twister* abound.

Brands that have tapped into a new weather fixation include Oakley wrap-around sun-glasses, sunscreen cosmetics, all-weather and all-terrain cars for city dwellers and the ubiquitous fashion themes of survival gear, from hiking boots to snow jackets to diving watches. Isn't there something of a new 'Noah's ark' mentality? Or is it just me being paranoid?

◈ Non-human intelligence

Arthur C. Clark said that 'any truly new technology strikes us as magical'. And a time traveller from the past would probably be most struck by the number of apparently sentient machines around us, from speaking watches to Microsoft's Barney – a cuddly dinosaur toy which interacts with computers and TV. Not to mention all those ghoulishly realistic baby dolls. And not forgetting the on-line psychotherapist that asked questions by computer algorithm ('Tell me more about...') but which most patients swore was real.

These features are becoming integral to technology brands and most digital age prophets say that many currently dumb devices will soon interact with each other. Science fiction has spent a century or so telling us what life will be like when we share the planet with thinking, feeling robots.

The latest brand to mine and mythologize the same territory was the Sky Digital TV launch. The commercials featured a message purportedly from your own television ('Let me show you what I can really do'), which was very intrusive in ad breaks of dumb films. This may be the beginnings of a mythic interactive advertising where brand personalities come to life.

Beyond Painting By Numbers

People adopt these kinds of myths – and the brands that go with them – as ideas to live by. It reminds me of the story a psychoanalyst friend told me of a man who kept saying 'I'm a control freak' as if he was proud of it. On probing, he tied this back into the Volvo commercial where a stunt man says this as a heroic expression of how he lives through such high wire stunts!

There is another possibility beyond 'painting in' these new ways of living. And that is sketching out a possibility from scratch. I have worked on two campaigns in ten years that have moved people in fundamentally new directions. IKEA where we challenged people's taste and genuinely changed the 'décor culture' (and nearly doubled IKEA's sales in the process). And five years earlier the campaign for the milkman, featuring a Mary Poppins-like milkman and his computer animated dancing bottles. This revived a homely family life myth, (halting the decline in milkman customers overnight and making £20 million in extra profits).

Twice in ten years says to me that it is rare but acheivable to fundamentally reshape the way people live. In both cases 90 per cent of the credit must go to the creative people, the myth makers.

My favourite story about this kind of snowplough strategy was Punk.

Punk rock brought in the DIY 'white label' music culture, a rejection of authority, the dirty realism trend in fashion and film and so much else besides. And it was started, the story goes, by two people as a marketing ruse for a single shop. Malcolm McLaren and Vivienne Westwood had a shop called 'Sex' that resold fetish clothing as fashion on the King's Road. The ruse (or 'Great Rock and Roll Swindle') dreamt up by McLaren was the Sex Pistols. They were only intended to be a kind of publicity stunt. And judged against its original aims, punk did make Vivienne Westwood's fashion career!

This kind of path-making creativity is often a happy accident and also often takes great courage and creativity. It is also the preserve of people, like Malcolm McLaren, who have the kind of cultural antennae to not just spot trends but to make them. Not many readers will have the task of reinventing fashion. And reinventing other markets that are less creatively competitive can be as simple as the round teabag of the last section.

From marketing to climating

One thing that I believe holds marketing back from tackling these huge tasks of reinvention is that it doesn't have powerful enough tools. Like movies for example.

When *Educating Rita* was shown applications to the Open University doubled. *Top Gun* had a similar effect on applications to the US military. And it's well known that films and programmes have that sort of effect on tourism – for instance *Ballykissangel* and Ireland.

One big next wave in marketing is likely to be advertiser-funded films and programmes. When this happens we are going to have the most powerful tools of mythologizing life at our disposal. Of course if the result is drossy films and programmes or plonky product placement, not much will have changed. But if we start to see brands being marketed through ideas like the classic *Herbie* films (featuring a VW Beetle) then we could be in for an exciting time.

CREATE TANGIBLE DIFFERENCES IN THE EXPERIENCE

The One-Minute Summary

This rule is about 'experience marketing'. This can involve new media experiences, but it is most applicable to more integral elements of your basic product or service or venue. Because it is about tangibility and trust.

Marketing has been through an 'emperor's new clothes' re-evaluation. The old marketing created wildly different personalities for what were often very similar products and experiences, but now consumers are inclined to believe that if it looks, tastes, smells, feels and sounds the same, then it is pretty much the same. Differences have to be tangible. I call this the 'Doubting Thomas' society.

Brand preference has always been a function of perceived difference. Now marketers have to work much harder to create perceived difference.

Give Me an Example

The beer market. For decades, this was the market that epitomised selling similar bland products through creative positionings and presentation. Since the late 1980s, it has been a market in which tangible differences in the experience are what has counted – limes in the top, Ice beers, Widgets, waiting for the Guinness to settle. 'Give me a (tangible) point (of difference) and I will move the earth'.

Create Tangible Differences in the Experience

In the last chapter, one of the trends listed was the move to a more physical, sensual culture. This chapter explores this new culture in detail. As you'd expect there are quite a variety of implications of this, both for the consumer culture and also for brands.

Sensorama Culture

Sensorama was the title of a report I produced for MTV's 'Word of Relevant Mouth Conference' several years ago. The original Sensorama was a contraption made by Morton Heilig, an early pioneer of virtual reality. The Sensorama offered a realistic motor-bike ride through New York, complete with realistic rumbles, sounds and even smells. The report was subtitled *The New Youth Culture of Intense Experience*. If you're interested you can find an updated copy of it on St. Luke's web site (http://www.stlukes.co.uk).

The central theme of the report was that to get a handle on modern youth culture you needed to recognise the shift from a visual-image-led culture to one where the other four senses took the lead. For example:

- **Sound.** Music obviously – this was at the height of rave culture.
- **Smell.** Scents were ascendant, from CK One to Aveda Chackra.
- **Touch.** From massage to body piercing to comfort clothes.
- **Taste.** Gourmet coffee, exotic foreign cuisines, ice-cream in bed...

There was also a general shift to immersive peak experiences – lurid, visceral films in surround sound cinemas, festivals and live events like funfairs and football, skating, bungee jumping and other physical 'rush' sports – and of course mind and mood altering drugs.

Meanwhile the visual world of fashion had become blunt and subjective, with strong, simple colour themes (acid green and orange), replacing details and styling. The clothes matched a more subjective 'doing your own thing', 'anything goes' ethos, and the key fashion theme was (and still is) comfort.

I've found that following youth culture is quite a good way of spotting emerging trends. Not because they are the adults of the future – that would be too long range, nor because they are in themselves particularly innovative. They are not the instigators, fifteen year-olds do not generally create great art, music etc! However, because they are open-minded, impressionable and early adopters of broad sweeps of social change, they are a kind of 'early warning' system.

New Media: Cause or Effect?

At the time of the Sensorama report, I was very into new media, and very influenced by the writings of Marshall McLuhan. In the report I went as far as to say that new digital media had caused Sensorama – a classic change in sense ratio's as McLuhan would have put it.

Looking back now, I'm not so sure.

The reach of the internet was fairly small at that time, especially in Europe. And particulary among school age (as opposed to college age) kids. So logically Sensorama culture – the heart of which was the Rave scene – could not have been caused by the internet. If you had to pinpoint a single cause it was much more likely to be to do with drugs like Ecstasy, and the music that went with them.

A similar claim was made in Don Tapscott's book about the 'Net Generation'. It described features of youth culture – individuality, non-conformism, taking personal responsibility – which rings true in my experience. BUT, even on the most optimistic of estimates, the people it was talking about have on average never used the internet (as in much less than half of the sample).

Generation insights are supposed to reflect common experiences and values. In the 1950s, most young people did listen to, and were influenced by Rock and Roll music. Admittedly the Electronica scene in the States was too small to account for this shift either. I think we might just have to acknowledge that cause and effect may be too simplistic a model for generation shifts!

I don't believe media *caused* the shift to a more tangible culture of experience. Any more than they *caused* interactivity, as some authors have suggested. New media and music and all sorts of other things are part of a system of change, which also involves moving to more sensual, experiential culture.

I now think the roots of the Sensorama shift lie in the move to a more subjective, personal, intimate society – away from traditions and institutions and authorities. Our red thread of the post-traditional society once again!

Society has become more inward and about the experience of individuals, for instance, we have more 'real' tastes and less 'acquired' ones. We got into fresh juices and organic foods and rich coffees and spicy or juicy cuisine's because they taste good, rather than being what we're supposed to eat. Gourmet foods were once what only the rich were 'supposed to eat'. And which only the rich could afford.

The Doubting Thomas Society

In the New Testament, Doubting Thomas was the disciple who did not believe in the Resurrection until he actually saw Jesus was risen and could put his fingers into the wounds from the cross. He did not believe second-hand reports. He had to see and touch for himself. I think there is a big Doubting Thomas syndrome in our relationship with culture and brands now. This attitude is a scepticism born of lack of trust.

We have learned not to trust authorities. The 1960s and Vietnam was a crisis of trust in the American 'Father Figure' of government. The Risk Society described by sociologist Ulrich Beck is a similar process of consumers learning not to trust the experts, for example the scientists who told us beef was safe, margarine was good for us, etc.

We tend to trust familiar people with whom we have repeated good experiences, for example, pharmacists are the most trusted of all professions. Friends, colleagues and family are who we trust most as sources of information and advice. Of course this has to do with those who have our best interests at heart but also with proximity, or closeness to our real lives.

In markets where trust or lack of it is the issue, contact can be the most powerful answer. Look at the politician who, close to elections, is out kissing babies and shaking hands!

We are adjusting to an unfamiliar, changing world. A world different to the one we were prepared for. Where trust in anything is a rare commodity. In situations of unfamiliarity and low trust we innately trust our senses. Like the toddler who picks everything up and puts it in their mouth. There is something about touching things that makes them real. And something about things that touch us – like music or taste – that has a real anchoring effect.

What does the Experience Culture Mean for Brands?

The fundamental implication of this sensual culture for brands is that *the experience* (not just the image) should be unique in tangible, physical ways. A corollary being that if your product and service is intangible then a powerful way to brand yourself can be by creating tangible experiences.

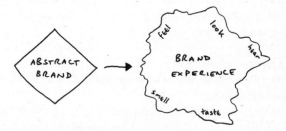

This takes us back to the meaning and purpose of branding. In the 1960s it was conceived of as creating subtle image-based reasons for preference among very similar physical products. Like the boxes of washing powders. Marketing textbooks quoted Fredkin's Paradox as justification. Fredkin's Paradox is that the more similar two objects are, the harder they are to choose between – but the more similar they are, the less it matters. Branding was there to make shopping choices easier!

Contrast this with the detergents market now. The action is in creating physical differences in experience and form of products. We've had liquids, concentrates, balls to put in the tub... Unilever this year gained back some of the ground it had lost after the Persil Power fiasco when it launched detergent tablets. In the last section we looked in detail at the success built on a simple change in product shape – the round teabag.

These product improvements may well bring about marginally better washing but I believe they are mainly part of the Doubting Thomas phenomenon. If it doesn't look, or feel, or taste different, then how different can it be? It's as if marketing has been through a mass Emperor's New Clothes moment. The Emperor's New Clothes syndrome in consumer markets happened around the turn of the 1990s. It was partly a reaction to some of the hollow image marketing excesses of the 1980s. Consumers suddenly pointed at brands which were all image and no substance. And laughed them off.

Ten Examples of Moving to Sensorama Marketing

My own induction to experience marketing largely came through working with alcoholic drinks companies. I'm going to start by going into the beer market in some detail as a case in point. It is one of the best examples I know of the Emperor's New Clothes syndrome.

① The Emperor's New Beer

In the late 1980s the beer market went through a crisis of industry and consumer change.

For most of that decade the beer market was dominated by the advance of bland and indistinguishable lagers. Bland and indistinguishable for two reasons – because lager is served cold, which dulls flavours and because the main brands were weak in alcohol, which accentuates flavours.

The brewery who was my client at that time (Courage) held a blind product tasting among the lager marketing group. Only one member of the department correctly identified their own products. This had not been a big problem in the market-place thus far. Lager was originally drunk as a refreshing cold drink but it had become adopted as a 'session' drink. A group of lads would get together for a session, the main aim of which was to drink a lot of pints. Standard lager, being weak and bland, was almost purpose-designed for these drink-all-you-can contests.

Another reason why indistinguishability was not a problem was the trade structure. Every brewery chain had its own pubs. And every brewery chain had its own lagers. And as long as any pub's brand of lager was acceptable i.e. well known, with popular advertising, young men were happy to drink it.

This set-up led to the heyday of great lager advertising (Carling Black Label, Heineken, Fosters...) It was some of the most popular advertising on British television – judged by many members of the public to be better than most of the programmes. There was a whole theory of beer advertising built up around this status quo. Lager was a sociable choice. The popular ad campaigns stimulated pub chat and conferred 'good bloke' status. It was 'love my ad, love my brand' (because of that brand's badge value).

Then everything changed. From all directions at once.

Firstly the government's MMC (Monopolies and Mergers Commission) report recommended that breweries should not be allowed to also own the pubs. Which meant the parallel distribution of 'our beer in our pubs' was going to come to an end, so the lager brands were likely to have to compete for the market rather than simply achieve comparable acceptance. Secondly the off-trade was growing as a source of business, which meant lots of similar brands competing for each purchase in supermarkets etc. and thirdly, and most importantly as it turned out, product quality and taste became an issue.

New bottled lagers with very different packaging and quite different, distinctive tastes were taking off. Brands like Budweiser, Beck's and Grolsch. Also the ales market – with Boddingtons and John Smiths leading the charge – was gaining ground. By the early 1990s British ales had regained leadership, capturing more than 50 per cent of the market.

In retrospect the monopolies report was not the main issue. It wasn't practicable for pubs to have deliveries from several different suppliers, so pubs still, even if they were independent, tied themselves to one brewer, meaning they would still benefit from discounts and the simple logistics of ordering and delivery. So what was feared – three or so similar brands from different breweries competing on one bar top – never came to pass.

The main issue was consumer-led. A demand for better tastes, more choice and more unique experiences to fit with different moods and occasions and physical needs. People became more flexible about drinking a repertoire rather than having a wholesale allegiance to lager or bitter. The same drinker would want a foodie, comforting pint of Guinness or ale for a quiet winter drink with girlfriend, and then a trendy, portable and not over-filling bottle of premium lager on their way to a club with mates. And of course, by now there were lots of girls drinking beers too, often in bottles, but also in pints.

The social pressure to drink endless pints in a session with the lads (favouring the bland, weak lagers) receded as social lives became more mixed-sex, mobile and open to individualism (rather than herd behaviour and conformism).

All of this is stark evidence of our more inner-directed, less aspirational culture. People stopped drinking things which labelled them. They stopped being boxed into categories like 'lager drinker', and started drinking brands that brought the right experience, mood and atmosphere.

At the time the breweries completely misread this. They took their lead from the MMC problem and drew their inspiration from other consumer goods that often had a 'product usp' (unique selling proposition). They scrapped their popular advertising campaigns and replaced them with campaigns emphasising *intangible* differences in products which everyone could tell were bland and samey. The airwaves were suddenly jammed with lager advertising proclaiming that this lager was 'brewed with Czechoslovakian yeast' or that lager was 'brewed at 4.1 per cent'.

To no avail. The brands that thrived from that day to this were those with real uniqueness: Becks (a unique taste – slightly sulphury), Budweiser (a unique taste – rice brewed and light and clean), Boddingtons (half-way between lager and bitter) and Guinness (smooth, dark and creamy).

The first innovation that I think really understood where drinkers were coming from was 'Ice beer', which had a tangibly different product experience to mythologize upon. Also Alcopops (like Hoopers' Hooch), which were basically a weak vodka and lemonade in a beer bottle. As a package they were really distinctive in what they offered and much more in tune with the non-conformist, easy-going ravey times.

I believe there is a key lesson in this for all marketing people: Don't just say you are different. Be different. Be different in tangible ways that the customer can experience. A good indicator is being outstanding in blind as well as named product tests. Your customers should be able to tell you with their eyes shut.

It could be objected that some products do unique things that aren't discernible in experience – they have invisible differences, and that a lot of services such as insurance are by definition fairly intangible. I believe nonetheless that tangible experience differences are critical in our Doubting Thomas times. A point which some of our other case studies will make.

② Direct but Distant

In many ways First Direct is the perfect bank. The world's first telephone bank, open 24 hours, courteous and efficient and with a clean slate compared with the negative vibes surrounding existing banks.

Everyone has at some time had a run-in with their bank that they have never quite forgiven or forgotten. And because of this, as well as the opening hours, banks are the only high street retail outlet where service is considered a big problem.

First Direct is not only better, it's cheaper than using a high street bank, because it does not have the overhead of branches to run, or the inefficiency of staff who are slack most of the day. But First Direct never really quite took off. In its first ten years it gained only a few per cent of the market, by which time all the main banks had launched their own version. So why did the 'perfect bank' not catch on?

One problem was inertia. People move their bank account slightly less often than they change marriages! It is generally too much hassle to re-organise all those standing orders, etc. plus the fact that banks have always been seen as pretty similar. But the inroads made in other similar financial markets by the likes of Virgin suggest that this can't have been the only problem. And nearly ten times as many people had switched their current accounts to the previous big threat to high street banks – the building societies.

First Direct used to be a client of mine. In research groups, one thing that non-customers always worried about was intangibility. There was something secure about knowing where your branch was – being able to touch it, to stand in it. It was safe as houses. It was real. The insecurity about First Direct was that your money would disappear.

First Direct got over this with existing customers. They had a very solid, tangible design style – in slabs of black, with typewriter-style white type. And the security questions you are asked every time you ring them become a very familiar ritual (right down to the fact that all the staff have Leeds accents). But for those who have never encountered First Direct there is a bit of a void, which may be why their main source of new customers was from recommendations from existing happy customers. Through contact.

Looking back, I think the simple New Marketing trick which we all missed was creating real points of physical contact for people to see and experience. Not bank branches – that would defeat the whole point of being a branch-less bank. But perhaps something like British Telecom's phone boxes and multimedia booths. It would have been great to have bought the Mercury telephone boxes when they were up for sale, and to have added just one button that put customers straight through to First Direct. Or we could have created something for the home. Like an electronic statue that glowed red when accounts became overdrawn and deeper and deeper greens when in credit.

A move very similar to this (down the telephone wire into people's hands) has been announced by Lloyds who are relaunching their phone bank service with its own dedicated mobile phone.

The internet banks would do well to learn from the First Direct experience. Given the psychology of money – broadly speaking we're happiest when it is under the mattress, virtual banking could well hit many of the same snags.

③ Going to Town

A pioneer in creating brand experiences is Nike. The Nike Town stores were created not to sell the product (that would have alienated all the trade customers) but to give people vivid tangible experiences of the Nike brand. The stores were invented as a walk in media – in the tradition of Disney's theme parks which are walk in versions of their films. And Disney has even built a real town in Miami as an expression of its social values.

The theme of experience marketing has become a popular hot topic recently. While there is fairly widespread disillusionment among marketing people with the early performance of some forms of new media, such as the internet, the interest in 'experience media' continues to grow.

④ Ironic Iconic Retailing

Calvin Klein commissioned fine art students to design vending machines for their perfumes; as a tangible expression of their 'innovate don't imitate' campaign.

Tesco's won design awards in 1998 for a new visual merchandising system. Instead of written signs – saying things like 'Cutlery' – they designed larger than life objects – like giant knives and forks – to signpost the different areas of their store. Which makes shopping at Tesco's more fun and tangibly different.

⑤ Pocket Books

Penguin had, I suspect, an unexpected hit on their hands when they published Penguin 60s to commemorate their 60th anniversary – 60 page extracts of famous Penguin samples for 60p.

These were pocket size books and ideal in length for journeys. A fact that Scotrail seized on in an inspired service surprise when they put a free Penguin 60 novel on the pillow of their sleeper beds.

⑥ The Brand as Café

Waddingtons announced recently that it is to open 'Monopoly Cafés'.This is the latest in a series of theme/experience cafés that has given the pub sector a run for its money. From internet cafés and launderette bars to cafés that encourage browsing in retail spaces like book shops.

⑦ Cool Events
Back at Youth Marketing, Evian has built a waterfall installation in a Leeds night-club, Rizzla took a chill-out tent on tour with the festivals and Levi's have launched a custom-fit jeans machine.

An earlier version of the 'first impressions' strategy so superbly executed by Red Bull, was that of Playstation. What they did (which Sega and Nintendo hadn't done) was put the home console into public spaces, so people could get a feel for the actual console experience, not just the games. They also chose much cooler 'arcade' settings like night clubs, creating a more exciting ambient context. And reaching people in a more 'receptive' state!

⑧ Packaging a Nation
The New Labour government commissioned the Powerhouse exhibition to merchandise the best of New Britain's creative industries. It was an exercise in making the idea of Cool Britannia tangible. The first visitors were the heads of state who came over for a European Union conference, which made it a pretty impressively targeted medium, that enhanced Britain's profile, through the resulting global media exposure.

⑨ Art and Whisky
Who says a sales force can't be creative? The 'Adventure' sales team at the then United Distillers (now part of Diageo) did some amazing things to bring brands to life in bars and events. They built a model whisky distillery and bar for Bells at the T in the Park music festival which was a great hit with the punters, including Noel and Liam Gallagher's mum apparently! They built a futuristic wrought iron dog statue as a display for Smirnoff in London's fashionable Dog Bar. And a 'chemistry set' spirits dispensing system for The Medicine Bar.

And all of this was several years before hiring visual artists became fashionable among bars and clubs.

⑩ Your Brand in Other's Hands
There's nothing like a great gin and tonic. And what you got a few years ago in a pub was nothing like a great gin and tonic! No wonder no-one drank it.

Until United Distillers embarked on a very successful UK marketing initiative – the Gordon's Gin 'perfect gin and tonic' campaign. They made this work by providing bars with nice graphics, branded glasses and cocktail stirrers and they trained the bar staff. All this was backed up by cinema advertising educating customers to insist on a great G&T. What they had spotted was that the delivery was letting their brand down – so they focused their marketing on improving this area.

The Experience Economy Comes of Age

I think by now, many marketers have come to realise the importance of tangibility and experienced quality, so it was not a great surprise when an article appeared in a 1998 *Harvard Business Review* entitled *The Experience Economy*. Their argument was that the economy had moved on to a new stage of added value; from products to services to experiences. I think this is consistent with everything this section has been saying.

My one reservation about the HBR piece was the examples it used. They were all of the slightly plastic 'theme park' variety – from theme cafés and parks to malls and casinos themed on ancient Italy. It might be a Europe-America thing. After all the Fashion Café in London went bust. Could it be that America is more open to the 'hyper-real', as Umberto Eco called the America of Disneyland and 3-D reproductions of famous paintings? But the authenticity movement (e.g. gourmet coffee shops and microbrew beers) started there in the States. My guess is that they are wrong – plastic reproducible, mass experiences are not where it's at.

A key thing about valuable experiences is authenticity – something we'll look at in detail in the next section. The kinds of ultimate experience-as-theatre that I think works in this market are the human, behind the scenes, hand-made, backstage variety. In the next section we'll look at some outstanding UK high street examples of this – Oddbins, Pizza Express and Waterstones.

An American example that I do think is truly outstanding is the Ian Schrager hotel chain. These create a unique and memorable experience from the moment you walk in the door, for example at the Royalton in New York where you walk into a narrow space with an incredibly stylish and buzzy cocktail bar and not a reception desk in sight. I think this sort of unique and surprising experience is far more valuable than the fast food chain feel of predictability that haunts some of what is vaunted as experience marketing in venues and retail spaces. But being creative and surprising isn't the exclusive province of the one-off hotelier. What about the on-board head steward picking from one of the twenty service surprises they have at their disposal on a Virgin Atlantic flight? – Today they might hand out ice-cream bars with the movie. Tomorrow it could be popcorn.

Like brands, meaningful service experience is about surprise, exceeded expectations, little thrills and flash gun memories. Which ultimately comes down to people. And getting up close and personal again. One real smile is worth a thousand perfunctory 'have a nice days'.

Does Sensorama mean that all marketing should give up on general communications and focus on specific experiences alone?

Not at all....

Communication and Brand Experiences

There are two ways that creative communications can add to experiences:

① Creating expectations

Building expectations means pointing out things to notice in the experience. Like when a wine buff friend says 'notice the hints of vanilla and oak'. And you do. And you can't wait to buy that wine and spring this insight on another friend.

An example from Volkswagen's advertising that gets fed back by customers (as part of their product experience) is the solid 'clunk' of a VW door closing.

② Conditioning the experience

Conditioning the experience is about adding a creative idea. Like when your wine buff friend produces a bottle with an air of solemnity and tells you they won it in a bet with a Chateau owner on holiday in the Loire last year.

Ideas can weave associations of romance and specialness into an experience. And they will genuinely make the wine taste different than if your host apologised and told you it's a 'cheap plonk'. Every experience comes with a story. There were some great studies in the 1960s on the effects of narcotics. They found that the key factor in how someone felt was what they were *told* they had taken. People were quite capable of getting high on placebo tablets. And people reported the effects of marijuana taken 'blind' to be similar to getting a mild cold. In our experiences, what we think we're getting – what psychologists call the label – is all important.

It's conditioning (rather than just reflecting) experience that a lot of marketing misses. The literal approach taken by many is to show or talk up the experience. In some American ad agencies they pride themselves in 'category leading product shots'. You know the sort of thing – the camera lingers lovingly in close-up over a chocolate bar that is being pulled open. We then cut to the eater's face, rapt with enjoyment as they chew slowly. More fool them. They might just as well show the product being digested!

The better approach, seen in roughly one food, or holiday, or airline, or car ad in a hundred, is to create an entrancing imaginative idea – like the Loire chateau story – that literally transforms the experience that we have. That was the secret to the great UK Volkswagen ads of the mid 1980s. They created a driver fantasy-experience around the car.

Remember the famous 1985 commercial where a woman storms out of a mews house throwing away expensive gifts from her sugar daddy. She gets in her *Golf* to drive away to a life of independence. And just for a moment she pauses, smiles and pats the steering wheel affectionately. The ad ends with the slogan 'If only everything in life was as reliable as a Volkswagen'.

When I worked on the VW account we had an unwritten rule that the car never be shown for more than three seconds. The *Golf* didn't look that different from every other hatchback, but it felt like it was in a different league. Part of this was the inherent qualities of the product, but these were drawn out and enhanced by conditioning.

Conditioning was what St. Luke's did with our Boots No7 advertising when we zoomed in (up close and personal) to moods and thoughts prompted by different types of products, with no beautiful model to show people what they'd look like with this mascara or lipstick.

Conditioning is why Ice beer took off. It did have a different experience, (cleaner, lighter tasting). But it was the Ice idea that created rich associations around this experience. Dry beer had a very similar taste profile through a different process. But it didn't have this feel. And it didn't sell.

To Summarise

What have we covered under this rule?

- We live in Sensorama – an experience economy – where Doubting Thomas consumers demand tangible differences. These can be part of your media or retail strategy, like the perfume vending machines, or they can be built around a product experience. By adding an idea.
- A lot of the examples have been in areas where experiences were formerly very poor and very undifferentiated – like drinks and retailers. I think what this suggests is that we have a generally heightened set of sense-expectations; as part of a general shift to valuing quality of life. It's a general shift from style to substance.
- It's such a simple rule. But in a world where everyone copies each other, it takes a lot to keep your experience different. And in our novelty culture it takes even more effort to keep your experience fresh and surprising. I was delighted to see recently that Guinness – one of my favourite experience brands – had launched an 'extra cool' version. That's the way to do it.

CULTIVATE AUTHENTICITY

The One-Minute Summary

New Marketing is about a real engagement with people, rather than a falsified and plastic projection of ideals. To paraphrase the *Bible* 'we do not worship false goods'. Authenticity is the benchmark against which all brands are now judged.

The old marketing drew its validity from the traditions and conventions it quoted. It was like the Old Testament Pharisees quoting scripture. Which may be why it was so derivative creatively. The formula for advertising in old marketing was to steal a creative film clip or character.

New Marketing needs to have its own intrinsic authenticity. Strong, new and relevant ideas have this quality. And there are new creative conventions of more authentic marketing too – like real life scenarios, hand-writing, truly personal and idiosyncratic service.

The standard for marketing now is quite a Taoist one. For it to truly succeed it must not be seen as "marketing". But rather as something compelling, and close to, and natural within everyday life.

Give Me An Example

MTV Unplugged created a more authentic connection between the audience and performers and their music, and hence differentiated MTV from all those new music television stations that just played pop promo's.

Cultivate Authenticity

The modern cultural hunger for ideas to live by, gives brands in today's society a new relevance. It also imposes a burden on brands to be sufficient to this task. The burden for brands in this new situation is authenticity.

The old kind of branding was all about attaching brands to authentic traditions of aspiration. The new brands have to have their own innate authenticity, which I have portrayed in this diagram as a kind of buoyancy.

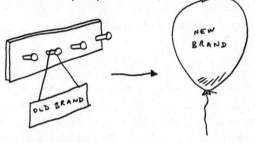

Beyond Crass Marketing

Critics talk about the new global media culture as a bland and shallow uprooting of a more natural way of life. About marketing creating a desire for things we don't need. New Marketing is partly an answer to this common complaint – that marketing is creating a crass and commercialised society.

These complaints are about the perceived inauthenticity of marketing relative to the traditions which it is seen as displacing. The French 'Cultural Chernobyl' outcry about Euro Disney was against the planting of a 'false' Disney theme park in French soil. It was seen as a symbol of the Americanisation of France and the loss of local traditions.

I agree that some marketing is crass and demeaning to the human spirit, but the problem is that portion of marketing which is shallow, unimaginative and repetitive. In many of the examples in this book marketing has added to people's lives, giving them inspiration, validating choices which tradition does not provide for, or simply making the world a more charming place to live. The acid test for marketing now is not whether it adds value to products by giving them a more appealing image, but whether it adds value to the lives of the people it is aimed at.

I don't think any marketing is of itself bad. Nor do I believe that the past ages with all their oppressions were better than the society we have now. Alarmist books talk about television corroding the public's minds, about 'affluenza' and addiction to spending. These are arguably nice problems to have when compared with breaking the backs and spirits of workers with filthy hard labour and an unrelieved grey, gruel-like existence in a society held together by cruel force and manipulative superstitions.

Many of the critics of crass marketing are snobs. Their creative reference point is high culture. Their real agenda is elitism. They are advocating tastes which run counter to popular culture.

Why Brands are Getting More Authentic

Brands are taking on the role of traditions.

However they are surrogates and this creates some defining differences. They do not have the weight of history – of 'having been tried on for a few generations' before they were accepted. Their role is to light the new path ahead. Brands as ideas are future facing – something to grow into. This makes them more ephemeral – they are cultural experiments and many experiments fail. It is the confident brands that do best – brands that create their own authenticity. Confidence compensates for their provisional nature.

The need for brands to compensate – to be super-authentic – has had an interesting net effect, which I think will silence the critics in time. Earlier forms of marketing were slick and image-led. Now there is a greater value in brands which are closer to natural, human everyday life.

New Age brands like The Body Shop have this character – they are more organic. I'd also cite brands like Muji and IKEA which are 'no brand' brands and substitute big savings for the old image premium. Also brands like BT which are part of the general downshifting to authentic human values and behaviours.

There are lots of examples of marketing successes due to bringing more authenticity to bear. This often means re-writing the rules of your market and to grasp this point, we are going to take a detour into what 'authenticity' means.

What is Authenticity?

Authentic is one of those words that, while we know it when we see it in practise, is quite hard to pin down in theory.

It can mean but does not necessarily mean:

- having a long history or heritage
- being associated with some local regional or national provenance
- more natural or human, and less technological
- something which is a one-off – like the Mona Lisa – but can also be a property of things that are in very wide circulation – like Coca-Cola.

Authenticity and traditions

Traditions are ideas that come to us from others – from history, from village elders etc. That is what makes them authentic. In coming to us through other people, traditions are opaque to any full understanding. Often they are a bit arbitrary and they do not yield to us as individuals. A good illustration of this is the way that we inherit traditional ideas.

Many of our traditions were passed on to us by our parents. We were born into families where things were done in a certain way, which we had to learn. These ways were largely imposed upon us and were not often explained. If challenged, parents would answer *'because I say so'*. Or if they were explained, they would be rationalised – certain foods were 'good for you' etc. rather than really explained in all their historical context. After all they were traditions for, and opaque to, our parents too.

There's a great story about how these ways of doing things become set in stone, which I've borrowed from a sociology book (*The Social Construction of Reality* by Berger and Luckman). It goes like this:

Shipwrecks and Sushi Sandwiches

Two people are shipwrecked on a desert island. One is an English man. The other is a Japanese woman.

At first they don't have any language in common. But they gradually develop a shared language which is a pidgin version of each.

Similarly they develop ways of cooking, dressing, hunting etc. that contain elements of each's past tradition but that also suit the island they find themselves on.

Their lives are full of discoveries, compromises and inventions.

Unsurprisingly, given their situation, they end up having a lot of children.

And as the family are never 'rescued', these children carry on their way of living on the island, passing on the new traditions to their children.

The point of this Island story is the contrast between how the founding couple thinks about their way of life, and how their descendants think about it. For the founding couple it is all made up. They might invent a dish like 'sushi sandwich' made from raw fish covered in coconut. But they'd have loads of other ideas to draw on and invent together if ingredients were scarce. For the descendants however, no matter how many stories from the outside were passed on, they would only ever have lived the island tradition. Things would be done the way they were done. They wouldn't have the sense that it was all made up, they would feel that was the proper way to do them. In sociology this process is called institutionalisation.

The key point the story makes is about authenticity. The authentic traditions which aren't challenged are those that come from other people. The founders would live a playful, inventive, flexible lifestyle. The descendants would live by the rules which they founded much more rigidly. Because the ideas were not theirs to adapt as freely. They would be like a code to which the original key had been lost, which could never be fully deciphered. In French psychoanalysis they call this realm of other people's rule The Other *(L'Autre)*. Ideas strike us as authentic when they come from this Other and do not yield to our own understanding and will.

My wife is Korean Japanese and I am currently learning Japanese etiquette by watching and copying how things are done. I may be picking up habits that are particular to one family and set of friends, but I am absorbing it as *the* way – from the mysterious Other.

Brands, Traditions and Authenticity

All of this has a bearing on creating authentic-seeming brands. In the past brands connected with the real traditions that people followed. For instance, many household brands connected with the unquestioned role of the housewife and mother. Persil was 'mothers care for clothes'. Now we live in a time when many traditions and sources of authority have receded as the guiding force in our lives. When we are making it up as we go along. And when new creative ideas that fit our current situation are welcomed. Like career woman.

For these new ideas to be accepted as valid they need a certain authority and authenticity. They need to come to us through other people. This mainly means the media and the people around us – our milieu. These vital new carriers of culture are covered in the next rule, Create Consensus.

Why do they need to have the force of authenticity? Well, because we need to believe in them. A lot of which is in turn to do with the reassurance that we won't look mad. Man is still a social animal. And culture is still our main guide to what 'goes' for our fellow human beings. If we are to switch from eating with knife and fork to eating with our fingers then we need to know that that is how most people eat Peking Duck!

I remember a woman in one of my research groups for IKEA saying all of this very eloquently. The group was in an IKEA manager's house, as we wanted to see how people react to IKEA décor *in situ* and she was staring at a rather creative arrangement of twigs and red apples in a modern vase:

> 'See that. Now that looks great. If I saw that in a magazine I'd think "That looks great". And I might well even copy it. But it's not something I'd ever come up with on my own. I might just as well put on my wedding dress, tuck it in my knickers, put a bowl of fruit on my head and run down my road singing.'

That's the theory – lets look at it in practise in a real marketing situation.

The Beer Market Revisited; Authenticity Evolving

In the beginning the beer market was local. There were genuinely traditional beers and equivalents (like scrumpy in the West Country), which were what working people drank in that community. Yorkshire ale was for Yorkshiremen. These brands came to people through their fathers and elder brothers.

The beer market lacked strong national brands until lager brands arrived on the scene in the late 1970s and early 1980s. The brands which thrived in this second stage were those presented as 'how they do things' somewhere credible and foreign:

- Carlsberg, Becks, Stella Artois etc. came from places known for brewing (the way that France is known for wine).
- Fosters, Budweiser, Guinness etc. came from places known as 'cultures that love their beer'.

In either case they were brands that had authentic reasons why they must be good, due to the brand's foreign country of origin. With this reassurance of authenticity, these lager brands offered a more modern identity to the drinkers. Not simply taking up their place in their fathers' seat in the pub, these drinkers would enter a dynamic world of change, where young men were allowed to be brash and dismissive of traditions. These lager lads were the original 'Men Behaving Badly'.

The next wave of beers into the market were the packaged premium lagers. The key brands offered new authenticities:

- Sol and Grolsch were physically unusual – manifestly part of someone else's traditions, in the same way as different countries have subtly different types of houses, with different shaped roofs.
- Becks and Budweiser continued the country of origin trend, but using bottle designs that reinforced their 'jeans like' earthy authenticity.

These packaged lagers gave men fashion cues and linked with the so-called new man and also male grooming. A bottled beer was a statement or badge – it was 'wearing a label'. The bottled lagers were, along with fashion labels, the embodiment of the designer 1980s.

Then in the 1990s some of the local British beers went national and established themselves in a backlash to designer lagers. Like Boddingtons (The Cream of Manchester), John Smiths and Tetley's. These brands came back with the same cultural logic as football coming back. They re-established some of the male traditional culture, in a reaction to the widespread feeling of loss of power relative to women. It was the time of the New Lad. As represented for instance by Jack Dee in the ads for John Smiths. New Lad was not 'Lad' though – it was more of a retro masculinity.

Then a thunderbolt struck the beer market in the form of a new drink called Hooper's Hooch. It came in a beer bottle, but actually contained something more like a weak vodka and lemonade. And it appealed to the "rave" generation. I believe that the very key thing that Hooper's Hooch had which virtually no new brands achieve is a sense that this wasn't just made up. It is opaque – The brand not the drink. Why that name, that taste? The only thing that grounded it was that it came in a beer bottle, which is a key thing about authenticity too – something old and something new combined.

I think Hooper's Hooch is a model for developing authentic new brands. It launched a completely new category (alcopops). A category that was so rapidly successful that steps were taken to curb its appeal to the young. There are two movements at play in this story of a rapidly evolving market:

① each successive entrant brought a new authenticity to bear;

② each new entrant was more relevant to the prevailing culture.

These two are intertwined. Each on its own is necessary but not sufficient. Relevant launches could look 'made up'. And the most authentic product in the world could just look dated. These lessons are even clearer when we look at a couple of examples of launches in the beer market that failed largely on the grounds of authenticity (just two out of the hundreds of failures – these were better than most, which were just bland me-one-hundred-and-two's!):

- Fontainbleu: lager for women, with a light taste and more refined design qualities (champagne cork).
- Miller Lite: lighter to drink and in values – the new man beer

The problem with these brands was, in my view, that they were too strategic. You can see right through them. You can see they are marketing, which makes them made up and inauthentic. In fact Miller Lite *was* real – a successful brand in the USA – but the launch didn't mention this.

The latest hot properties in the Beer market are continuing to come from somewhere original and authentic. Like Ice beers (an authentically different way of making it), Microbreweries (authentically more handmade) and new 'undiscovered' beer provenance's like Japan and Belgium.

Another route to authenticity in many markets (it hasn't happened in beer yet but it will!) is the Rule 1 idea: get up close and personal. This takes the form of realism – as in dirty realism in fashion and film making. Like the popular soap documentaries and like Bridget Jones' Diary compared with most novels for young women. In beer could this mean a home brew revival?

Brand Names and Authenticity

Hooper's Hooch was a great name. Fontainbleu was a bad one. As a rule of thumb it is a very bad idea to have a name that means something nowadays. This instantly says 'made up'. Which means inauthentic. You can see Fountainbleu coming a mile off! There are exceptions, but they have survived their name. The best you can do is choose a name which will resonate with your brand. Like 'Apple' (natural computing).

A good example of naming strategically was Inca Cola – a success story from the soft drinks market in Peru. As a competitor to Coca-Cola it draws on nationalism and the low level anti-American/capitalist mood of the country (whose extreme wing was the Shining Path guerrilla's!) Inca Cola's authenticity comes from rediscovering and valuing a past heritage as an anchor in a changing world. In the UK we had Margaret Thatcher, Merchant Ivory and Laura Ashley. Peru had Inca revivals in folk music etc. Inca Cola also has a local flavour – and so it goes very well with the spicy food of the region. In retrospect it was obvious why it would be a winner.

Developing a Brand's Authenticity: MTV Unplugged.

So far we have looked at authenticity as something almost genetic –
Markets being over-run by fitter, i.e. more authentic, brands. What if
you are trying to defend a market leader position, rather than being the
new kid on the block?

MTV is a great case in point.

MTV in the early days was very authentic in contrast to 'establishment
TV' which gave little airplay to pop music and youth. It was the only
music television in most of its markets and it pioneered the music video
– from performance promo to something of an art form.

But five to ten years ago the MTV brand was in trouble. In most of
its markets it now faced competition from other music TV stations, so
the music videos it played were generic and gave no reason for the viewer to prefer MTV. And the *local* competitors were often local; featuring
local presenters, the local language and local music tastes – making
them seem more authentic. MTV had become a victim of its success. In
appealing so broadly to youth, it felt like the establishment. Conversely
they had to appeal to such a broad audience that it was in danger of
being the lowest common denominator. MTV did a number of things
which seem to have tackled this problem of becoming a commodity.

The first was pioneering ideas for how to brand a television
channel, through the development of the MTV identity. Using those 'inter-
stitials (spaces between programmes) more creatively than anyone has
before, or probably since. One of my favourite strands in this identity was
the space they gave to issues. Surveys of young people across the world
show that one thing that unites them is their idealism (the other two
things that unite youth being music and sport). Their major concerns
included the environment, AIDS and racism and MTV made short awareness films about these issues and dotted them through the station. In doing
so they gave the station a voice and a view. Throughout all their identity
work, MTV created a more hand-made and closer to youth feel by using
young and experimental directors. This is an example of marketing being
more authentic and at the same time genuinely adding to the culture –
through airing issues and supporting new talent.

The next attempt to tackle the generic problem took the station two
steps back. MTV lifestyle programmes. 'Music videos are generic', their
argument went. 'The true value of MTV over other stations that also
play music is that we have a greater connection with youth culture. So
we will create more programmes that are for/about youth, without the
music focus.' The result was a series of youth lifestyle programmes
including dating shows and travelogues.

I often think that the best marketing comes from a very blunt kind of common sense. This was a good example of sophisticated planning arriving elegantly at the wrong answer. MTV is *MUSIC* television. Anything which went away from music into general lifestyle would make it less authentic and as more and more bland lifestyle shows were produced, MTV became more and more like other television.

What MTV did next was probably a creative fluke. Nothing wrong with that – it worked wonders, and has become a template for a certain type of marketing manoeuvre in this kind of situation. They created 'Unplugged'.

Unplugged is the music show where famous stars perform live without the amplification, high production values and huge audiences that usually create distance. And 'famous' means really famous like Nirvana (which at the time was the biggest rock band in America) who played simple acoustic sets to a small studio audience. Unplugged was a great success.

Firstly it re-established MTV as bringing a more exciting and original form of music than other media and secondly the stars underlined the stature of MTV. Only MTV could have got these people to do this. Which given the relationship fans have with these stars is like going from producing souvenirs to producing a fanzine – being 'one of us'. Thirdly, a crucial element – as covered in a later rule on participation – was that the Unplugged albums were a successful product in their own right. As Virgin have shown, the best forms of marketing are so valuable people pay for them, i.e. another business. But most importantly Unplugged was the most authentic music television.

There are a number of reasons why it was more authentic. It was partly because:

- it was so original and unexpected
- it took people 'backstage'; it was more intimate
- it was more basic and hand-made
- it is truer to musicians, lives – rehearsals, demo's etc.
- it used traditional ways of playing music.

Unplugged re-established MTV's claim as the authentic music television station.

Radio 1 Gets Real

Here's another case of authenticity to the rescue. It's the story of another music medium – BBC Radio 1 – one of St. Luke's early successes. Five years ago Radio 1 was officially naff. It was characterised by cheesy ageing DJs, as satirised by comedian Harry Enfield in the creation of two 'poptabulous' ageing transatlantic DJ bores called Smashey and Nicey.

The new controller, Matthew Bannister set out to change all of this. Firstly he changed the DJ line-up, moving out the old timers and bringing in genuinely credible talent. Like the dance music DJs such as Pete Tong and Judge Jules who were DJ superstars on the club scene. And by bringing in a 'new music first' policy. Matthew Bannister is one of the people who is credited with creating Britpop. 'New music first', meant that the new indie sound got loads of airplay on Britain's biggest radio station, when the talent – like Oasis – was small and unlikely otherwise to break through. And it was obviously to Radio One's benefit that 'you heard Oasis here first'.

This was the new Radio 1 when we were briefed. But the image was so bad that it was still losing a million listeners a year to the new competitors. Lots of people still listened to Radio 1, but it wasn't something you admitted to.

The solution we came up with was simple marketing common sense. We would short-circuit criticism by projecting the reality of the station. We argued that anything which promoted a cool image would backfire, but the new reality was genuinely cool without trying. So we made documentary glimpses behind the scenes of Radio 1: cinema films and TV trails showing the DJs at work, posters catching some of the back-chat and banter. This approach worked really well for Radio 1 because it established authenticity very directly.

However, lest we take all the credit, one other thing happened soon after our marketing campaign and that was the arrival of a DJ called Chris Evans – post-modern comic, prankster, shock jock and a hero of today's youth. This is the man who for a week told everyone listening to tune out of the station. And encouraged them to do so by playing the same boring record again and again (his plan was to get the listenership down to one hundred, at which point he was to have them around for a party!). This is the man who recently announced on his show at his own station that he'd 'decided to be gay for a year'. Chris Evans was a big dollop of authenticity for the station in a different way than just getting back to basics – he is authentic because he runs against the grain.

Transgression and Authenticity

New ideas naturally arise among the young in traditional societies as a rebellion against the old ways. Teenage itself was defined by this kind of rebellion and authenticity in teenage markets since has been largely defined by transgressing – breaking taboos and adult rules. That it is a big part of the appeal of drugs – the more they are the subject of a tabloid moral panic the more appealing they become.

In the music business nothing succeeds like getting banned. Making a video which is banned from terrestrial TV, like George Michael's kinky video for the *Fast Love* song, is a short cut to success. He then went one better by getting caught cottaging by an undercover policeman. In the following weeks his single and album flew to the top of charts across the world. As George said in a subsequent interview, if he had been smart and brave enough, he would have contrived to get caught in this way years ago. It was the best marketing ploy for his records ever.

I've drawn quite heavily on music examples because authenticity is such an accentuated necessity there so the examples are more stark. I think all consumer culture is headed the same way – as I said earlier the great thing about studying youth markets is that they show emerging trends.

Generally, going against the grain is the authentic way to establish something new. Too many marketing launches try too hard to please so they play by the rules, whereas things that break the rules – like calling a margarine 'I can't believe it's not butter!' – are instantly more authentic.

The Underdog Strategy

The David and Goliath strategy is another way of going against the grain. 'Against the Establishment' automatically says 'on the side of the people'. Richard Branson is a great proponent of the David and Goliath strategy to win people over, take for example the BA dirty tricks campaign. Virgin generally breaks more than its quota of market and marketing rules. The thing Virgin has to watch out for the most is becoming too much part of the establishment to stay a rebel.

To Summarise

I think everyone in marketing will realise that customers are more demanding and 'literate' these days. One of the ways in which they are more demanding is of things that feel authentic, and not synthetic or 'made up'. There are many ways to tackle the same issue. However you do it, the rule is the same – be one step more authentic than what's gone before.

RULE 7

WORK THROUGH CONSENSUS

The One-Minute Summary

This rule extends the idea of brands coming to us through other people. Surveys show that people are more likely to trust ideas that come to them through their immediate circle of friends, family and colleagues, and are quite likely to trust the news and free-standing media but unlikely to trust and follow advertising and manufacturers.

What the old marketing did was try to influence audiences directly. Sell to them. And 'as advertised on TV' was proven in this bygone age to make a product 70 per cent more valued!

New Marketing works in more mysterious ways. It is about launching ideas into general circulation. It is the domino effect of word of mouth and good PR that surrounds marketing activities which makes them work. In other words it is about enlisting advocates. A bit like a lawyer, who has to give a jury the arguments to persuade themselves. And a lot like a political spin doctor who does this kind of advocacy work out in the public media.

Give Me an Example

The most successful phase of the Government HEA/AIDS campaign, to persuade young people to practise safe sex, was a series of very human and funny cinema commercials designed to break the ice and get new couples talking about condoms.

Work Through Consensus

The main idea of this chapter is that 'selling' is very much less effective than getting recommendations and ideas into circulation. Things that succeed in our times spread from person to person like a cultural virus, not through 'thought rays' beamed from direct marketing companies.

Who We Trust

It is a well known finding of a number of surveys over recent years that people are less and less inclined to trust institutions – like the medical profession in general – but are increasingly inclined to trust people they have contact with – like their doctor and especially, for some reason, their pharmacist. In surveys in the UK and US, pharmacists emerge as the people we trust most. This is partly the Doubting Thomas society where we only trust through direct experience and encounters with people, not abstract ideas. There is no doubt that we also increasingly place our trust in our chosen circle of people close to us, as this survey data shows. A survey of sources of information ranked how much people say, 'I generally agree with them'.

Source of information	Percentage of people who agree with that source
Husband/Wife/Partner	90
Friends	82
Work Colleagues	69
TV News	50
Retailers	27
Manufacturers	27
Government	14
Adverts	14

(Source: Henley Centre, Planning for Social Change)

The reader will note that the best way to get trusted information to people is through other people and the worst way is through adverts (although ads do have other uses!). This has completely changed the way I think about the way that advertising and other marketing works.

It is usually thought of as having a direct effect on individual members of a target audience – like a missile. I see it more as getting ideas into circulation – like launching a satellite into orbit. So that people's close advisers and the media can work on them.

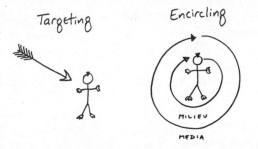

How can you build a brand around something as informal and outside your control as word of mouth?

Planning to Get Talked About

This is something that is difficult for the control culture of marketing to take in. You can control what you say, but you cannot control what people say about what you say. Nonetheless it is possible to plan communications relying on word of mouth, as later examples will show. And one great thing about word of mouth is that it is free.

A simple place to start is to ask what kind of marketing gets people talking? Wonderbra achieved very high levels of media coverage with 'Hello Boys', the headline from a poster with an 'up-front' photograph of Eva Herzegova, wearing only a Wonderbra and an attitude. That PR must have been a factor in getting the Wonderbra itself talked about. It was particularly apt in this case to create a flutter of media interest which would leave buyers of the Wonderbra feeling that it would get them noticed, like the posters. Wonderbra got all of this going without a heavy national coverage of poster sites, which would have cost millions. They originally bought only a few sites in places that would get noticed and written about.

The Fall of Authority

In the mass marketing heyday, we still trusted authorities and institutions like the church, banks, the police, scientists and experts.

Confidence in these has been falling steadily over the last thirty years. Some say it was the Vietnam War that first taught us not to trust authority figures but I suspect it was a whole series of these kinds of public test cases, for example the recent BSE crisis similarly taught us not to trust health advisors.

For all its supposed ills, we may in the future look on television as a revolutionary force, liberating the masses from authority. Far from creating a world where everyone believes in Father Christmas, it has created a world where people are aware of all the alternative traditions and also aware of the mass marketing event that modern Christmas is. And of course it deals with bigger issues too.

The Domino Effect and New Labour's Landslide

The people we do trust are those in our immediate circle of contact and experience. An analysis by the Henley Centre showed that New Labour's victory in the last election could be accounted for by existing supporters convincing their floating voter friends. Labour supporters told everyone they knew to vote Labour, whereas Tory voters were much less likely to have advocated their party.

Readers in the UK must have seen this in action. I certainly did. Tory supporters presumably felt as strongly about their party winning, but the climate created by the media would have made them feel much less confident about recommending them in public. It was simply not a time when Tory voters felt like standing and being counted.

This is why political campaigners put so much emphasis on controlling the agenda. The media tend to focus on certain issues on the principle that people can only take in about three new things in half an hour, so the TV news doesn't want to be too broad-ranging! Rather than examine each party's manifesto in detail, the media tend to follow an agenda. The previous election was wrested away from Labour because the Tories successfully created an agenda around what might happen to the economy.

They used media in a very similar way to the way Wonderbra did, with sparing use of high impact sites, designed to be reproduced in the media. The most successful was their first poster 'Labour's tax bombshell' showing a big old fashioned bomb with '£1,000 on tax' written on it. The pollsters conclusion on that previous election result was that while people in their hearts felt Labour was right, a lot of them voted with their wallets.

Labour controlled the agenda from start to finish at the next election. There were no great talking points out there for the Tory supporters to seize upon, but plenty in 'New Britain' and hardy perennials like schools and hospitals. Not to mention the anti-sleaze campaign and the number of Tory politicians like Neil Hamilton who had brought the party into disrepute and into pub conversations.

Brands in Different Media Traditions

Brand as a word of mouth idea – perhaps a sound bite or an event that gets relayed – is from a different tradition of human communication than the classic TV-advertised brands. There are three archetypal media through which human beings communicate things to each other:

- conversation
- displays
- writing

This is a very useful way of categorising the history and current developments in media, as the book called *Mediamorphosis* by Roger Fidler shows.

If you think about TV, it is largely a display medium, similar to the original displays like cave drawings. It is largely visual and has a passive audience who come to it, whereas the internet is a much more living and conversational medium – especially when it involves e-mail and chatrooms. It seems to me that the majority of ideas about branding are in the middle realm of displaying – image, metaphor, one message for many etc. This goes deep into the heart of marketing.

On a more subtle level the concepts of marketing are presented and conceptualised in the visual register. Positioning is something we only do in the visual sense, other senses are about intensity not geometry. New Marketing is part of the other two realms – of written reports in the news, – and of personal conversations.

What marketing needs to find is ways to fuel word-of-mouth recommendations as richly, humanly and evocatively as display advertising fuelled metaphorical added values. One of my clients calls this finding 'The Killer Applications for Marketing of New Media'. I think there is also still potential in using television advertising (which still reaches more people more powerfully than any-thing else) in new ways, rather than literally using the new media.

A Prototype for Viral Marketing

An idea we worked on recently for a pitch, was just such an exam-ple of using TV as the medium which would 'launch a thousand conversations'. The client in question was launching a digital TV service and our strategy was getting digital TV to people, through conversations with other people.

The idea was to show someone explaining digital TV by using everyday objects. For instance, in one script a butcher picked up a string of sausages to explain that digital signals come down your aerial. This idea tackled worries that the Middle England could have about new-fangled digital TV. These people generally don't like change and this wasn't any old change. It was the television, the single thing that fills our waking non-working hours, the corner-stone of the modern home. If TV changed, what was sacred?

Our 'everyday life' approach set out to diffuse this. It would put the digital set top box in the context of everyday life – of sausages and lawnmowers and aerobics classes. It would tackle the authenticity question because it was being down to earth and catchy, and coming through other people. But an approach that was naturalistic, down to earth and altogether no fuss, would run the danger of lowering the profile of the launch. The reason people usually go in for big budgets and razzmatazz when launching some-thing is that they want to be noticed. Rather than going for the usual fireworks display (message to middle England; this is an assault on our culture) we designed something that would work in a more subtle way. The device of using everyday objects stood a good chance of catching on as part of everyday banter. Imagine the kids at the breakfast table saying, 'So mum, this cereal packet is the TV set...' It was also very funny, which would have helped. This was TV after all, our light relief medium, not brain surgery.

After all that – and after the client had chosen us over several other agencies – they then decided that they didn't have the budget. C'est la guerre!

Getting Them Talking

The AIDS cinema commercials from the HEA (Health Education Authority) a few years back had a similarly self conscious strategy of creating consensus.

They were conceived to act as an ice-breaker for conversations among newly dating couples. Couples who would otherwise be too embarrassed to raise the subject. In one ad, an eighty-year-old man talks about his trusty pig-skin sheath which he'd nick-named Geronimo. The commercials were filmed with glorious naturalism. It was a very accomplished approach to starting an authentic conversation out there in the real world.

I suspect that there are killer applications out there in the realm of conversational media. BT's 'Friends and Family' promotion (which I'm sure each participant explains to their mum, who then signs up) is tending in that direction. This is surely where e-mail must come into its own? If someone can work out a marketing equivalent of chain letters, they could be the next Bill Gates!

Getting Them Selling

One company that has experienced phenomenal growth through getting to people through friends and contacts is Nu Skin. Nu Skin is a network marketing company selling skin care products and vitamins. They have no retail outlets or distribution facility but instead work through a network of sales people who sell directly to their own network of contacts.

This network of little sales operations adds up to a global operation of over $1 billion dollars. It has just taken off in Japan and while it has none of the traditional marketing presence of billboards and TV commercials, people out there talk about it. It is a word of mouth business. Nu Skin have experimented with internet e-business models, but I believe most of their multi-level marketing is still face to face.

Getting Them Searching

Marketing on the internet is much bigger in the States (where two-thirds of current internet users live) than in Europe. A typical big player is a New York internet agency called Yoyodyne. They claim to be the biggest receiver of e-mails on the net. How do they get such full post bags?

They pay people to take part. Not en masse but through amazing big jackpot incentives. When they launched a new web browser (for Yahoo!), their promotion was a treasure hunt through web sites, using the browser. People got to test drive the service at the same time as looking for clues. Another scheme of theirs involved offering to pay the taxes of people who took part in a detailed learning quiz about high rate taxes, for a tax accountancy product requiring high levels of knowledge to appreciate its finer points.

My guess is that there are ways other than bribes to get people to interact with knowledge and pass it on. The Tory 'Tax Bombshell' poster did not necessarily reflect anything that the Labour party would do, but it was a great scare. Underhand, but effective.

One thing that would be interesting to explore would be using jokes as a medium to convey ideas and knowledge or, similarly, juicy rumours and gossip. In that way people would be 'paid' in other, more authentic ways than jackpots and incentives. Having said that, gambling and big prizes are one of the hot themes of the moment and Yoyodyne's approach is to old-fashioned junk mail, what the National Lottery is to Littlewoods' football pools.

Consensus and Customs

Another way of creating consensus is to work through the medium of shared rules. In our post-traditional time we feel like we've lost the instructions to life. As a result 'the rules' is a vibrant area in diverse media – self-help books, political correctness, packaging instructions and so on.

The international best seller *The Rules* (temptingly subtitled: Time-tested secrets for capturing the heart of Mr Right) contains valuable rules of behaviour in the historically new situation of being a single and slightly desperate girl in the great Metropolis! Advice like:

Don't call him and rarely return his calls.
Don't accept a Saturday night date after Wednesday.
Let him take the lead.

This type of creative idea works through consensus. If you found a book like this in the attic from the 1950s with exactly the same copy it would have a completely different impact. The most important element of *The Rules* is the flash on the front saying it is a best-seller. Saying, in effect, that these are the rules that a lot of people follow. Similarly *The Rules* is always popping up in television shows like *Ally McBeal* furthering the impression that there are a lot of people out there following these rules (which apparently there are).

Other self-help hits of recent years include, the *Celestine Prophesies* (ten new commandments), the *Code* (of American chauvinism), *Men are from Mars, Women are from Venus* (do's and don'ts in relationships for men and women). All of them are highly prescriptive about what you should do. And all of them have gathered momentum as they have become famously widely read and discussed. We meet the rules, like all good traditions, through other people.

A movement that was more about what you shouldn't do was the political correctness (PC) drive, starting on American campuses. Political correctness in its original form was do's and don'ts – and mainly 'don't do this'. Campuses would literally print leaflets advising men of what did and did not constitute acceptable behaviour on dates, and high profile law suits have taken this same code into offices. It's hampered by the same problems perhaps as any very rigid code, but thirty years of gentle persuasion had left women still the target of male chauvinist taunts and advances.

In the UK, PC has not been so extreme, and has mostly been about what you say, more than what you do. There is a kind of very carefully chosen wording that characterises membership of what here is more of a PC sub-culture. 'Differently-abled' programmes are careful not only in their description of their issue but also use words like notified, instead of told.

Recipes for Lifestyle

A crude but effective example of this comes from *The Observer* newspaper. They have a very successful strand within their lifestyle listings to edit choice and also – like Waterstones book shops – to suggest a shared set of interests and values called, 'If you do one thing today.' Not only 'here's what's on this week', but 'here's what you should do'. Also worth noting is the popularity of 'recipe' activities; not only cookery, but gardening, DIY, the latest health fad or diet. And the popularity now of gadgets with a lot of functions and big instruction books.

The message of these activities and devices is that, at least in this part of our lives, if we follow the rules everything turns out OK. This is very therapeutic to people experiencing chaos and stress because it creates a space where things can be contained and order enacted. Most people with this kind of hobby talk about it in these terms. It puts them back in a grid for a while.

'Acting out' is an important concept in psychology and highly applicable to the world of brands. It means venting tensions and feelings in physical actions. The classic example is spinning the wheels of your car as you drive off after an argument. In more constrained times we were acting out pent up passions and emotions. And now – despite the media moral panic about things like road rage – I believe that far more people are 'opting out', into little bubbles of order – like their hobby at the bottom of the garden or their football trivia.

Finally, an example of the rules transforming a fickle market.

Why is it that in a world where we know that fashion is just convention and hype we readily accept that 'brown is the new black'?

Perhaps because fashion doesn't matter to us as much as it used to. We just want a workable convention to wear out today. In the group world everyone has the same overcoat – but out of convenience – whereas in the grid world people eagerly awaited the next big thing in coats.

Crowd Power: the Big WE

The 'big WE' is a feeling of being a part of one big humanity. It is the feeling we got when we saw the first pictures of earth from space. When we saw the Berlin Wall come down. That 'whole world is watching' feeling. But it isn't about being part of the whole world necessarily, just being part of a big inclusive group as opposed to grids which create exclusive groups.

One form of big WE event is the Lottery. This example highlights an important point about WE crowds. People watching the lottery draw are nearly all holding a ticket. This is a true WE as opposed to the old US psychology where individuality was lost in the crowd. WE collectives are never less than the sum of their parts.

Similarly football is always shown live wherever possible because the role of televising it is to make the audience part of the crowd. Hence the popularity of group viewings in pubs, work-places or friends' houses. Talk to any modern fan and you find that they feel part of the match – even if only on the level of willing their team on. The novel *Fever Pitch* is a fascinating dissection of this fan psychology. Similarly, big football events are now crowd events. From the dumb but nice Mexican wave, to the less polite but often very sharp and funny football chants.

The urge to join in is evident in fund-raising events like Red Nose Day and sponsored walks. They are such long-standing successes that I think they are undervalued. In two centuries time a historian of media will probably say that the sponsored charity walk in the 1970s was the prototype of what we now know as group-media. It is pure 'group', working through participation and contact with people in your close milieu. Just because it wasn't invented in MIT Media Labs doesn't mean it's not the shape of things to come.

In a few years time we will have fully interactive TV and movies on demand and home shopping and more but they are bringing up the rear. Society went digital a long time before television. Media are slowly adjusting to the Culturequake. So slowly that I wouldn't be surprised if TV was a news-only medium in future – and the main entertainment medium was computer games.

The Word on the Street is ... Tommy Hilfiger

Once Tommy Hilfiger was a poor man's Polo, with the result that it seemed quite inauthentic and struggled in its middle American heartland. All of this changed when Tommy Hilfiger's nephew took up the cause with his friends at Def Jam recordings. Def Jam is *the* record label for black American rap artists. Through his contacts the nephew got some of the label's major artists to wear Hilfiger clothes, which got them into pop videos and publicity and came back to the brand's heartland as something authentic and cool from the world of gangsta's and rap stars. Now Hilfiger is a booming global brand – because rap and hip hop in particular is a booming global phenomenon again. A case of right place, right time.

In the future there will be more and more cases like Hilfiger. Cases of product placement in cultural ideas (rather than just in films) and they will have to obey all the rules of authenticity – to appear just as much of a happy accident as Hilfiger. The Hilfiger example highlights one of the key differences between the old sort of marketing idea and the new sort. The old sort of marketing idea was window dressing – putting things out facing the world, which would attract people. The new sort of marketing idea is all about the word on the street. The connections which new marketing makes are all about creating this sort of conversation and live interaction. 'Run DMC wear it' is a great sound bite.

To Summarise

The whole of this chapter has been about getting brands into circulation through ideas – advertising stunts, codes of conduct, rock stars, whatever.

We've looked at three ways to do this – creating word of mouth, creating a framework of 'the rules' and creating a WE tribal following.

This style of indirect marketing underlines one of the key points in the whole book. Strong brands are made out of ideas in people's minds, everyday lives and conversations. They are ideas in circulation, not frigid stand-offish essences.

Which brings us to the next rule.

RULE 8

OPEN UP TO PARTICIPATION

The One-Minute Summary

An important distinction these days is that of being a partner versus being a supplier. How close are you to your customers. How much do you interact with them and they with you? Marketing used to be some sort of great impressive screen or facade. Now it is ideally more of an open door.

The old marketing used to broadcast culture – brands and messages – in a sterile form which people were supposed to receive passively. Marketing did everything for people – it was in a ready-made, finished form.

New Marketing is not finished and sealed off. It is half-made and ready for customers to pick up and use and be part of. It is open to participation.

Give Me an Example

Sainsbury's recipe marketing. They worked from recipes in TV adverts and Delia Smith recipes in their magazine, right down to recipe sheets and promotions in store. This created a more participative way of shopping than simply stocking up the larder. In doing so Sainsbury's were helping people with a big post-traditional dilemma: what to cook tonight.

Open Up to Participation

Marketing people are by and large control freaks. I don't necessarily mean this in too bad a way. The creative parts of marketing are a big leap in the dark and anything one can do to minimise the risk and anxiety that that risk causes is quite sane.

There is a style of marketing management which has grown around 'proven formula' which is inimitable to New Marketing. That approach is trying to over-determine the outcome of what, these days, ought to be a conversation not a lecture. It's like people who think too hard about what they are going to say next and never listen. The trick with New Marketing is to relax a bit and let customers have their say, their part in the process. This is because we now have *A new culture of participation*. People expect to have a part to play and, when they don't, they feel shut out. The New Marketing response to this new culture is *Let customers participate as co-creators of the brand*.

What is this Shift to a 'New Culture' all About?

'Culture' is one of those words that is used to mean a lot of different things, from artistic productions to traditional unwritten rules. I understand culture in the sense it is used in this book as:

- the creative and expressive part of...
- the ideas that people live by.

New Marketing considers brands as part of this broader system of meanings rather than as just the meanings attached to branded goods. Brands are one way for people to create meaning in their lives.

The metaphor that is often used for modern culture is that we feel like we are living in a film. We are playing parts that we have cobbled together from films, advertising, brands. When we decide to be a new lad, or a career woman, we are indeed living in a film in this sense if not in the literal sense explored by the brilliant allegorical movie *The Truman Show.*

But living in a film is in some ways too one-sided. I think a better metaphor for the way we create our life stories now is the computer game, which may also explain their current high appeal (the global market for computer games is bigger than music and films added together). The kind of computer game I have in mind is the role playing game or RPG. A classic game of this type is *Myst.*

In *Myst* you find yourself on an island where everyone has disappeared. The game consists of exploring this island and finding clues and also resources, for instance keys to open doors. Unlike the simpler 'shoot-em-up' and 'platform' games, the player determines their own route through the island and gradually creates their own interpretation of what has happened there.

There is a special moment when playing these games when the player feels themselves slipping into the character. The game players out there will know what I'm talking about. It is the sudden sensation of being the character and being in this parallel world. In classic media terms it is the suspension of disbelief, but in computer games it comes in flashes of identification rather than a gradual immersion.

If any reader wants to quickly understand how this media works at its outer limits I cannot recommend too highly that they try *Resident Evil.* This is the nearest thing I've ever seen to an interactive movie. Some games have better graphics, but none has that heart in the mouth sense that you are actually in the game. It is literally the most terrifying bit of media I have ever come across and not for the faint-hearted. The key moments in the game are when you open a new door and step into a room that could contain anything from zombie's to giant spiders. This is the stuff that nightmares are made of.

The difference with this sort of game is that, while it looks a bit like a film, it is really a film of the players' making and each game is utterly unique. The old culture was more like a film with a big passive audience in a cinema. The new culture is more like a game in your own Playstation. It's more dynamic, participative and self-directed.

Interacting with Static Media

This participation is not limited to interactive media. People's relationship with all media has changed dramatically. Fast forward. Change channels. Chat through the movie or even applaud. The passive audience is long gone.

A great early example of people becoming more involved in media was Channel 4's *Right to Reply,* the TV programme where viewers give their feedback – usually complaints – on TV programmes. There was an earlier counterpart of this on the BBC, but letters and disembodied actors voices kept the audience at a safe distance. *Right to Reply* uses the video booth and TV producers being grilled by members of the public (rather than letters) to give a much more real sense of the public joining in and television responding.

From TV to the high street. The Architecture Society recently invited public participation in development of the Hammersmith shopping centre with a video booth comments box. This became part of a public debate in local TV news about priorities in the area, but was mainly there for direct feedback. Also in West London there are a couple of craft cafés, catering to families with younger children. The customers get to make their own crockery and have it fired in a kiln. A dramatic leap forward from café self-service!

Great Happenings

Another way to grasp the participative culture is to look at what kinds of 'happenings' (as the media called them in the 1960s) are luminous in our culture.

The things that used to glow were organised rituals of tradition. For instance a Royal Wedding. Or other public ceremonies like May Day or the Harvest Festival. Or religious rituals. Or organised demonstration marches. These were pre-scripted 'films' which people participated in passively. There was no room for much individuality because that wasn't the point. The message of these events was that we should all stick to our allotted place in society – we were dressing up in its uniforms and playing our part. Which usually meant waving little plastic flags or placards.

Compare this with recent cultural 'happenings' that have been luminous. These are much more about the individual participant and their creative role. One example of this is the music culture which has shifted to the audience being the performer – as the dancer in the club or literally, as the performer in karaoke.

The Tamagochi Craze

Another example is the Tamagochi. Not only is this a particularly interactive toy but it has encouraged a very creative, participative user culture to grow around it. Restaurants opened crèches. Schoolgirls changed the rules of the game to 'how quickly and ingeniously can you kill the baby'. The Tamagochi gave business executives the chance to be maternal – to have broody conversations etc. And at the same time gave the Girl Power generation a way of symbolically killing their maternal instincts.

These meanings are powerfully linked to modern changes in gender role. They mythologize the new, and they were invented by the people who used the game, which was probably originally intended as a virtual 'doll' for a very young market of mainly girls – a more feminine counterpart to the *Gameboy*.

The Tamagochi is a great example of the rules in action. It taps deep human needs and also new life situations. It is utterly personal, participative and authentic. And its wildfire growth was fuelled by media stories and word of mouth not conventional promotion.

There are lots more examples that we'll cover as we go through different marketing applications of the rules. The point here is to underline the idea that *we are living in a culture where the most powerful trends and crazes are associated with giving people a creative and interactive role.*

The effect of this on branding is quite profound. Marketing which is not interactive is less valuable. Customers sit back and let it pass like the title sequences of the game. When we are not participating, we feel cool and remote – we don't pick up meaning and stimulation.

The New Value Equation

It used to be that the more you did for people the more they valued you. Marketing was like the domestic staff in a big old country home. You only had to lift a finger and they were there providing everything you needed. Of course life in a house with a staff of this size was expensive and there was also some mutual resentment. Now marketing is more like having friends to stay – the more you let customers do, the more at home they feel.

This doesn't quite mean more value as in charging premiums. It means a different value equation. Where, as IKEA say, 'the customer does more of the work and saves more of their money'.

Retailing Lessons in Participation

IKEA was one of the first to create a high participation culture in retailing. In retail markets, the customer has a high level of interaction and involvement in the basic product and service and this involvement has increased over the last forty years. From full-service shops to self-service. But I think the key shift more recently is towards a 'New Retailing', where the brand is created by interactions in the shopping experience.

A key split in shopping patterns that has guided much retail development in recent years is that between:

* convenience versus leisure
* buying versus shopping
* following a list versus browsing, etc.

A common assumption is that this split depends on whether the products in question are high interest or low interest. We want to enjoy shopping for pleasure indulgence goods – it is part of our leisure time – but we want the quickest most convenient way to buy basic essentials like groceries.

This distinction, the theory goes, is becoming more important as our leisure time is squeezed by longer working hours. Retailers must offer value for our time. Low interest goods must be quick and easy. High interest goods can be part of a longer indulgent experience.

I think this a rather self-fulfilling prophesy. These ideas are valid in relation to old ways of retailing. But as we will see, it is quite possible to buck the trend and make any retail experience – however low interest the products are – a valuable part of the brand.

The New Book Shop

One area which has been through a revolution recently is book retailing.

The old book shop was a prime example of fascinating products in a dull shop. They were like small public libraries. Places where people picked up books based on pre-existing preferences. Perhaps they had read a review, or followed a particular author.

The new book shop has opened out into a browsing space. Books are stacked on tables with the store recommending titles and new areas of interest. People are encouraged to linger and to spend more time deciding what to read. Coffee shops and sofas are often provided where they can relax and dip into books.

A retailing client tells me that the number of books bought is a direct function of the time spent in store. Hence all the measures taken to compete for time – like the in-store cafés. This is a very different time-value equation. Most of the browse-as-long-as-you-like concepts are also deep discounters. They are competing for people spending time in the form of numbers of books chosen.

It may be just me, but for all the vaunted qualities of the on-line bookshop, Amazon.com, I think it has lower participation. It is like a very old-fashioned library where the assistant finds books for you on request and maybe suggests other titles you might be interested in. Despite being in an interactive medium I think it does too much for me as a book shopper and it is not something I can walk through and browse like a shop. I have to choose specific areas and I only see those books. Whereas at Waterstones I always go there for non-fiction; but I always linger in the fiction stands because they are on the way.

What Amazon badly needs in my opinion is a better graphical interface. One which is 3-dimensional and physically intuitive – like *Myst*. A virtual shop you can walk through. This would be the cyber-shopping equivalent of the invention of the desktop for PC working to create person-centred and intuitive participation. Another thing it could do with is fellow shoppers. How many times have you bought a book because you have first seen someone else pick it up and flick through it?

However, even with the above, an on-line bookshop will never have the tactility of a great book shop. I believe that a big part of shopping is picking up and holding objects, standing under big displays etc. A book's appeal is all in the weight, the paper, the binding and the whole way it is displayed, much more than a graphic of the cover and a blurb. The reason that the Penguin 60s were so great was that they were a new twist on this physical tactility and 'object-ness' of books.

I believe that creating a mail order business on-line is not necessarily the best use of what is supposed to be a completely new paradigm of media. And that the current stampede in that direction will lead to another wave of burnt fingers and ghost-town sites (following the first wave which was internet magazine publishing). A counter-argument in favour of Amazon is that it is an information-rich intermediary. It can, as a database, give each customer a lot more time and guidance. The value of the brand and the heart of the experience is knowledge. This is a theme we'll come back to later.

But books are relatively high interest. Arguably what new forms of book selling have done is spring their innate interest and involvement. What about low interest categories like staple groceries?

Supermarkets as Leisure Destinations

I believe that supermarkets suffer from a 'low interest fallacy' which can become a self-fulfilling prophesy. The obvious exception to this is food which has – through the cooking and foodie trends – become a high interest category. As a result, parts of supermarkets are involving and pleasurable – the fresh fruits and vegetables, the delicatessen and the in-store bakery. Even in the low interest product areas I do not believe that the experience needs to be vacuous and uninvolving.

Because housework is a chore, it is assumed that the shopping experience should be quick and easy rather than involving. That competing for more time would be suicidal. However, this is not borne out by actual retail success stories.

The best practitioner of participation in UK retailing in my view is Tesco's. And they must be doing something right because they have taken the number one spot and kept it. One example I mentioned earlier was the giant knives and forks idea. A Tesco's spokesperson said that because all supermarkets are the same in product and service, Tesco's felt that the best way to compete was to make shopping more fun. This is the same strategy as that used by parents when they get bath-time toys for their kids!

No experience has to be boring and negative. Another of Tesco's other great innovations was taking the sweets away from the checkout counter – saving mothers from the spectre of a screaming confrontation with a sweet-toothed toddler. Both moves are highly symbolic gestures made in a way that people participate in. They used the experience as a medium.

Quinn's stores in Ireland have done more than most to make shopping (as opposed to what is bought) involving. One of my favourites is their 'singles nights'. Who says supermarkets have to work like a cold bath – quick in and quick out?

Sainsbury's created a different in-store medium: recipe's. They hitched themselves to the foodie-cooking boom in general and to Delia Smith, the leading TV chef, in particular. When Delia Smith started an autumn TV season with recipes using cranberries, Sainsbury's sold out of cranberries the next day. This is a good example of a reframing of the experience. At the height of this campaign, when Sainsbury's had in-store recipes with the ingredients in linked promotions, they were a place to go for ideas of what to cook this week not just a place to buy food. They changed the way that people shop and made it more participative and meaningful.

Recipes are adding value through adding knowledge. A good example is the modern gallery. In the past galleries assumed you knew about the art, and had just come to see it. In the new gallery the main exhibit is the information you are given – a reframing from art temple to art class. A great recent example was the Warhol exhibition where visitors were given audio CD ROMs. When you wanted to know more about a particular painting you punched the number and could choose to listen to recordings of critics, art historians or even Warhol himself talking about the painting.

The added knowledge approach could apply to any retail experience. Supermarkets could very usefully have multimedia kiosks to help people with frequently asked questions such as how to tackle different kinds of stains in clothes. Domestic science (like art history) is one of those areas where there is a huge knowledge gap that people want to fill. They wouldn't have to sell products. The great thing about retailing is once you get more people coming in to the store more often, the products tend to sell themselves. That must be why Boots The Chemists are building in-store cafés.

Participation Through Self Service

Another form of meaningful participation is self-service. This was introduced to save money on staff and time, and to fit with a more informal, open plan, self-service home and work culture. But I think its main value going forward is getting customers to do meaningful, positive things.

Take airline service. The classic model says the more service, the better. First and Business class were positively tripping over themselves with extra cabin staff to take care of your needs. But British Airways have found out what every frequent traveller knows. That airline service is oppressive because you are 'belted in' – to their timetable, their menu, their range of movies. Most airlines have moved to more choice and control. BA took it a stage further with their 'Raid the Larder' food concept for Business class. The concept is simply that you get the food you want, when you want it. It's interesting, isn't it, that the more upmarket, expensive airline classes are getting into self-service? It's yet more evidence that value comes from being allowed to participate.

Authority of Range

Another conventional wisdom that is dubious in the new culture is the value of simplicity. 'Don't confuse people with too much choice'.

This was great news for big brands like Dulux – they took up market share (and hence power) as small brands were delisted. I don't think it was such good news for the customer (less choice and less competition) and there is growing evidence that it is no longer the best thing for the retailer either.

The phrase that booksellers use is 'authority of range'. In the great American chains such as Barnes & Noble, they don't just have a selection of titles – they have a mountain. If you want a Western novel for instance, you'll find a selection, not of a few hundred but of thirty thousand titles.

Authority of range is a pillar of IKEA's business. Their stores generally do about ten times the business of a typical competitor superstore and they have an enormous range on offer rather than concentrating on a few key lines. Rather than getting people through the store quickly and conveniently they literally march people past every item. They have everything for the home and an incredible depth of choice and they rightly regard this as a key part of their brand. At IKEA they say 'the range is our identity'.

IKEA is still the most participative retailer. You don't just select furniture, you find it in the warehouse, you deliver it yourself and you make it yourself. The displays are designed to get you interacting – they encourage you to touch, to bounce on the beds etc. IKEA use their catalogue for added knowledge – to teach people about home design and to pass on valuable inside information of the 'this chair's great to look at but if you want one to watch TV and eat dinner on there's a cheaper chair that might be better for you' kind.

At the more creative end of participation they have done all sorts of incredible things. Children's IKEA is highly interactive. There is a chute for kids to enter through and loads inside to play with and in. They have in-store events, from furniture construction competitions (a great hit with German men apparently), to getting animals in from London Zoo for half term. When they first launched their beds range they got customers to sleep in the stores overnight.

IKEA is a great example of retailing as leisure destination. Families often go there for a day out. Not because what they sell is necessarily higher interest than everything on the high street but because it is a whole day out with lots of participation. It's a way to spend a Saturday. In Stockholm, the IKEA store is one of the major tourist attractions!

The Gadget Society

Another example of 'authority of range' leading to high participation is gadgets. Again the conventional wisdom in product design was to make things simple and user friendly and I think this is an idea that has got out of date. What people want now is an incredible range and depth of function.

Japan is always coming up with gadgets like the watch-phone-and-personal-organiser. Things that can do ten times as much for you. These offer not just more convenience or good value. They offer control. Gadgets are a means to practise mastery over the physical world – climate control in the car; thousands of editing options on the Minidisc Walkman.

And the more control is at your fingertips, even if you never use half the functions, the more powerful you feel. Ultimately a piano is much more satisfying than just pressing the play button on a recording device. Devices are moving in the 'piano' direction.

Participation is about People Not Buttons

I prefer the word 'participation' to the more common 'interactivity' because it highlights a key difference. Participation means taking part. It's a word about the participant not the machine and it points to a creative, human engagement.

A great example of the difference between participation and interactivity, was a Saturday night special on Channel 4. All the TV programmes were on the theme of 'Disco'. With the launch of the films *Studio 54* and the *Last Days of Disco*, this was a topical theme. The participative fulcrum of the night – at least in my house – was my wife and me sitting (or singing, or dancing) through a long selection of classic disco videos like *Boogie Wonderland* and *I Will Survive*, and having all those nostalgic discussions about the 70s we grew up in. The TV could hardly get a word in edgeways! In comparison, the station's Interactive strand was in my view clumsy and highly disposable – a phone poll on which single the audience at home thought should be the 'all-time disco number one'. Who cares? When this strand came on, there were suddenly urgent things to do in the kitchen!

Until interactive TV improves to video game levels (and beyond into voice and mood operation), we are stuck with pressing buttons and limited choices, like phone polls. They are great for a few things (like election night polls), but they don't add much to most media experiences. The example often quoted for the future of interactive TV is being able to choose the camera angles while watching football. I don't know about you, but I'd rather concentrate on the game and to be honest, I don't have a problem with a skilled director choosing angles for me, just as I never really have a problem going to a match and standing on the south stand and only having one point of view. It's interactivity for its own sake and it's no great advance.

The kind of participation I have in mind comes from leaps forward like the Steadycam that gives you more of a sense of being in the scene. If interactive TV could give me options like the game from Zola or Di Matteo's point of view I might get a little more excited.

Back to 'Living in a Film'

Someone who used hand-held cameras a lot recently was Stephen Spielberg in *Saving Private Ryan*. Interviewed for a pre-film publicity, Spielberg said he had learned over the years to give the audience more credit for piecing together the film for themselves and to avoid the temptation of trying to do it all for them. There could be four hundred people in the cinema who have effectively seen a different film, because they have all got something more personal and meaningful out of it. Films that have this kind of effect fit the new culture much better and with this sort of film in mind, maybe the 'living in a film' metaphor isn't such a bad one after all.

To Summarise

Participation is about redesigning the spaces where people touch your
brand. Redesigning them so that they do more and you do less. In a
way it's just the old 'Betty Crocker' cake mix idea – let them add the egg
themselves.

It's a paradox of New Marketing economics that the less you do, and the
more they participate, the more you are worth.

Every category will have an IKEA in the 21st Century that realises what this
rule can do for their sector first. Even the supermarkets.

RULE 9

BUILD COMMUNITIES OF INTEREST
The One-Minute Summary

A core concept of marketing is that of the target audience.

In the old marketing, target audiences were classified by habits and allegiances and also by great and valid social categories. These were the passive target audiences of marketing messages.

New Marketing also works through audiences which collect around brands but they are active audiences who have *chosen* to gather. Half the battle in building a strong brand now is creating these communities of interest.

Give Me an Example

Oddbins, which has reframed the role of a high street off-licence to something more akin to a wine club with hand-written selections and recommendations and tastings, and a 'jazz shop' style of shared enthusiasm service. Like a wine club, but also accessible to the everyday punter like you and me, who wants a bottle of plonk for a drinks party and something to say about it when we arrive. No wonder Oddbins has been the trade magazine's 'off-license of the year' for eight out of the last ten years.

Build Communities of Interest

This rule is a prime example of brands taking on the role of tradition. The instinct to form communities is a powerful human drive (one of the fifteen basic instincts identified by the American psychological survey quoted earlier in the book). Brands are providing non-traditional communities to belong to, from owners and hobby clubs to social causes.

The Pack Instinct

In the past, this drive found expression in the real communities people were part of – the extended family and village or neighbourhood or the firm which gave you a job for life. Now people are more uprooted. Social, geographical and work mobility are a central feature of most people's lives. Sociologists say that in this sense we are all homeless because we have no fixed point as our emotional origin. This creates a hunger for communities which we can belong to. This community hunger has put a completely new twist on the old concept of the target audience. The New Marketing response is to create active communities of interest.

Some businesses have been based on a community of members for a long time, for instance building societies with their mutual status. What this rule is saying is that all businesses should now consider very seriously what 'community of shared interests' they are creating with their brand.

This is not as drastic as it sounds. I'm talking about surrogate communities, not building actual towns like Disney has. You don't have to be a community in the full civic sense, for example, all strong media brands are communities of interest. A strong newspaper is a 'community' in the sense that I mean. Strong media brands create a sense of belonging to an audience with shared values.

A good way of seeing the role of other brands in future is to see them as media. You don't need to go as far as literal club-like organisation. Just to tap into a sense of belonging to a group who share your interests. It's time for brands to see themselves as media owners. The logical conclusion of this of course is to produce their own media, rather than advertising in others.

Community Glue for Brands that Otherwise Fall Apart

Why go to all that bother you may ask. Surely most businesses just need to make and sell their goods. They don't have to become a social club or launch a magazine into the bargain. The main answer has to be that you bother because you can. You don't have to do this. But if you don't somebody else will – and they will benefit at your expense.

The gulf between weaker and stronger brands is widening. As the opportunities offered by New Marketing are taken up by some brands in a market place a community of interest can be a vital advantage. The volatility in people's lives and relationships that makes communities of interest and belonging powerful, also makes relying on brand loyalty and habit doubtful. Because when people's lives are fractured, their brand loyalties become fractured too.

And the great unknown looming is how many brands will survive the marketing Millennium bug. Will your brand become something your audience leave behind as a 20th Century brand – part of their old lives and selves? Involvement in communities does not totally insulate a brand from this kind of change in any individual customers' lives. But collectively it gives them some more stability.

If Nike as a brand was grounded in local community sports clubs and activities people would have had to give up exercise and friends to leave it behind, rather than just giving up on a badge. Communities of interest make brands less disposable. The old marketing relied on identifying passive target audiences whose only connection with the brand and each other was purchasing. New Marketing aims to form a much more active and bonded community of interest.

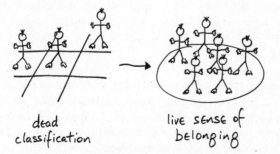

dead
classification

live sense of
belonging

Partnership and New Brand Economics

The last rule touched on the difference between being a partner and a supplier. Forming a community of interest is forming a partnership.

Membership of a community repays people in a sense of belonging and identity. It is a part of life that we invest time and feelings in, not just money. The main point of this rule is one of involvement, not the ability to charge premiums. Which brings us to a point that has run throughout the book. Generally marketing – at least brand marketing – used to be there to add value. Meaning that the cost of marketing the brand was more than made up for by the premium that could be charged. Studies across many markets show that brand leaders typically not only have the lion's share of the people and purchasing, but they also charge a premium compared with other brands that are similar in function and quality, etc. I believe this was largely phoney economics. People are paying for the advertising and packaging and promotions by a kind of indirect taxation.

The growing strength of own label brands in grocery markets shows what a precarious position this may be. Especially if you consider that own label goods are disproportionately bought by under thirty-fives. The same 'Emperor's New Clothes' witch-hunt that hit the beer market, may one day soon be gunning for branded goods in general. There are already murmurs on the fringes, like the recent global 'no shopping day'.

New Marketing is also about making brands more valuable. But this does not mean making them more expensive. It means, in the words of Sergio Zyman, former head of marketing at Coca-Cola and a New Marketing guru if ever there was one, making them 'worth more than they cost'. A good example is The Body Shop.

The Body Shop

The Body Shop community idea was that of *business as a social cause*.

Staff and customers were involved in campaigns like 'against animal testing' by buying products which were sourced in more ethical ways – trade not aid and all that, but also through direct actions like petitions and even demonstrations. People who bought The Body Shop products were doing so partly to feel part of the thriving green consumer movement. Obviously The Body Shop was aiming to further the cause rather than cynically take it up just for profit. But it was a perfect virtuous circle.

Surveys of the Green Consumer phenomenon in the late 80s, such as Mintel's, found that concerns were highest among teenage girls and mothers of young children. These two groups are the core market for basic and cheap rather than aspirational and expensive cosmetics. The no frills approach created enormous cost savings. One container shape for each size was used for all the products. Not only did this create incredible savings but it gave customers a tangible unique Body Shop product experience.

When I recently met with the Roddick's they told me that the original business idea for their company was to spend the money on the products, not the packaging. That alone would give them a crushing cost advantage in the excessively ornate market for pots of cream and potions.

This same communing model was taken to its ultimate form by a Body Shop supported project called *The Big Issue*. *The Big Issue* is the magazine sold by homeless people. It gives the vendor a business – not only an income but a step back into a constructive role in society and the vital self-esteem and impetus to take further steps. It gives commuters a great read, with city relevant topics and listings. And it's well suited to packed trains and buses (compared with a heavy glossy magazine or unwieldy newspaper). It also gives the buyer a more constructive response to the homelessness we see all around us than giving what may only be alcohol or drug money.

In business terms, it created a unique distribution platform. Most magazines fail because they compete for shelf space and attention with so many other titles. *Big Issue* sales are opportune. I don't think it's a title that would race off the shelves at WHSmiths. And for all the stakeholders it gave alienated city dwelling more of a village community feel. It created a community of interest. Vendors of *The Big Issue* have become an icon of the community. In London they are now as familiar as red buses and black cabs.

Strategic Philanthropy

Another cause-based marketing idea came from my favourite supermarket retailer, Tesco's. The Computers for Schools initiative was a loyalty scheme with a difference. It put back some of the 'shops as cornerstones of community' feeling that was lost when supermarkets gobbled up the grocery market in the 1950s and 60s.

Quite a few community of interest ideas fall into this ethical role in society area. In America they call it 'strategic philanthropy'. The idea behind this is that most companies give money to good causes. In the past this was often done in a haphazard way where the donations may simply follow the causes and interests of the Chairman. Often the sums of money are quite large and the strategic approach is to focus these funds on really doing some good – in a way that is relevant to the core business and brands.

Examples of strategic philanthropy from the States include *The New York Times'* literacy drives, the food companies banding together to supply homeless centres with surplus food and Microsoft's donation of billions of pounds of computer equipment to schools. There are many others. The reason this form of community marketing is increasingly common is that it reflects a broader shift in the role of business. Companies are taking on some of the ethical role of fading institutions in society.

Perhaps this will fix the problem identified by Charles Handy, which is that capitalism is all efficiency and no driving cause-like passion (the reverse of communism) – all head and no heart. The Third Way political tendency puts a big emphasis on public-private-citizen partnerships. Communities of shared interest in other words. This is the formula that Tony Blair's welfare programme is pursuing in transforming the welfare state into a welfare society.

Virtual Communities

Communities of conscience are just one way an active audience of belonging can be built around a business – and they are more likely to be corporate rather than brand level activities.

Tesco's has recently launched another community-like scheme – the Tesco's internet service. This obviously dovetails into their home shopping service but it also gives them a powerful place in people's lives other than when they shop. At the moment it is just a cheap gateway to the internet but I am hoping that they will develop it into something more unique and brand building – like America On-Line.

Much has been made of the internet as a venue for new virtual communities because it groups people by shared interest, not by accidental location. According to *The Guardian* newspaper's New Media Group, the key factor for success in any internet web site is the space for like-minded people to meet and chat. And they should know. Their Euro 96 soccer site contained one of the only places in the world where fans could meet across continents to discuss minutiae. Their research showed that while people may initially be drawn to a site by fancy production values, strong branding and promotion, they go back to meet people and participate in their chosen interests.

I once went along to an internet pirate radio broadcast. The difference between this and other radio stations was exactly this virtual community feel. It had a global audience of around 500,000 people with exactly the same taste in music as the DJ's. And listeners were in touch with the station by e-mail or a chat line. Answers to messages that were being sent in were being beamed out again with the music. This community use of the internet is a genuinely new paradigm, compared with the corporate leaflet, the billboard and the mail order businesses which are the three standard uses of the net.

The Jazz Principle

You don't have to know many people to feel you belong. Being part of something can be more of a cultural thing. I live in Camden, a scruffy but trendy part of London. I know maybe ten other people who actually live around here and am on nodding terms with maybe twenty or so people in local shops and bars. There are tens of thousands of neighbours I'll never know, but I've lived here for four years and I feel part of Camden as an idea.

Brands can work in the same way. Madonna fans can feel a tribal affinity as can shoppers in outlets with a highly defined culture. It works best when the staff and customers are bonded by some shared passion. I call this the 'jazz shop' model. Jazz shops are the ultimate retail business. The people who work there are incredibly motivated enthusiasts as are the customers. There is no barrier between the business and these people and very high value in time and money can be invested in their passion for jazz.

Oddbins is one mainstream retailer which works in exactly this way. It's a great example of how New Marketing – using all the rules – can create outstanding businesses compared with more conventional businesses. The rest of the wine market falls largely between supermarkets and off licence retailers. The latter aren't that different from supermarkets in range and value. If you shop for wine like I do, then whether you use a supermarket or local off-licence depends on whether you are stocking up with the groceries, or buying for a specific occasion.

Oddbins is different. The basis of its success is that it is a wine enthusiast's shop. Its great achievement is that it has kept as up close and personal as a village wine merchant on a big scale. Wine enthusiasts want information about the wine they are buying. I'm not talking about wine club members as a niche. I'm talking about everyone who's arrived at a dinner party primed with a few notes on their choice of wine to get conversation going. Oddbins gives them these notes, hand-written (up close and personal) for every wine in the shop. They have also created a jazz shop staff culture. Probably mainly through hiring people that fit the bill. The impression given by most off-licence staff is either that they feel this job is one up from a petrol station or supermarket, or that it's the small business they could afford. Oddbins staff come across more like the student actors who work in theatre box offices. They are great for advice or just a chat while buying.

Oddbins also artfully uses massive discounting to build, not cheapen the brand. Its model is of being one big bin-end sale, i.e. from the world of wine merchants, not supermarket plonk but also accessible, familiar, welcoming not intimidating. As with Pizza Express (the 'high street Conran', see case studies) it does this partly through great design and shop-fitting. Of course lots of people just go there for a bottle of wine but all the branding adds value to that wine.

Vocations, Enthusiasms and Crazes

Hobby vocations are a powerful branch of 'ideas to live by'. An interest in wine is just one example of what hobbies are in general – which is a movement of 'work' into 'leisure'. Wine buffs are home sommeliers. Anglers are home hunters. Enthusiastic cooks are home restaurateurs. And so on. That's why I call them vocations, because I think that the vibrancy of hobby markets is linked to people searching for their calling. I've included vocations under communities of interest, because like causes they are only one option. But like causes they are a big social trend and you'd be mad if you haven't looked really hard at your business to see if it could be either a hobby or a cause. They are two of the main 'bigger things' in people's lives that business can tap into.

Most businesses which start small, start with this enthusiast mindset. The most common way to start a business is extending an existing hobby. Even Microsoft started as two kids at Harvard who'd spent their whole puberty punching into the school mini-computer. And who were so excited about the new microcomputers that one of them (Bill Gates) left college half way through to get started on it.

Great companies like Microsoft never lose this mindset. It becomes part of their cultural DNA. Like the adventuring spirit of Federal Express that came from being, in its early days, staffed by ex-fighter pilots.

In our parents' time even the basic white goods were wonder-products of convenience and home improvement – liberating people from the drudgery of housework. If they have become commodities, it doesn't mean they have to stay that way. Cooking was fairly low interest to most people ten years ago.

The most powerful thing that can happen in any consumer market is for it to gain 'craze' status. This sounds like the province of hula hoops, or currently yo-yos but the secret history of many markets is that they were built by just these sorts of crazes, i.e. by cultural luck. So it was that jogging and then aerobics built the trainer market. Before jogging Nike was a $1 million marathon shoe specialist. They were lucky that their business model was not to own the factories as they could respond much faster to changes in demand.

- Playstation did everything right to put their brand at the heart of a new wave of computer game enthusiasm.
- Dulux and other brands were catapulted into success by the post-war DIY revolution.
- Booksellers currently are riding the self-improvement end of the new knowledge economy.

And so on.

New Social Networks

Another form of community as brand builder is the social network. The biggest club in Britain is the Neighbourhood Watch scheme. It has six million members. Car boot sales and LETS (local economic trading schemes) are a similar booming feature of the new unofficial community economy. Inventing a social network idea like these – that is part of people's lives and relationships with people – is another way of creating a community.

A classic example is the Anne Summers (sex goods) business. Most of the selling is done at Anne Summers parties rather than the few city centre shops. These are held among friends by hosts who work for commission. It is an incredibly vibrant community culture. And ever more relevant in this 'Full Monty' society of strip clubs and other sex industries for liberated and independent women.

Another thriving UK network organisation is the National Childbirth Trust which as well as information and training to be a mother, provides a community of social contact for young mothers. Two other community of support and socialisation organisations are Alcoholics Anonymous and Weight Watchers. In the past these kinds of network have often formed around specific problems like the support groups that exist around particular illnesses but they don't have to be this heavy or specific.

Saturn, the revolutionary American car company has an owners club. Tens of thousands of people turn out for their Saturn Owners Rallies. There's a lesson in this. From the outside Saturn looks like a fairly bland range of modern cars – not exactly Love Bugs or Harley Davidsons. An objective, cynical marketing person might not have considered an owners club because the car wasn't a classic. But look at it from the inside. Having an owner's club *makes* the car special – it's a powerful medium for the brand. And everyone who buys a car wants it to be this special.

This is an example of what we'll cover in the last rule – having a vision to grow into, rather than being too constrained by the leaden boots of current reality.

Community Centres

Another way a business with retail premises can build a community brand is by being a venue for a community, which, if you think about it, many retail spaces already are. If you run a coffee shop you could be a school common room at some times, a work canteen at others, a drop-in community centre for mothers or senior citizens at others.

The new café in Boots The Chemist stores is destined to make Boots one of these community spaces, rather than just a place to pick up some aspirin. It suits the leisure side of the business. I've already mentioned it as an exercise in added participation. One of Boots' main markets is indulgence. Beauty products are often bought as what the research industry calls 'self gifts', and most others would call treats. Putting a café in the store is saying 'we think this is an important place in your life where you want to spend quality time browsing'. Or for other types of shoppers it is a service oasis in the busy day of a stretched and tired mum.

Venue ideas are like the 'experience ideas' I covered earlier. Ideally, something creative is added into the space to make a unique, relevant difference. The development of the café sector itself – from struggling to compete with fast food joints, to vibrant focal points in the modern shopping areas – is a great example. Venue ideas which have animated this sector include:

- the internet café
- the news stand café
- the record shop/DJ behind the bar café
- the board games café
- the book shop café
- the craft café
- the philosophy café
- the launderette café

Surely many cafés are 'just cafés'?

Well, if you think about it, many of these have strong venue ideas. They are just a bit more familiar. So an Italian café is really ciabatta with a bit of Mediterranean gusto. Just as Seattle-style American coffee chains are coffee and a little visit to 'the States'. Then there are all the English cafés that are like *The Sun* newspaper – full of cabbies and brickies eating chips.

Also, the flagship outlets have done a great job for the category, moving us back towards a 'café society'. Restoring cafés to the kind of central social role enjoyed by the Lyons tea houses forty years ago. Of course you'll always be able to name lame, bland examples. But if you think about it, they aren't doing that well really, are they?

Media-Brand Convergence.

Becoming 'a surrogate community' is very close to becoming 'a medium'.

The whole point of media after all is to gather a like-minded audience by espousing their values and interests. Economically, the point of this is to gather these audiences for advertisers. One short cut into New Marketing is to stop buying space in someone else's medium and start making your own. That way you can have an honest transaction. People will pay for good media and you won't have to load your brand with the hidden extra of advertising costs. And if your media is any good, other less enlightened marketing people will pay for space in it. Sainsbury's Magazine is one of the biggest lifestyle magazines in the country and I'm sure is more than self financing.

Procter & Gamble are a constant revelation at the moment, in their transformation from a boring, formulaic advertiser to a company with breakthrough ideas. They have launched a parents' internet site as their form of community marketing. Apart from anything else, it's great for research purposes to be able to be part of real parents' conversations. I believe that this is the future of media and marketing – they will become one.

Sony – ever the visionary – bought Columbia and founded Sony music for exactly this reason of synergy between their product lines and creative media products. It's the model Disney has always followed. Where does the media stop and the product begin?

The reason I believe that brand and media convergence will take over quite quickly is that the current system is in crisis. Media owners are constantly strapped for cash despite charging ad rates that mean that effectiveness in advertising is becoming the exception not the rule – and viewers are tired of being interrupted with commercial messages from the crass, repetitive brands.

New Marketing offers the prospect of more creative, more meaningful interaction with customers in a way that is rooted in a new business model at a fraction of the cost. All it takes is balls and brains. The only reason that not everyone will be a Virgin-style marketer may be that not everyone will have a Richard Branson at the helm.

I think this convergence of media and brands is one of the exciting frontiers for creative business. One of my ambitions is to come up with something as creative, socially useful and strategically brilliant as *The Big Issue*.

Seeing Through Community Lenses

Careers in creative marketing are full of 'ones that got away'. One of my own favourites was a New Marketing idea we pitched to a spectacles retailer.

Our idea, which would be executed in free media, from the shop windows to a new TV series, was based on the little truth that glasses make you look clever. Their category could not dumb down any further 'quality two-for-one in about an hour with a service promise', with all the soul and charm of a fast food chain. Our intention was to create more of a Waterstones feel and environment and correspondingly to tap into a growing community of knowledge workers, whose glasses are like the 80s stockbrokers' braces.

One of the great things about this idea was that it transcended any media. It was a genre idea – in that it fitted any media, including conversation and other effects. Coming up with ideas like this is the subject of the next chapter.

RULE 10

USE STRATEGIC CREATIVITY

The One-Minute Summary

This is the rule where New Marketing most collides with New Media.

The old marketing's conventions were largely defined by the media they used. Trademark brands like Coca-Cola and Marlboro grew out of what you could do with the mass advertising media of posters. Aspiration brands came into their own with the dramatic, personality-led medium of television.

New Marketing is not necessarily about using New Media. It is not like a river that has cut a new channel. It is more like a river which has burst its banks. It uses freer form multimedia ideas. If it uses the old media, it uses them in new ways. The creativity is strategic rather than media-led.

A key concept in New Marketing creatively is that of the 'genre idea'. A genre is a creative form that transcends media. Romantic fiction, for example, can exist in pulp novels, in TV soaps, in magazines, in internet chat-lines, and conceivably in computer games or retail experiences.

Give Me an Example

The genre that was used by Gap Khaki's was that of modern dance. The TV advertising conveys everything you could say about the physical experience and the values of this sub-brand, in a way that speaks to our bodies. Now every time I see skateboarders I think Gap – and vice versa.

Use Strategic Creativity

I hope by now you have got the impression that New Marketing is about a spirit of ingenuity and opportunism. This is the subject of this rule. It is another convergence – the coming together of strategy and creativity. The spur to this is a much wider range of options, for instance a much wider range of communication media. So that the strategic choice of how some marketing will work has a massive defining effect on the creative content.

The range of creative branding media has expanded recently with the launch of digital television. And the growth of other new media like the internet has been rapid throughout the 1990s. This explosion of different possibilities has had a very beneficial effect on the creative side of marketing. Just as the recent advances in the availability of global ingredients for cooking has had a positive, creative effect on what and how we cook.

This has woken marketing up from a long slumber of complacent convention. Now even the most conventional media spaces are looked at as an opportunity to do something different and the communicative media around a brand are looked at more holistically – from packaging to publicity. And also include parts of the brand not seriously treated as media before, like the store or logo or service script.

Before, what could be done for a brand was very much conditioned by what a conventional use of conventional media could do – create awareness, communicate benefits, add personality. This led to an ornamental creativity where the question was at best 'how could we use this media differently?' And to a strategic morbidity. My first agency taught me that there were only six basic advertising strategies, from direct responses to seeding attitudes with non-users that might later cause them to re-evaluate. So much of marketing in this time was routine and because the form of marketing did not change very much, there were routine approaches to most tasks.

The range of media now mean that most marketing is 'multimedia' and this has led to a shift in emphasis, to ideas that transcend their media and to much higher order strategic questions requiring creative answers.

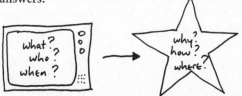

The (Limited) Creativity of Media Choice

Somebody claimed a few years ago that media people are the new creatives. The media people they were talking about were the advertising agency media planners. And the media they were mostly thinking of were New Media. At that time there was a new emphasis on experimenting with the form of media used, as well as being creative with the content.

I think the principle was partly right. The explosion in choices (of media within which to build brands) means that the initial choice of media and genre can outweigh subsequent decisions. But in practise, I'm afraid that many of these media people were not creative. As a result a lot of the new uses of media turned out to be sponsorship of existing TV programmes. TV sponsorship in the early 1990s in the UK was a good idea because few advertisers were using it and it was cheap. So small brands which did use it early on got good exposure with high quality programmes and they stood out because sponsorship was new and interesting to viewers. One brand which benefited was Beamish.

Beamish was a little known stout. The company sponsored a very popular programme called *Inspector Morse*. The creative idea behind *Inspector Morse* was to put modern crime fiction in a more sumptuous setting – of Oxford colleges and stately homes, with the lead character being a connoisseur of things like opera, classic cars and real ale. Sponsoring this programme gave Beamish both a high profile and a big slice of authentic heritage by association. That is how sponsorship is supposed to work.

The problem with sponsorship – now it is neither a bargain nor an open field – is that by definition it is hitching a ride on something whose creative agenda has nothing to do with your brand. It is buying a media answer that may have nothing to do with the strategic questions your brand faces. Creatively you are limited to making a link between your brand and the programme; a last-ditch attempt to minimise the extent to which your name seems just 'stuck on' the programme. Occasionally sponsorship of that programme is exactly what the brand needs but more usually it is a case of not only putting the cart before the horse, but the horse pushing the cart on a journey you didn't need to make.

Transcending the Limitations of Media
(Why, How and then Where)

The best New Marketing approach is the opposite of sponsorship. It involves working out from first principles what the question is and then finding a creative answer. Or more precisely, figuring out what the key problem is that your brand faces and then how a solution could work. This dialectic is what I mean by strategic creativity. It's not just strategy because the 'how' usually involves some sort of creative lateral leap. And it is not just creative new media because it is grounded in the needs of the business.

I went through an exercise in this type of thinking with an international team of people at IKEA responsible for the development of the IKEA catalogue into new electronic media. What they had done up until that point was work out how the existing catalogue could be replicated in new media, either as a place to browse IKEA's product range before visiting the store, or as a mail order tool. What we did in our workshop was ignore new media for most of the day. Instead we talked about what the IKEA business needed and what the existing printed catalogue did. We debated distinctions like 'new or existing customers?' 'more visits or a greater depth of purchasing?' and 'growing the market or increasing IKEA's share?'.

Having agreed the tasks the new catalogue should tackle in order to grow the business (it was going to add to the cost so it had to grow the business) we then set out to explore how New Media could be used to meet these aims. This led to some very creative new media ideas. New ways of using the internet that would engage potential customers outside the stores but which would also include IKEA's product range integrally. At the time of publication of this book the details are confidential as it is a live project. Suffice to say that the ideas touched on many of the themes in this book like education and building communities of interest.

This approach is so simple. Work out what the problems are and what answers to those problems would do. Then brainstorm the beginnings of creative answers. If you work this way you never have to be self-conscious about innovation – it comes naturally.

In my experience the reason why marketing teams don't do this all the time is that they get locked into conventions and assumptions. Working from first principles is simple – in IKEA's case it was just a day's work. But it is a scary process compared with writing up marketing plans drawing on known predispositions of management. Thinking outside the box means going beyond not just the obvious, but beyond past consensus.

Isn't it the case that a lot of business planning works like the law in that it is judged against consistency with past decisions? One of the reasons for this of course, is the decision-making hierarchy. In my experience, one of the critical factors for success in any creative marketing venture is regularly involving people who will make the decisions in the development. Otherwise, no matter how right the answer is, you will always hit that barrier of showing them what they hadn't expected.

The Power of Genres

I now want to explore in more detail what the New Marketing alternative to following conventions entails. In practical terms, this means you need to learn to think in what I call genres. A genre is a particular creative form, within and also across media. Documentaries are a genre that can exist in television and cinema. Romantic fiction is a genre that exists in these two media and also in books. Existing genres can be applied to new media too. So romantic fiction would be an interesting genre to apply to computer games. The reason I have found that genres are the best tools for creative strategy is that they get you thinking at the right level – specific enough, but not *too* executional.

Creative genres are specific enough to think about how New Marketing will work. Romantic fiction works through escapist identification with a lead character. It could be a good genre for instance for a brand that needed to be more of an indulgent escape – perhaps a perfume. But genre ideas are also general enough to judge as a general approach compared with other general approaches. Choosing a new creative genre for your brand and market is an act of reframing. Most perfume marketing is already romantic fiction. A reframing idea could be to work through documentary instead. Leading to a brand that was more up close and personal – and more authentic.

Avon Calling

Something like this was tried by Avon cosmetics. Their advertising a few years ago used the documentary genre. The ads featured close-up observations of emotional moments in womens lives. Their waterproof mascara was featured in a commercial where a mother was having a sentimental cry on a friend's shoulder; because their children had gone to their first day at school. Avon cosmetics are sold through a network of people who visit customers' homes and form personal relationships with them. This kind of personal contact and real relationship was reflected in this advertising. I have no information on whether this campaign was a success. It seemed quite short lived, so it may not have done all that was hoped. Whether it was right or not, it was at least a very clear and strategic choice of genre.

Khaki's Rock

Another example of the genre approach is Gap. Gap's main brand advertising is nothing that new. It features music performers and improvisation. The message is 'original' (or authentic). It is in the same genre as most jeans advertising – that of pop videos. The best exponent of this, Levi's, made such good pop videos in the 80s and early 90s that nearly all the singles they used went straight into the music charts.

Gap's ads, compared with Levi's, are more 'Unplugged' and spontaneous and so more in tune with 90s culture but they didn't break the mould in genre terms, they just reshaped it slightly. Gap's Khaki's advertising, on the other hand, does feature a new genre for clothes advertising and is devastatingly different. That creative genre is modern dance. In these commercials dancers perform in Khakis – from skateboarding to jive. The ads speak to the body about comfort and also physical movement and prowess. It works in the way that going to see dance performances makes the audience come out feeling lithe and full of vitality. These commercials speak to a different part of us, about a fundamental human drive (physical activity) and a different relationship with the brand meanings – of being comfortable with yourself in their casual loose fit clothes.

The strategic question which this Gap Khaki campaign tackles is how to take a nearly passé niche fashion (combat trousers and khaki colours) into the mainstream as a timeless 'classic' that will last a good few years. Like retro fashions, it needed an added creative twist to pull this off.

The genre approach works particularly powerfully when it reaches out of the media into people's experience of the product. People may not jive in their Gap Khakis but they certainly experience freedom of movement.

Global Blockbuster Genres and Coca-Cola

Coca-Cola stepped out of conventional advertising genres when they appointed Creative Artists (Hollywood directors working for Coke directly) to write ads to the brief of 'Always' (authentic, anchored, iconic and so on). These ads were a breath of fresh air for the brand and like Coca-Cola, Hollywood movie makers have a very broad global creative vision. I particularly like the global cute polar bear spots.

Another powerful genre Coke adopted was football. Football that is, from a fan's perspective as in the 'Eat, Sleep, Drink' commercials for successive World Cups. Football reaches as many people as Coca-Cola, with the kind of exuberance for life that Coca-Cola has always embodied. It's the perfect marriage.

The Diet Coke Break idea – work-time breaks and career girl camaraderie – helps a negative brand (no sugar) carve out a positive role in the soft drinks market. It works for me because it reaches out into people's lives, although I do find the execution a bit bland and predictable. I appreciate that it's a global campaign but Hollywood manages to turn out global films that hit this audience and situation with far more edge and originality. Perhaps Coke should go back to CAA for this brand now?

It's Good to Talk

Another great example of genres in action is BT's focus on the self-help medium of (better) relationships through phone conversations. The ads, as described earlier, all centre around using the phone more effectively in everyday life. This creates an awareness in real telephone conversations of a different quality of conversation and different behaviours so people get to notice first hand that it really is 'good to talk'.

Reality Bites

Our genre idea for St. Luke's Radio 1 advertising was documentary realism. The reason this was a good choice is that the station was seen as plastic and inauthentic even though the backstage reality of the station – for instance the DJ line-up – was actually very cool and credible. This campaign was branded 'As it is'. A low key approach that short-circuited the satirists of the old 'poptastic' Radio 1.

Another genre which Radio 1 have used is live events; mainly festivals like Glastonbury and Tribal Gathering. Radio 1 is at the events and interacts with people there in meaningful positive ways. For instance, at Glastonbury they brought showers to one of the smelliest events in the music calendar! They also broadcast live from the events. The live events genre is a development of the station product and of its brand profile. The question it tackles is how can something which is so big be good? The live events are both big and good, answering the question rather directly. The phrase we coined for this strategy was 'One Nation'.

An Animated Example

A classic example of this kind of genre approach is Disney.

Disney stands out more as a brand within cinema compared with any other studio. Only Stephen Spielberg can rival them in drumming up an audience for any film venture and I believe this is more than a set of values and consistent expectations. It is because Disney own the genre of cartoon films and characters. It is these characters which translate into theme park attendants and merchandising toys.

Many people think that animation will be the key creative form of the next century's media as it is already in children's films, computer games and quite a number of TV hits, like *The Simpsons*, *South Park* and *Wallace and Gromit*. In the future even the news could be presented by animated characters. Creatively, you can do more with them. They can change not just their expression but their very being and they can also respond in interactive environments better. Just as we have modelled ourselves on film stars for the last one hundred years, we will increasingly style ourselves to look like cartoon characters – a tendency already strong in Japanese fashion and grooming.

So far we have considered only advertising and media examples. But the genre idea is not advertising – or even media-specific.

Once Gap decided that their genre for Khakis was dance, they could just as easily have gone into completely new forms of media. There is an arcade game (*Beat Mania*) I've seen in Japan, which follows up on the disco craze. The player has to follow dance step instructions in a rapid sequence by stepping on different pressure pads. These would have worked great in stores and public spaces like bars as Gap's lead media.

Whenever a company uses media that are this new, they tend to get publicity. People expect you to try to be creative in advertising and so it is very hard to pull a stunt here that surprises people – just as it is hard to startle people in an art gallery. But put the same idea in real life… .

Gap could have done all sorts of things with modern dance as their genre. They could have invented the next aerobics (another dancercise). Or they could have had Gap Khaki-only nights at famous night-clubs (Levi's revival was started by exactly this sort of door policy at London's night-clubs in the early 1980s – the right classic 501s with the right stitching). The possibilities for creative new marketing are usually many and fairly easy to think of once you have a strong genre idea.

A Post-Advertising Pioneer

A real example of how non-advertising genre ideas can work powerfully is the cigarette market. Personally, I wouldn't work on a cigarette brand, but I'm quite happy to learn general marketing lessons from them.

A 'shock finding' of a long term study into the effects of cigarette marketing, was that the number of people smoking had grown faster in European markets where advertising and sponsorship was banned, than in markets like Britain where it is allowed. There could be all sorts of reasons for this. One key factor might be that in markets where advertising is outlawed, the cigarette brands have been forced onto more creative forms of promotion than trademark posters.

Camel has launched a genuinely fashionable range of clothing, shoes and bags. Their creative genre is mostly brown leather goods. Marlboro have done the same and these brands – as the Cowboy or Desert archetypes suggest – are linked with rugged machismo and the great outdoors. The kind of boots they made – like Timberland's – were one of the key fashion themes of the early 1990s. The key growth area in their market is young women. Women took to Marlboro Lights for the same reasons that they drank more bottled beers and wore more masculine fashions: they were experimenting with the trappings of masculinity.

The Genre Mindset

A genre idea contains three related ideas:

Where? Which creative media to use in what way;
How? How you expect the communication to work on people and how it might pass into real life experiences; and
Why? Does it directly fit your needs for marketing?

When you have a strong, original and strategic idea that answers these three questions, then you are most of the way there. Finding ways of executing this creatively is often the easier part. That's why creative genre is a good level on which to think about strategic creativity – it is at the intersection of these elements of 'a good answer'. It is still simple and inspiring because it brings to mind creative things that move people.

Becoming a Genre Collector

If you want to think in genres you obviously need a big storehouse of examples. Marketing people need to spend more time at the movies, in games arcades and book stores. My client at Coca-Cola, Nick Hahn, spends part of his time as New Strategy Director trying to find and learn from new cultural happenings. For example he has:

- Visited the UK to find out about the wave of public emotion following the death of Princess Diana.
- Visited Japan to learn about the cultural impact of the Nagano Olympics there.
- Studied the launch of *Godzilla* (the movie) in the States.

Every marketing company should have people who think and explore like this.

RULE 11

STAKE A CLAIM TO FAME

The One-Minute Summary

Here's something that hasn't changed that much in a hundred or so years of marketing. Great brands tend to be famous.

But the idea of fame has shifted somewhat.

The old fame was about memorable, stable essences. Old marketing got this by repeated, engaging expressions of the brand identity. For brands, as for movie stars, fame was about putting on and maintaining appearances and the brands and movie stars of these eras were distant and idealised.

Now fame is a far more unstable concept. It is about currency. About doing something interesting. It fades rather fast. Which means brands have to do something interesting rather regularly. And 'interesting' now means something that connects with ordinary people's lives.

Give Me an Example

Richard Branson.

He repeatedly attempts to fly around the world in a balloon. He turns up in a wedding dress to publicise 'Virgin Brides'. He has his memoirs serialised in The Sun. He takes a lottery company to court for trying to bribe him. And he gives his name to a brand that positively glows with all this currency.

Stake a Claim to Fame

Widespread recognition has always been a key feature of branding. The great iconic trademarking campaigns of the print years of marketing achieved this through posters – the Coca-Cola Script signs, the Marlboro Cowboy and so on. Then came the radio age of slogans and jingles and the 'sophisticated' era of television commercials featuring famous presenters and branding characters and other devices aiming for memorability. Now, the equivalent is 'Fame'. Which is a far more free-standing concept and which puts brands on the same playing field as movies and presidents.

Brands on the Bigger Stage

Fame in past marketing was brand awareness that you could buy through repetitive memorable advertising but this is getting too expensive nowadays. If half your advertising money was wasted in 1955, then media inflation figures suggest that 90 per cent would be wasted by 1995. Also advertising awareness is a worn currency. Being a well known advertiser is being a big fish in a small and stagnant pond because advertising is literally, as we saw earlier, the last medium that people trust. To achieve real fame, not just brand awareness, you have to be news-worthy.

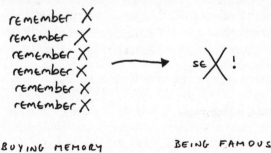

Being Known for Something

Branding now is a more dynamic idea – the by-product of your marketing rather than an end in itself. The following story illustrates this well:

After a tampering scare, the American division of Johnson & Johnson withdrew all stock of Tylenol at a colossal cost to the company. They over-reacted to the potential risk to ensure that no further harm would be done to any member of the public and rather than leaving a faintly negative image, which on the theory that a brand is supposed to guarantee basic safety would have seemed likely, the whole episode created an incredibly strong bond of trust between the American people and Johnson & Johnson. It was a living demonstration of their commitment first and foremost to their public service mission to alleviate suffering. It was the best branded activity this company could ever have done and they are still reaping the benefits.

The thing about staking a claim to fame, rather than trying to be well known, is that it means doing something that makes you famous. And doing things like this regularly. Because as every music and film promoter knows, fame tends to fade fast if it is not topped up with regular publicity.

Branson's Publicity Machine

That is why Richard Branson is such an asset to the Virgin brand. People assume that he is involved closely with every Virgin venture. Which is natural, I suppose, given that he is the public face of the company but the reality inside Virgin is very different to this public impression. He has assembled a team of exceptionally talented and dynamic young managers and has given them free rein to run the different territories in the Virgin Empire, many of which are franchise-like deals.

Richard Branson is a real asset because he always finds a way to be in the news in a way that is relevant to the brand. He is the brand in action; exploring and adventuring, taking on BA's dirty tricks campaign or corruption in the Lottery, or simply telling his own life story as an inspiration. Long before the Labour Party spin doctors, Richard Branson was out there using claims to fame for the Virgin brand.

A key feature of all this Virgin publicity is that it is much bigger in scope than the products and services they have on offer. It is national news, not a story for the trade press. It is the brand on the public stage rather than in that little pond called 'paid-for media'. One reason why the Richard Branson approach works so well in modern media is that famous people are a key feature of what we regard as public news. Celebrity is one of the key forms of modern media culture. It is the public arena getting up close and personal.

The Personalising of the Public Realm

The public realm used to be the exclusive preserve of traditional institutions – the monarchy, the government, the nation, the law, industry, the universities and so on. The news was the official and impersonal account of the continuation of the history of these governing bodies. It came in the official language and manner of the ruling classes and had a formality in presentation and a distance from the key actors as people. They were presented as holders of office, not individuals.

The public realm now is up close and personal to an uncomfortable extent for politicians like Bill Clinton whose private lives have become a matter of rather embarrassing public record. The people are still there largely by virtue of holding offices but the news is about them as individuals and it is reported in an informal, close-to-the-audience tone and manner. Rather than getting news about the continuation of our shared public history we get the reflection of our own little psychodrama's and moral dilemma's for example infidelities, personal tragedies, and battles against illnesses.

The British Royal Family has been one of the most compelling soap operas on television for the last five or six years – from the royal divorces and *annus horribilis* to the tragic death of Princess Diana. This tragedy was an example of how powerfully the news media connects the lives of the famous (and once distant) to our own lives and emotions.

The Agenda as a News Story Brand

The Princess Diana story was a prime example of how news media have their own sort of brand called 'the agenda'. An agenda is a topic which has an established familiarity and acceptance. The news works primarily through linking new stories to old agendas. It is how we assimilate things as a society, so the hard-to-take-in news of Diana's death was reported successively as, 'being hounded by the media', 'drunk driving', as well as referring to archetypes of famous people who have been 'taken from us' like Marilyn Monroe. This is a kind of media conditioned reflex. These media conditioned reflexes have been used for marketing purposes. Not just by creating brands or activities that tap into bigger things that are going on but occasionally by creating the reflex for the brand to tap into.

The Pre-Publicity for Playstation

One example was the UK launch of the Sony Playstation, the end point of which was a television advertising campaign from the fictitious organisation SAPS – Society Against Playstation. These ads featured a presenter from SAPS who is a pastiche of a 1950s American TV moralist – the type you can imagine in a religious programme talking about 'saving yourself for marriage'. He warns the viewer that Playstation can have harmful effects in a way reminiscent of the arguments put against television and its effects on children – with the slogan 'Beware the power of Playstation'.

All of this is obviously very flattering to the product – it's not just slightly faster home arcade games, it's a huge jump in media akin to the launch of TV. It tapped into every adolescent's desire for things that their parents wouldn't approve of. In doing this it was a very good fit with the kind of game that works well in the console market – like *Resident Evil* and *Grand Theft Auto*. It gave Playstation a forbidden allure and authenticity. What came before this was even smarter in staking a claim to fame.

Long before the campaign was launched, the trade fairs were leafleted by an unknown organisation called Society Against Technology (SAT). There was already an ambient 'new Luddite' news agenda containing disparate stories like the Unabomber. But SAT (covertly from Sony) created an apparently real agenda for the SAPS campaign. This underground, authentic backdrop to the TV campaign was continued by using stickers and flyposters from SAPS, just like a political fringe movement would have done. When the TV campaign was launched, it seemed a natural extension of what was already a hot agenda.

Previous console games had used more traditional brand building methods and were simply displaced by the 'power of Playstation'. It is a very good demonstration of how the New Marketing rules are simply more effective nowadays.

Even the Nintendo 64, twice as fast as Playstation and hence overturning every claim of the SAPS campaign, could not compete with the street cred that Playstation had established. Playstation is simply a very strong brand of the new kind, from the 'claim to fame', illicit appeal launch to the informal 'Playstation clubs' that exist among groups of friends who share games and get together to compete.

Of course it helped that it came from Sony but, as raw material, this was not necessarily going to beat the console specialists like Nintendo any more than an Apple or Technics new computer game system would. And the Sony brand itself has been built on New Marketing principles, right back to the Walkman, (which twenty or so years later is still one of the most up close and personal media ever invented).

It's a very simple point, but the difference between Playstation and its competitors is that Playstation made itself 'newsworthy'.

Managing Your Publicity

The PR agency usually gets briefed later than the media buyers (and that usually means very late!). In a world where fame counts for everything, this has got to be wrong. Look at how successful the companies run by natural publicists are; the Virgin's and The Body Shop's. Look at the transformation of New Labour in the hands of the spin doctors. The fame factor has to be a key part of your thinking from the outset.

If you start with the premise that what you do will have a claim to fame, then you are likely to get masses of free media. Given that being in the news is a key brand attribute these days, and given that news coverage is free, it seems much better to start out here and work in. Perhaps you could start by having some meetings with editors to find out what's on their minds? People high up in the media can usually tell you more interesting things for your next year's marketing than hundreds of thousands of pounds of trend research. And they don't charge either!

Whether you meet them or not, the point is that it is their agenda not yours that will make or break your claims to fame. 'Are computer games bad for our children?' is newsworthy and '32-bit processing for superb graphics' is not.

It is this kind of thinking ahead that starts to make sense of the 'integrated services' agency. Whether the synergy exists in one company or not, if you are going to launch multi-media ideas like SAPS then you need a PR agency and an ad agency and some other agencies too that can not only talk each others language, but which can collaborate.

One of the most successful agencies in consistently turning out what they call 3-D Marketing in London is HHCL. At the heart of the company they have a fifty-person unit devoted to PR stunts called 'In Real Life'. They are able to work on genuinely multi-media campaigns in concert because their teams contain all the relevant skill sets. Only this kind of organisation could have come up with promotional ideas like the Tango Voodoo Doll.

Enlightened marketing clients are increasingly assembling their own multi-disciplinary teams. And enlightened agencies are increasingly finding that the ability to work in open collaboration is key. As in so many markets, alliances and "co-opetition" is the way forward.

Taking the News Personally

We have looked at how the news favours famous people and existing hot agendas. Another trend which is relevant to New Marketing is the way that people now take the news very personally.

We used to be insulated from the news by the fact that it was very public and hence removed from our lives. Everyone seeing the news could take comfort in the assumption that 'it will never happen to me'. Now the opposite seems to be the case. Perhaps it is because the news is absorbed as a kind of 'village news', where we get to know the personalities and see behind the scenes into private events and emotions. News now is watched with the feeling that 'it could be me'.

Sociologists call this reflexivity, which is the tendency of news to shape society. For instance, a report about increasing divorce rates tends to increase divorce rates and opinion polls about how people intend to vote, when publicly reported, tend to affect the way people vote. Through reflexivity, news is another source of 'new traditions'. It gives us ideas in the form of agendas; it tells us how we could or should be living.

A serious example and moral dilemma for broadcasters is copycat crime. A commissioning editor for documentaries at one of the main UK stations told me that when they ran a serious and well-meaning programme about rape within marriages, they had a call from a woman who had watched the programme with her husband, who had then raped her. Given that a story in media can be taken as a prompt or even a kind of implicit justification for personal acts, there has to be questions asked about the booming television trend for 'true life crime' programmes.

The 'it could be me' news is usually bad news. When one batch of walnut flavour yoghurt in one UK factory was infected with listeria in the early 1990s, sales in the whole yoghurt market fell to half their previous level and took three years to recover.

'It Could Be Me' Turned to Branding

The reflexivity of news media was used to create the powerful brand of the UK National Lottery, which exactly caught this psychology. The National Lottery had a number of powerful claims to fame to start with:

- It had its own news medium, through prime time television draws, when the nation sat down together to effectively play a massive game of bingo.
- It had a massive jackpot which ensured that anyone winning would be catapulted to fame and reported on, especially in the tabloid news.
- It also has in the funding of public arts and charity projects, an ongoing supply of 'good news' stories.

The Lottery brand had a great launch campaign that took all of this very up close and personal, with posters and television advertising featuring a great, pointing hand in the sky and a booming voice that says 'IT COULD BE YOU!'

According to a witty statistician at *The Guardian* you have more chance of being hit by a meteor than winning the lottery and that is a great example of the old public objective view. The irresistible logic of the lottery in an age when we take the news personally is the feeling of certainty, every time, that we have just bought the winning ticket.

Another part of the Lottery's appeal is the bigger awareness that we are personally wired into an information age lottery called the economy. The fact itself isn't that new – people in the 1930s were all too affected en masse by the Great Depression but the mass awareness of this lottery economy and its potential impact is new. We take the financial news very personally.

Studies have shown that many ordinary people base big decisions about their life (like whether to move home or job) on their current assessment of how the economy is doing. Which is a feedback loop of consumer confidence that tends to make economic news as self-fulfilling as election polls can be. This insight could be a key factor in marketing big life decision products like mortgages and new cars. It's certainly something we have been very aware of when working with The Midland Bank. Money matters are no longer low interest.

The Company as a Brand

There was a popular theory a few years ago that people no longer buy into and trust product brands and that instead they increasingly buy into and trust the companies behind the brands. This was a fallacy.

Most people don't want to know more about the companies they are buying from – their values and operations – to any great extent. Whenever I have researched brand ideas about this, unless they have a strategic angle like Radio 1, they have tended to get a big 'so what?' reaction. It is true that more of the successful brands now have company names but that is because of the type of business that is succeeding now and not because of any burning consumer interest.

Many of the successful names now are retail, media and service companies who tend to go under a company rather than product portfolio brand because they sell a range of things under one promise. Not because people 'buy the company', or have any knowledge or interest in its internal workings.

However, one aspect of a company which I think is a vital part of the brand – because it is often the claim to fame in public news of that brand – is the company as a news story. Success is a key part of a brand's charisma. Perceived success that is. Virgin Atlantic only started making money a few years ago and Amazon.com has yet to make a profit. But they are held up as success stories. Failure stories have a powerful negative effect. A kind of widow complex develops around failing brands and enterprises and no-one wants to go near them. The media follow the 'failure agenda' looking for new examples.

Managing your company brand, whether it is also the product brand name or not, is a key part of modern marketing and is all about managing your success story. Microsoft is a great example of doing this really well. And this is perhaps the area where Procter & Gamble has most out-stripped Lever Brothers in recent years. Even if no-one knows who Procter & Gamble is, they know that Persil

Power was a humiliating public failure.

The other factor is that a rather important community of interest called 'shareholders' is also tuned into the news and the reputation value of the company is often more than ten times its actual worth. So success in this area can have more than ten times the effect of most marketing. Some senior managers counter that this is a very small audience, who know the company very well. They can be reached very economically by phone or meetings. But this belies the way companies as brands work. One to one communications do not create the grandeur of reflected glory and success.

When Saatchi & Saatchi landed the advertising account for Margaret Thatcher's Conservative Party twenty years ago, they became one of the strongest business-to-business brands because they had a claim to fame and were part of a bigger success story. And because they were now a club many senior managers wanted to be part of.

Celebrities as Brand Ideas

Famous people like the Saatchi brothers are brands. They are 'ideas to live by' insofar as they are held up as providing role models or 'lessons for us all'. However, the Saatchi's are not the best example of this. They are famous for their company and an art collection rather than *really* famous celebrity brands.

Pop and TV stars are better examples, as are high profile politicians. The role model side of stardom was covered in the "Up Close and Personal" section – for instance the 'I'm Tiger Woods' ads. Here I wanted to digress briefly into the slightly subtler role of public figures as actors in meaningful stories.

Much has been made in America about the raw power of celebrity. Everyone wants to be famous and everyone has their fifteen minutes of fame. Fame is the new morality.

Celebrity Turned to Branding

An advertising campaign for Martini some years ago tried to rebuild this once glamorous brand by using the fame principle. They made the campaign very participative. It started with public and widely publicised castings for 'beautiful people' to appear in the ads. This gave them a great implicit promise, like the National Lottery, as a brand that could make you famous.

The side of the campaign I was less convinced by was its take on fame because we no longer live in a time when people in our society want to be Great Gatsby's or Greta Garbo's. I know the aspiration in Martini's ads was ironic, but I think it backfired. It's a time when the distance and impossible beauty of glamour no longer really works. We do have very strong emotional ties with stars and heroes but it's the time of inner-directed fame which is personally resonant. Famous people are getting uglier – they are realistic models of ourselves, rather than godly archetypes.

The Moral of the Stories

Most important now is *why* these people-as-brands are famous. The claim to fame comes from doing something that tells a relevant story. It has a 'moral' to use an old fashioned term.

An interesting example is the world of politicians. Politicians exist in a kind of 'living Shakespeare play' for news. Tony Blair has to keep in the saddle as Henry V with his tough kindness and not get drawn into a cabinet battle of King Lear dimensions.

A French literary theorist once demonstrated that there are only twenty-seven basic dramatic stories. If like a politician you are a brand-as-a-person-as-a-story, then you need to be constantly aware that a story always has a point and that yours should point towards success against all odds, rather than heroic failure, or even deserved come-uppance. This is just one way in which 'story-telling' is important for marketers.

Story-telling is one of the three forms of human communication – the other two being visual signs and conversation, so it's a pretty big topic. Stories are a powerful part of modern fame – from spin doctoring to rumours – to success stories to how a product or service fits into my life story.

Story-telling is a more informal creative form than the tightly controlled 'science' of marketing using signs. A story is a way of putting things in up close and personal human terms and to present new ideas in a manner that is very easy to grasp.

There is a whole book to be written on this subject so I won't go deeper into it here, except to say that a good exercise to try early in planning some New Marketing, is to write the newspaper reports that in a few years' time might result from this. Which is an example of working with vision and values.

Which takes us onto the last rule.

FOLLOW A VISION AND BE TRUE TO YOUR VALUES

The One-Minute Summary

There is one aspect of New Marketing we have left to cover: The power of brands to lead and transform companies from within. Old Marketing was external, while New Marketing deals with ideas – brands – that are change agents both outside and inside the business.

For this to be true, then there is another kind of authenticity which marketers need to embrace. As Shakespeare wrote, 'To thine own self be true'. New Marketing must be true to the vision and values of the company.

Consider what will happen if otherwise powerful marketing is not true to your company. It could be one of two things. Either the company will change – a powerful effect, or the company will get 'found out' – and crucified by the consumer media and by word of mouth. Even great companies like Virgin only need one poor train service that runs against all their values to get torpedoed.

Give Me an Example

IKEA. When we show them ideas their big question is 'Is this true to IKEA?' In the case of 'Chuck Out Your Chintz', apparently it was.

Follow a Vision and be True to Your Values

To recap:
- New Marketing is a third age of branding.
- Brands are ideas that people live by.
- Great brands can light the path in front of us, rather than simply shining a torch at our feet.
- Great brands are true to the culture of their company, rather than just a flattering reflection of what consumers want to hear.

The Value of Brands Inside Companies

A consultant I work with called Terry Finerty tells me this is vital now because the key competitive advantage a company can own is not its enduring and appealing brand values, but
  1. their unique vision of the future of its marketplace and their role within it; and
  2. their unique culture and values.
This is obvious in the case of service companies where people deliver the brand. If they are not caught by some human vision and set of values it is hard to see how they can do this but I believe it is a rule that applies to other brands too. Branding for anything nowadays has to address these internal culture issues. The New Marketing approach is something I would summarise as: branding-as-change-agent, inside and outside the business.

Another enlightened management consultant, Christie Franchi, once described this process to me as a great spiral, linking the smallest actions and thoughts of an individual employee to the broadest external branding. If it is not linked in this way, then discord will arise in a company. No matter how strong a marketing campaign is for an external audience, if it does not strike a chord with the reality of the company as it is lived, then it is heading for a great fall. It could turn workers against a desired transformation, or promise things which won't really happen. Service businesses are an obvious case in point. But if factory workers haven't caught a vision of a certain type of quality, won't the same be true?

I've been working with Terry and Christie (both of Arthur Andersen) to find creative marketing approaches to company transformation: ideas-led ways for companies to grasp and move towards some future business model. We are applying all these rules of New Marketing inside 'the factory' and trying to find ways to engage people's hearts and minds as well as their hands in constructive change. What we are trying to achieve is strong internal ideas that link to the external brand. Ideas that people in the company can live by. So I would say their spiral should be more of a tornado that sweeps people up. And they would say, 'You would say that'!

The two terms which the good people of Arthur Andersen people have really helped me to grasp, both very current in management, are **Vision** and **Values**.

What are Vision and Values?

Everybody in business has heard of the importance of 'the vision thing', and they have probably received the latest copy of the mission statement from the board of directors. Everybody will also have read stuff about 'values' – perhaps a grandiose booklet of ethical values, but the true potential of vision and values in companies is only realised when they infuse the company exactly like brand ideas out there in the general population. Like live yoghurt.

A strong vision and set of values is the internal version of the company brand. It is the set of ideas that employees of the company live by and it is what psychoanalysts call 'the theory in practice' (as opposed to 'the theory in theory' – ideas we espouse but which don't necessarily run that deep). Building that strong internal brand is an important part of New Marketing. It has traditionally had little to do with marketing departments.

Another idea in this area that has a lot of management guru currency is that of the 'company culture'. A company's products and services and operations can be copied, but its culture is unique. It is the positive aspects of this culture that make the rest of the company work – because results are ultimately achieved by people. According to stud-

ies of company culture there are a number of different ways that are
commonly used to establish a strong company culture.

Telling Stories and Paying your Taxes

One method we have already touched on is story-telling – shared
human examples of how the vision and values work in practise. The
Andersen people told me a great story that was used to show how
committed a company was to the idea that honesty was the best policy.

> The chairman was told that due to an oversight by the Australian
> government they had unpaid taxes from three years earlier. Because of
> the time delay and because it was the Inland Revenue's mistake, the
> proposal was that the company be let off these unpaid taxes. The chair-
> man said no, the company owed this money so it should pay the taxes.

That level of honesty, whatever the cost, was what the company
expected. You can see how employees lower down in the company
could readily understand from this story the kind of behaviour that
was expected of them.

Role Models and Chairman Mao

Another classic method of building strong models of internal culture
is the role model. In many sales and service companies this takes the
form of the 'employee of the month' award.

My favourite, more creative, example is that of the *Diary of Lee
Feng*. This was a book used by Chairman Mao to illustrate the ideal
attitude and behaviour of a worker in communist China. Lee Feng
was a selfless army private who thought only of the greater good. He
was a model citizen. Only later was it discovered that the diary was
actually a work of fictional propaganda.

I think every company should consider hiring novelists and play-
wrights to weave their company mythologies, in the same way that
the old royal courts had their storytellers.

Shared Identities and Little Dragons

Another model of strong cultures is the idea of a shared identity. A person's identity is the deep-rooted sense of who they are: a Catholic, a woman, a member of the working class. Strong internal cultures can create a strong company identity, which people feel part of, 'I'm a Fedex employee' carries a lot of weight and pride.

These identities often have roots that stretch out into the community. The strong cultures of the 'Little Dragon' companies in South East Asia were largely predicated on a dented national pride at being so left behind by their neighbour Japan.

BHAGs and Crusades

One part of culture that was emphasised in a recent book on what makes strong companies (*Built to Last* by Collins and Porras) was having 'Big Hairy Audacious Goals' (BHAGs). The book showed that this factor distinguished the great, e.g. Disney, General Electric, IBM, from the not quite so great, e.g. Columbia Tristar, Westinghouse, Texas Instruments. Having a company goal in mind is a way for every employee to relate their efforts to some overall effect and also to feel part of some adventure.

This is tapping a deep human need – to have a crusading cause in life. Companies that don't have this, leave their employees to find their own causes. Which can range from benign community work and hobbies outside work, to dynastic politics and in-fighting!

Brands and the Great Spiral

These internal culture ideas relate to New Marketing in both directions along the 'spiral':

On the one hand New Marketing has to follow the old precept 'to thine own self be true'. Its consistency has to come from always being true to the vision and values of the company, because:

- otherwise it is very likely to be inconsistent – with other places customers have contact with the company;
- New Marketing is closer and more interactive with customers so any 'falseness' would be a greater problem; and
- authentic marketing feels like it all comes from one author – not a mercenary creative agency that could just as well have worked for your competitor.

On the other hand external marketing – as a creative projection of the vision and values of the company – can be one of the most powerful methods for developing the internal culture, because:

- the external marketing shows employees what the customer is being led to expect;
- it gives the identity of the company creative form;
- by virtue of being external and famous it gives more weight and validity to company culture. It seems important and real;
- great external marketing is inspiring and exciting. It makes the company a more attractive place to work, to talk to your friends about; and
- ultimately company culture is about connecting individual pride in your work to a collective pride and sense of purpose. I would go as far as to say there are no companies with strong internal cultures that do not have strong external brands.

Four Great Company-Transforming Brand Ideas

Virgin
One company where this spiral of culture and branding works especially powerfully is Virgin. The culture is applied to every brand decision: Does this venture give customers a better deal? Does it have that Virgin 'buzz' about it? Equally, the brand of Virgin makes the company exciting to work for. 'I work for Virgin' has a great ring to it, it says a lot about you as a person.

British Telecom
BT found itself through its external advertising. The 'It's Good to Talk' campaign has spiralled back into the company as a powerful mission to help people to communicate better.

As a private company it has discovered a much more altruistic public service cause than when it was a public utility. When I met BT to talk about their internal brand several years ago they were talking about building a 'brand centre' where employees could live the BT mission and ethos. And also about spiralling this back out of the company again in community and publishing ventures aimed at getting people talking. One early high profile production was a prime-time ITV show called *Look Who's Talking*.

IKEA
IKEA is a company with a similar mission – this time from its incep-

tion. They exist 'to improve the everyday life of the majority of people'. This mission has kept them driving for astonishing feats of low cost, great design. Like the minimalist metal bin that undercut the whole market, which they got by going to a tin can manufacturer. It has also driven their expansion across the world. And it is future facing – with loads of room to grow into. Or as their founder says 'Glory is in the future – much remains to be done'.

I have experienced the IKEA culture first hand, as they have been one of my main clients over the last three years. They are great to work with creatively because they always refer our work back to 'is this an IKEA kind of thing to do?' Telling the nation to 'Chuck Out Your Chintz' was apparently very IKEA – they've been doing things like this in Sweden for the past forty years.

IKEA also have one of the most intelligent cultures I've ever come across, not because they only hire geniuses, but because they give people at any level of the organisation the freedom to think for themselves. They give a lot of guidance in how IKEA has done things before, but they allow people to work out for themselves what IKEA would do next. A senior client of mine there told me that one of their most important functions is hiring the right people. Again not 'the best' in some general qualification sense, or the 'smartest', but first of all the most 'IKEA' people.

Procter & Gamble

The most inspiring recent change in a company culture I have come across – and one that has everything to do with external marketing – is the transformation of Procter & Gamble. The new chairman, John Pepper has brought in some very liberating changes in the company's style such as the move to casual dress for all employees, all of which are linked to one big new goal 'BREAKTHROUGH!'

The whole company is being geared to look for the kind of step changes which will double the company's sales over the next ten years. Like dramatic new product inventions that completely redefine their markets. It's too early to know if Oleastra (the fat-free fat) will do this, but Pantene is a great recent example – a shampoo with vitamins – which has caught the 'beauty is health' trend with a vengeance, to become a market leader.

The Implications for Marketing

This rule challenges marketing to go through a paradigm shift from the external creative communicators, to a holistic part of the enterprise.

In many of the more entrepreneurial examples in this book the companies do not have separate marketing functions and many of the other examples are total relaunches. This is the main circumstance under which true project management does seem to thrive, in even the most departmental companies. Marketing in the next century must be the heart of the company, not just its clothes. Or more controversially, New Marketing is Non Marketing.

This was a point we made when we were asked to produce an IKEA brand manual for Europe. The book that we actually produced was the *Not a Brand* book, produced specifically because the way that people traditionally do consumer branding (the aspiration and added value model) would be very dangerous for IKEA. The gist of our advice was: be a retailer. That's where your heartland vision and values are – driving down prices and improving people's everyday lives.

I think it's good advice for many other brands too. Many of the best already think like this: Virgin, The Body Shop, Boots, Clarks, and many other enlightened companies that we've come into contact with at St. Luke's.

There is a proviso to this chapter. If your company's vision and values stink then perhaps that should be your first priority, rather than ingenious New Marketing ideas?

PART THREE

WORKING WITH THE RULES
METHODS AND MINDSET
Asking The Right Questions

'I keep six honest serving men
(They taught me all I knew)
Their names are what? and why? and when?,
and how? and where? and who?'

Rudyard Kipling, The Just So Stories, 1902

New Marketing is about having ideas that change your brand. Ideas which reach out and change people's lives. New ideas. Often the newest thing about these ideas is not the execution in some new medium, but the strategy itself.

What I mean by a strategy is the answer to those six questions. For instance, the strategy for IKEA's 'Chuck Out Your Chintz' went something like this:

Question	IKEA's answer
Why?	Expansion into middle England (and two thirds of UK adults didn't like modern décor).
How?	Challenge and change people's tastes.
Who?	Women aged 25 – 45 – the key décor decision makers.
What?	Furniture feminism (if your décor were a dress you wouldn't wear it).
Where?	TV advertising – quick, direct and pungent.
When?	September – key sales period, launch of new catalogue.

The key question in this – and many other of the examples in this book is 'Why?' Why are we doing this marketing? What problem is the marketing setting out to solve?

You are much more likely to have a breakthrough idea, if you have an unusual answer to this first simple question. I guess I'm saying that the most unusual thing about New Marketing is often its purpose.

Here are some other great answers to the 'Why?' question, from the twelve case studies coming up in the next section;

BT	it's men who limit phone use (because they are bad at it themselves).
New Deal	not another employment scheme! (cynicism was the key barrier).
Friends	create an instant movie-like, appealing premise (sitcoms often fail before they've got going).

Having defined an unusual and simple purpose ('Why?'), the 12 Rules provide some guidance as to 'How?' you might solve that problem effectively for today's society and markets. This 'why? – how?' approach is the opposite of the typical marketing planning process, which usually starts with assumptions. It is typical to concentrate your thinking on how to *subdivide* marketing efforts between:

• different products in a portfolio;
• different types of activity e.g. advertising vs. promotions; and
• tasks – e.g. increasing usage vs. increasing users.

What is being asked here are the other four questions: What? (products, messages), Who? (target audience), Where? (media) and When? (schedule).

This is all very comforting. Everyone knows roughly what is to be done, and it comes down to the fine details of where, when and how much. Everyone can feel that decisions have been made and different voices heard. But it is the kind of discussion that was going on in every other tea marketing department, while Tetley was preparing to launch the round tea bag.

The lack of thought about 'Why?' and 'How?' is literally *conventional*. If you do not ask these questions you can only follow 'the usual strategy'. Once you have a good answer to the 'Why?' – How?' questions, then creative answers suggest themselves. With an innovative question, original answers are never hard to find.

This gets you away from the danger in New Marketing of being too executional, too soon. It is interesting and feels good to always be throwing out wild ideas but these are worse than useless unless they have a point. And that point has to be to tackle a marketing problem.

I'm sure the reader has seen plenty of New Media ideas which are just daft because they *start* with a way of doing things differently; like projecting an advert onto a building, or having an internet site, or advertising on condom packets. This is worse than doing a standard marketing plan, because at least the conventional approaches are tried and tested to do something for your business.

As a guide, when I have run workshops on marketing strategy I have found that it pays to spend at least half the time exploring the different 'Why?' ideas of what problem the marketing in sum total could address. And nearly all the rest of the time on finding a blunt and unusual 'How?'.

In many cases there will be some agency or creative group who will go off and work on this anyway. And whenever the brief is handed on in the process I have always found that a simple two line statement of 'Why?' and 'How?' is best too. This is the way to *talk* and *think* about strategy in a way anyone can grasp – from a finance director to a film director.

The other thing I've found when working on marketing strategy is that people are too inclined to take the first answer they think of whereas a good 'Why?' might only come from a new analysis of your market research, or the smallest chance remark in a meeting. Great strategy is often painstaking work.

My advice if you are sitting down to apply these rules is forget all the exciting New Media opportunities for a while and think deeply but simply about your business and market. And keep asking 'Why?'

The Nomad Ethos

New Marketing is and isn't new. It's a tendency that has been around in marketing for a while now – some of the case examples are ten years old. But it is also in its infancy. I struggled finding really pure examples for the book because it is just beginning. It will really take off with the growth of New Media, the new markets of the information age, the spread of a new doctrine of business innovation and another post-traditional generation.

I see the Culturequake as making society more like a postcard, with a generic universal image on one side, and a personal hand-written message on the other. New Marketing is one of those postcards. It is a movement towards marketing which is closer to real people's lives as customers and workers. At the same time it is a movement towards more holistic marketing – not as a separate function but as an organic part of the business and of society. That is perhaps why the entrepreneurial companies, with strong human values – like Virgin – do it best. It may be growing simply because our generation of business people are tending towards the Virgin way.

It is connected with ideas that are finding currency within business. For instance the 'Learning Organisation', which is part of the same sea-change. In the future, business is about people, their capacities, their collaborations, their values and aspirations. New Marketing is about bringing customers and other stakeholders into this loop too. What New Marketing can add to this general tendency in business is creativity. New Marketing is about the power of ideas to transform people. That is what a great brand is – a powerful idea. Ideas like those in this book can transform not only brands and markets, but people within the organisation as well.

New Marketing is a challenge to the pseudo-scientific age of business. It is a great human, subjective enterprise. It is an art. New Marketing needs New Market Research. Old market research was largely there to objectify and to justify – to support conventions. New Marketing is here to challenge and seek the unconventional. There is a place for research in New Marketing, but it is the place of listening and authentic conversation, not abstraction.

New Marketing has gained favour in some quarters simply because it is more creative and exciting. This kind of marketing will always attract the best people and the bravest companies. In my occasional role as a tutor on courses I find it is New Marketing that excites the new generation of people coming into our industry. This being the case and all other things being equal, New Marketing will win. All business now is about people and talent. But none more so than ours.

New Marketing is a gift to those of us who want to enjoy our work, but it is also a responsibility. The old marketing was responsible for repetitive, stereotyped, attempted brainwashing. With media bought on 'carpet bombing' principles, using crass commercials and store fronts and junk mail. Now brands can take a guiding role as new traditions. This is a responsibility. Marketing has a duty to make its activities human and enriching. The power is shifting to ever-more literate consumers. So this duty is becoming a cost of entry. I very much doubt that people will have their favourite media interrupted by selling messages for much longer, and then, when marketing becomes an invited guest, it is going to have to be far more delightful to its hosts if it wants to get invited back.

The new media that will emerge in this time will not, I don't think, be the New Media we have now. They won't be about pushing buttons, they will be media that engage people with exciting ideas. The successful media now will play a big part in this and if the internet and other digital media reach their creative potential they will be part of it too. My guess is that these are going to be primarily education and shopping (rather than entertainment) media, and that this is where they will find their core role in marketing. With these media assuming marketing roles, marketing strategy will become more of a conversation with customers than a public lecture.

Some people have said to me that they think all of this is great in 'times of plenty', but that with a gathering world depression it could all be put back ten years. As people get their heads down and fall back to the basic, tried and tested approaches.

They could be right, but I doubt it. Desperate times call for desperate measures. Most of the boldest moves in the book have come from companies who *had* to make bold moves.

New Marketing will not be lost on those whose budgets get squeezed. It can be far cheaper to have ideas that others propagate for you. You can even make marketing something people will pay for, like Disney's films, or Sainsbury's magazine. The economics of New Marketing is likely, if anything, to make it recession-friendly rather than just recession-proof.

Risk in marketing is a bit of a strange concept as it is in any creative endeavour. The really risky thing is to do something 'safe', and waste all your money because nobody notices, or it doesn't change their behaviour.

Above all New Marketing is a matter of temperament and ethos.

Throughout human history there have been farmers and there have been nomadic adventurers. Old marketing was like arable farming on quite a large scale – and quite tedious. New Marketing has something more of the nomadic 'Lawrence of Arabia' about it. Even if both approaches were equally valid and equally likely to succeed, I know which I'd rather do. And that is an important factor in the marketing of New Marketing. Exciting ideas tend to take hold of people, all other things being equal. And on current trends in business it's time for the nomads to step forward and run things.

All of this is my view of marketing. It's a result of experience, not general theory and it's worked for me and for many other like minded marketers I've known. It seems to have worked for many of the examples quoted in this book – whether the people involved thought they were 'doing' New Marketing or not. And if I'm right that New Marketing is the way of the future then increasingly all of this will just be marketing anyway!

I want to close this section on working with the rules, with three thoughts:

The first is that New Marketing is about wily ingenuity. It is about finding surprising new ways of doing things. Because that is what brings results in today's novelty addicted society.

The second is that New Marketing is about *doing* (not just saying). It is active, situationist, company- and market-transforming, headline-grabbing stuff.

The third is that – to paraphrase Raymond Carver – if it isn't *doing good,* then it isn't worth a damn.

The kind of crass marketing that we have had for a lot of the last hundred years isn't good enough any more. This doesn't mean necessarily that we have to be pious or moralistic, but the value that we need to add to our brands and industry is *adding value to people's lives.*

THE WILD FRONTIERS
OF NEW MARKETING
12 CASE STUDIES

Throughout the book I have used examples to illustrate what the rules mean and how they have been applied in practice. In this section I want to show how the rules apply in combination through some fuller case studies. The examples were chosen because they are on some sort of Wild West Frontier. They have broken new ground.

A lot of the best New Marketing has been done by those who would not consider what they do to be marketing – restaurant chains, music producers, politicians etc. There are some branded products and services here too though. New Marketing is not the exclusive preserve of those who have unusual products to sell.

These are all, to the best of my knowledge, accurate stories of New Marketing. But they may bear little relation to the way that those involved conceived their work. They are my interpretations. This section is more like journalism than 'case histories' proper. They are written from an outsider's perspective. Even when they are examples that I worked on personally I have tried to take this objective stance, because of course I don't want to give away all of my clients' secrets.

New Marketing is about having creative ideas to solve problems. It is probably seldom done as systematically as the rules suggest. It is often the work of instinctive entrepreneurs who would hate the idea they were following rules. Nonetheless the rules do seem to apply consistently to these case studies.

I hope that you are as excited by New Marketing as I am by now. But if you're not already totally blown away, now might be the moment to hold on to your hat. In my view, some of the cases that follow are about as exciting and creative as marketing gets.

Case Study 1: Friends

The hit TV show *Friends* is one example in this book that every reader should have seen. A few years ago it was the top rating TV series in the world. Just in case you haven't seen it – and by way of introducing certain key features of the show... .

Friends is a situation comedy. It is the story of a group of twenty-somethings living in Manhattan. The action revolves mainly around two apartments which they share and the coffee shop below. The dialogue and acting is very sharply funny and the characters well defined and developed.

Between them, the characters represent a number of types: a neurotic and obsessively tidy, wannabe career woman, turned failing waitress, the monomaniac actual career woman working in fashion, the sexily macho Latin type – struggling actor, the museum curator whose wife ran off with another woman, and sometime boyfriend of the career woman; the hippie new age woman and the straight man with a boring office job and a dry line in quips.

These don't necessarily sound a very promising cast of characters for a hit show. I can imagine the show being pitched to some television executive who said 'so basically you want to make a prime-time show out of a bunch of losers?' But the decision to make the characters flawed is a key part of the show. Their weaknesses and failings make them likeable underdogs who always need each others support and the audience's sympathy.

The casting over-compensates by making them all happen to be implausibly good-looking, even by American TV standards. And they also happen to have some of the best comic lines in TV to deliver. Cameo roles played by famous Hollywood actors like Burt Reynolds add to the glamour.

The problem *Friends* originally had was how to make a new hit comedy, in a market where most shows fail very quickly – too quickly for the old idea of building up characters across several series to work. This show had to have instant appeal. It had to grab its audience from the first episode, and like other recent hit shows (for example Ally McBeal and Seinfeld) the answer was to use a marketing logic – to follow the 12 rules.

The core idea of the show is contained in the title and the theme tune lyrics; *I'll be there for you*. The show is about a group of friends acting as a surrogate family. This is a very good idea for two reasons:

1. Many viewers are short of friends and use this kind of TV show to compensate by 'having relationships' with TV characters.
2. The premise taps a big trend in modern living – we do use our circle of friends to play the role that would traditionally have been played by our family.

I think its worth exploring each of these in a bit more detail, as both have potential applications to other marketing problems.

1. The solitary society

One of my favourite recent statistics from social surveys is that men in the UK over the age of thirty have *on average* less than one close friend. A close friend being defined as someone who you would confide in. This may partly say something about the reticence of older men to disclose their feelings and problems. But I think it mostly says we live in quite a lonely world compared with other ages.

Another statistic from the solitary society is that the largest household type in the UK is not the nuclear family. It is the adult living alone. This is forecast by the government to grow to over one third of all households by early in the next century. This is a symptom of the trends to greater mobility, independence, self-reliance and individualism. And reflects longer life expectancies. But it is also an indicator of loneliness. For those living in households with families, or with a group of flat-mates the trend is towards parallel lives. With each person having their own territory, their own schedule, their own TV set and even their own shampoo.

As a result of these 'lonely society' trends, a key growth market in media is solitary media offering surrogate relationships. We'll see this again in the Tamagochi case study. This is why so many big TV shows share one thing in common: they are about relationships. They offer the viewer a place in this circle. What used to be 'family entertainment to share' is now taking on the role of the family of close warmth and company itself. From shared entertainment to surrogate intimacy.

Friends is a prime example of this, along with soaps like *Neighbours*. In a world where we don't know our real neighbours, we enter imaginary communities.

2. 'Friendilies' – the new family

Friends is about what sociologists call an 'affinity ghetto'. In more traditional times, people lived in varied communities of all types of people. Every village had one of every type, from the wise old woman, to the blacksmith, to the village idiot. Now we increasingly only see and know people like us – people at work and people in our communities of interest. And as *Friends* shows, while we may know people from all sorts of different backgrounds, we increasingly only know people at our own lifestage.

The traditional unit of society is the family. Now many of us live at some distance from our families – geographically, emotionally and socially. Families are no longer bound by duty and ritual, and as well as being free from these duties and rituals, families are often split by divorce. In the place of the family we have the 'friendily' as depicted by *Friends* – a surrogate family of people with similar ages and interests to ourselves.

In old societies the concept of the 'friend' – a freely and accidentally chosen relationship – often did not exist. Friendship groups were made by the village. So, in rural France, for instance, pubescent girls were sent away together to learn about sex and sowing from an old woman in another village. These girls as a rule became lifelong friends, supporting each other through childbirth and widowhood into old age. Again, in most societies, men socialised as an extension of profession – much as they still do now in Japan.

Now we choose our friends to fit our current lifestyle, which is a volatile part of modern life. The friends in *Friends* are typical. They are all together because they have not – like their friends from home – settled down into stable careers and relationships. Any member of the cast is in constant danger of moving into this next phase of their life (e.g. getting married) and hence no longer being a valid member of the group.

Friends, like all great brands nowadays, is a myth for a new way of life. It is an idea we already live by, but which had not been so overtly branded and validated before.

The show that has come closest to this brand in the past was

Cheers, which was about a friendship group of similarly sad misfits but which really did see its characters as sad misfits who had become barflies. Instead of this, *Friends* says 'it's OK' in fact its positively glamorous, to be single in your late twenties and living in a 'friendily'. The casting and the way that the show loves its characters confers this acceptance on the audience.

Of course, the show appeals to many who are not at this stage of their life, but it offers an attractive template for everyone whose friends are closer than their family – be they in their teens or in middle age. And, because it is based in a great truth, it works against other rules like authenticity too.

Here is a summary of how I think the show used the 12 rules to create *Friends* as a powerful brand in general circulation.

How Friends **followed the 12 Rules**

1. **Get Up Close and Personal**
   Sympathy and empathy with attractive losers.
2. **Tap Basic Human Needs**
   Company.
3. **Author Innovation**
   In plot, famous cameos, locations, seasonal and topical references.
4. **Mythologize the New**
   The 'friendily' (friends as surrogate family).
5. **Create Tangible Differences in the Experience**
   Signature style and creative icons.
6. **Cultivate Authenticity**
   Insightful scenarios and uncomfortable moments.
7. **Work through Consensus**
   A show to share or discuss with others, or read about.
8. **Open Up to Participation**
   Everyone has their favourite 'friend' they identify with, or even copy.
9. **Build Communities of Interest**
   It's one of the few TV shows that attracts fans not just viewers.
10. **Use Strategic Creativity**
    It's a movie premise for a TV show – for a quick hit.
11. **Stake a Claim to Fame**
    The stars are real friends – at least for the purpose of endless PR stories.
12. **Follow a Vision and be True to Your Values**
    'We're all like that in real life, only not as funny' (Joey).

Case Study 2: IKEA

The first advertising account we won after we launched St. Luke's was 'Chuck Out Your Chintz'.

For those that don't know it, this was the advertising slogan in an IKEA television campaign launched in autumn 1996.

The main TV commercial features a housing estate where a crowd of women is throwing out all their old flowery and traditional furniture, curtains and doilies – to replace with IKEA furniture and furnishings. The soundtrack features a 1960s protest-style song written for the commercial which starts:

'Chuck out your chintz, come on do it today, prise off those pelmets and throw them away, those sofas are twirly, too silly, too girly, that flowery trimage is harming our image....'

Compared with most commercials on TV, the world it depicts is dowdy and ordinary except for the cut-away to an IKEA home – which, as the song says, is: 'spacious and airy and light, loose and informal and stripy and bright'.

This is using advertising in a different way than the great majority of brands. It does very little to present IKEA's virtues as a furniture store – its unique sparse Swedish design, its all-encompassing range, its dramatically low prices. It is an example of New Marketing being about *doing* not *saying*. It paradoxically tells you more about IKEA than any conventional brand advertising could.

Two things set this apart as a genuinely new sort of marketing – albeit in the old medium of paid-for TV advertising;

1. The strategy – trying to change people's taste.
2. The tone of voice – bluntly challenging and critical.

1. Changing the Nation's Taste in Décor

IKEA was in a unique position. It was the only major supplier of modern furniture in the UK (the only other one, Habitat, is owned by IKEA). It had very successful stores in major cities, and it wanted to expand into heartland middle England – the next two stores being in Nottingham and in the Lakeside shopping centre, Thurrock.

The one thing holding IKEA back was that most people in Britain didn't like modern furniture. We conducted a survey and found that only a third of people liked modern furniture, two thirds preferring 'traditional' English styles. If we could shift this in IKEA's favour, then everything else would follow (a larger market for modern furniture could only be satisfied by IKEA). Also, we argued, it was an outrageous thing to do that would get a lot of fame, which in a market where people get up on a Saturday and say 'we've really got to get a new sofa – now where should we look?' would be valuable in itself.

The IKEA we had come to know and love was the kind of company that does this kind of marketing. IKEA is a socially progressive company who likes to be the rebel and the catalyst for debate.

Why could we even contemplate trying to change people's taste, something that is supposed to be beyond marketing's reach? Because we live in a time when brands are the ideas that people live by. A time when 'traditional' things are very vulnerable to change, and new ideas that capture the imagination can change the whole culture of a market.

'Traditional' tastes might be held up as a counterpoint to all the arguments in this book about moving into a post-traditional age, (if we're in such a post-traditional age how come people are still trying to make their homes look Victorian?) but it is actually a mirage.

In the 60s and 70s the dominant taste groups in UK décor were very modern. Remember all those orange bean-bags and chrome light stands? Then, in the 80s, came Thatcherism, Merchant Ivory films and their counterpoint in décor – the dado rail and chintzy curtains. Old fireplaces were uncovered and reproduction ceiling roses glued in place. 'Traditional' furniture was part of the same movement as 'American Retro'.

Not only was traditional décor actually 'retro-fitted' but by the mid-90's it had lost its relevance. We were only a year away from the Blair election campaign and the country was in the mood to face the future but there was a deeper problem lurking. People weren't ready to give up their flowery flouncy homes as lightly as this historical perspective suggested. Or to be more specific, the women weren't.

At its heart, this flowery, crafty, nick-nacky, matching-pastels décor style was felt to be 'homely'. Which turned out to have its roots in the home as a nursery or nest. The dado rails had gone, but the traditional laces and soft colours and lines had stuck as a 'dolls house' décor.

These women had left behind nearly every traditional idea of the role of women – in their careers, their clothes, their relationships – but were still reverting to these quaint ideas in their décor. That's why we tackled them on feminist grounds with a slogan reminiscent of 'burn your bra'.

Which all makes perfect logical sense, and looking back we know it worked. The UK is now IKEA's fastest growing and most profitable market. A recent furniture retail survey described IKEA as a 'category killer'.

At the time however, it felt a very risky course. That is something that the rules applied to old case studies can't capture; the fear and excitement of trying something new; something that doesn't fit experience or conventional wisdom.

2. Marketing Assertiveness.

The campaign was intended to work through constructive criticism. It is very reminiscent of self-help books, like *Feel The Fear And Do It Anyway!* It tells you how to live your life. This is a common feature of quite a few New Marketing campaigns. Such as BT telling us how to use their phones to communicate better. Marketing is getting more assertive.

Marketing used to be this confident. Television advertisements from the 1960s told housewives what to do. One commercial for Kellogg's told women to 'Make sure your husband's had his Cornflakes'. (The story of the advert was that of a husband who skipped breakfast and as a result got caught in a mushrooming series of accidents, culminating in his losing his job!) This was one sort of confidence – the confidence of speaking on behalf of traditions. Of speaking to themes that everyone is supposed to agree with.

Then the traditions became less and less clear, and marketing became a shadow of its former self. In times of uncertainty, marketing did not know which side to take – traditional woman or modern woman, macho man or new man.

The beer market used to be incredibly confident in its portrayal of the pub 'good bloke'. Now it is more tentative. Eager to please, not to alienate – and it shows. Beer brands feel less confident and that is fatal.

Confidence is a key part of how New Marketing works. We gravitate towards ideas that have a certain assertiveness – like 'the rules' – because we feel uncertain ourselves. Strong brands exude the confidence that traditions had, while pointing us in new directions. The old marketing was preaching to the converted, the New Marketing is helping the uncertain.

Strong pronouncements have immense appeal to the media and their audiences, because there is so little clarity from them to draw upon. In a world where people don't follow fashion and are increasingly doing their own thing, pronouncements like 'brown is the new black' have paradoxically more appeal than ever.

'Chuck Out Your Chintz' became just such a new rule – sometimes vehemently disagreed with, but always in the foreground. It still features strongly as a phrase in a lot of décor editorial. There are literally hundreds of articles over the last three years that have led with this idea, and soon after the campaign was aired, when Britain went to the ballot box, it became a rallying cry for the modernist Blair supporters. One newspaper carried a profile of the Blairs at home with the headline 'Tony Blair – Tough on Chintz, Tough on the Causes of Chintz' (satirising the famous Blair policy – 'Tough on Crime, Tough on the Causes of Crime').

After the election was won a minister was interviewed outside Number 10 Downing Street, the Blair's new home. 'What's Tony doing now?' asked one reporter. 'I expect he's chucking out the chintz' came the reply.

New traditions need apparent consensus. If they appear true, then they become true. That is the role of confidence in modern marketing. As the voice says to Kevin Kostner in the film *Field of Dreams* – 'If you build it, they will come'.

How IKEA followed the 12 Rules

1: Get Up Close and Personal
Criticising people's taste. ('You can't do that.')
2: Tap Basic Human Needs
Belonging. (Social approval.)

3: Author Innovation

IKEA has never repeated itself.

4: Mythologize the New

'New Britain.'

5: Create Tangible Differences in the Experience

IKEA stores and product range.

6: Cultivate Authenticity

Assertiveness is always interpreted as authentic.

7: Work through Consensus

Two fat books of press cuttings ensued.

8: Open Up to Participation

Instructions for everyday life (to be followed/rejected/debated).

9: Build Communities of Interest

It polarised, forcing IKEA occasionals to take sides (usually IKEA's).

10: Use Strategic Creativity

Why? Change people's taste. How? By furniture feminism.

11: Stake a Claim to Fame

'Chuck out Your Chintz' – a 'side-brand' (like Girl Power for
The Spice Girls).

12: Follow a Vision and be True to Your Values

It is *very* IKEA. The founder, Ingvar Kamprad, phoned up to say so.

Case Study 3: The Tamagochi

Another term for New Marketing could be 'Craze Marketing'.

I suspect that crazes for games have followed the 12 rules for a long time – back to skateboards, the Rubik's cube or even the hula hoop. They are implicitly based on interactions, club-like groups, tangible new experiences etc. They are above all great ideas that tap powerfully into bigger needs and trends. And which spread like cultural viruses.

A way of describing modern marketing is that it aims to work in the same sort of way as these craze games. The Tamagochi is not the latest of these trends. It has given way to the return of yo-yo's and break-dancing among others. But it is in my view one of the best recent lessons in inventing new brands.

Tamagochi (for anyone who has been in solitary confinement for the last three years) are hand held computer pets, originally from Japan. The game is to nurture this pet, (or baby, or angel or other variants) to feed it and tend to all its needs. If you neglect it or mistreat it, it dies.

The Tamagochi's appeal in my view is two-fold:
1. It satisfies a human need to have nurturing, caring relationships.
2. It allows us to 'play god' which is a general property of great new media.

There is a third factor which is that it was hand-held and portable. This is a major trend in all appliances. Mobile phones, computers, Minidisc Walkmans etc. are increasingly palm size and still shrinking. This portability is a key part of the success of these gadgets which fit into our lives. Tamagochi would not have been one-tenth the success as a Playstation game. But I'm going to argue that this is part of 2: that the true meaning of this portability and miniaturisation is giving us even more 'god-like' powers.

1. Our Nurture Nature

Nurture toys are not new. Dolls are one of the oldest types of toys in human societies. Modern dolls allow their owner to feed them, change their nappies and comfort them when they cry. But apart from this increase in realism, they are not that different from dolls found in archaeological digs. There seems to be a stage in the development of human children when there is a need to rehearse this sort of attachment behaviour – playing at being a mummy.

What was new about Tamagochi was the breadth of its appeal. Businessmen in Japan became so immersed in caring for their Tamagochi that restaurants started providing crèches to look after their charges while they ate. Meanwhile the stridently independent teenage girls of Japan took to competing over who could kill their Tamagochi most quickly and ingeniously.

Both adaptations of Tamagochi are very revealing about modern society. Men are accepting more nurturing caring roles and relationships. They missed the stage when they learned this with dolls – they probably had an Action Man but probably never nursed it! Tamagochi were offering a second chance.

In the meantime, young women are rapidly embracing male patterns of behaviour. A *Cosmopolitan* magazine survey found that the majority of their readers rated career ambitions as important to them, but only a minority rated having children as highly.

I also think there is a general broodiness and interest in babies evident in our society due to the fact that actually having babies has become delayed or avoided altogether. Like Ally McBeal who is followed by a dancing baby to represent her maternal instincts thwarted, we are all haunted by the babies that our world would have been filled with on old population trends.

Real children and their nuclear families used to be the absolute epicentre of our social and media lives. Now surrogate babies, like surrogate families, are filling the void they have left. And like *Friends,* Tamagochi, as the most explicit and blunt and direct expression of this, became a major beneficiary.

It is obvious in retrospect that broodiness was a major cultural leyline of our times. Obvious because Tamagochi branded it and brought it into focus. Just as a number of brands have made it clear that we are feeling a bit sex-starved in the post-AIDS society. Or a bit hungry in our weight and diet conscious age. Denial is the mother of desire, and all that.

2. Prosthetic gods

Marshall McLuhan defined media as the 'technological extensions of man'. Sigmund Freud said the same thing more poetically in his late work *Civilisation and its Discontents*. The progress of human beings via technologies like media (and medicine and transport) is one of becoming 'prosthetic gods'. This sounds very grandiose and psychological at first. But it makes a lot of simple sense.

The gods, Freud argues, were an early cultural expression of our deep-seated human natures and desires. The stories of the Greek gods on Olympus, for instance, are those of a super-race of bored and rich playboys – compared by one classics scholar to the American TV series *Dallas*!

Throughout the rest of human history we have been using technologies to get towards what these Gods of man could do – we can fly, annihilate nations, see events anywhere in the world. And through modern medicine we are working on the last great god-like attribute of immortality! The prosthetic part of the equation is the catch. (Prosthetics simply means artificial extensions of the human body – from false teeth to artificial limbs.)

Machines and technologies can help us to fly, keep us alive etc. but we are increasingly like daleks, hooked up to technology without which we can barely 'walk'. The calculator is a humble example – undoing the progress over 7,000 years towards a human race that could count.

A more pressing example is the millennium bug, which according to some could set back human history fifty years and cause massive short-term chaos. We are as dependent on our technology as we once were on nature.

The Tamagochi is a prime example of technology making us prosthetic gods. God-like in the sense of playing god in the most fundamental life-or-death way. So 'prosthetic', we could carry a realistic life that depended on us in our pockets. Of course its only a game. Which is also part of how it works – we get the deep needs satisfied without the responsibility. I wish more media inventors and owners understood that their mission is to make us into prosthetic Gods.

Microsoft seems to understand this, demonstrated by their offering internet services under a slogan that could have come from Aladdin's genie: 'Where do you want to go today?'. And by producing a talking, laughing dinosaur toy that links to computer and TV. There are a few wonder drugs that tap the magic too –

notably Prozac and Viagra. Television was always a magic window on the world and videophones should soon join it in this. Computer games have this magic soaked into them – they even often look like medieval magical grimoires.

But where is the magic in the internet and digital television development? Until they discover that spark of magic, the world will go digital very slowly. As slowly as Singapore One – the most advanced and expensive multimedia network whose brand name took on an unintended meaning when it barely scraped 1 per cent of the population as a user base. If web-footed developers aren't careful, things with low bandwidth and high magic and inventiveness – like the Tamagochi – will continue to eat their lunch.

How can marketers who do not make technological gadgets apply these insights?

One implication of Freud's idea about the Gods representing deep seated drives and needs is that you can use old mythology to invent new brands. Rather than working from the list of fifteen needs you could just as easily get your ideas from a book of ancient myths and fables. I recently heard for instance that a company in Dublin is offering marketing services based on an analysis of characters in modern Hollywood films into ancient Greek archetypes.

How the Tamagochi followed the 12 Rules

1: Get Up Close and Personal
A pocket surrogate baby or pet.
2: Tap Basic Human Needs
Nurture and playing God.
3: Author Innovation
Variants. (But could have gone further).
4: Mythologize the New
The broody society.
5: Create Tangible Differences in the Experience
Unique size and functions.
6: Cultivate Authenticity
A cultural virus.
7: Work through Consensus
Created word of mouth and massive media coverage.

8: Open Up to Participation

If the Personal Organiser scored '5' and the Walkman '7', this was a '9'.

9. Build Communities of Interest

Spawned a virtual 'club' of Tamagochi-ites.

10: Use Strategic Creativity

A brilliant idea that took immersion in computer games to a new level.

11: Stake a Claim to Fame

The craze.

12: Follow a Vision and be True to Your Values

Only in Japan.

Case Study 4: Football

Football, as we British call it, is the most successful and fastest growing sport in the world. In some markets – like Brazil – it has always held a quasi-religious grip on the national imagination. In others like Japan and the USA it is undergoing slow development as a new 'exotic' sport. It has, through the World Cup, taken on a global importance that is related to its sheer scale. The whole world is watching: and therefore it creates media moments akin to the moon landing, linking us to one epic sense of shared humanity.

In England, where the sport started, football has been through a very interesting recent history all of its own. It has gone from being a negative, failing, marginal brand to one of the most powerful branded markets. With the recent attempted purchase of Manchester United for £600 million (blocked by the MMC) by Rupert Murdoch giving a small indication of the value that has been created. I have often used the story of the rehabilitation of football in the UK as an example of how there are no lost causes to New Marketing, and I think it deserves a place here.

Football, only ten years ago, was a negative brand. (A negative brand being one which is worth less than the sum of its parts.) Football had a fairly large following of supporters who went to matches and watched games on TV, along with many players in schools and Sunday leagues. It also had a very bad name, and a number of related problems.

Football hooliganism was held up as a symbol of society gone bad. It had the same reputation as gang crime in America, and played the same sort of role as a media shorthand for a general decline into chaos. This was more of a brand problem than an actual one. The great majority of fans were peaceful sports enthusiasts. It was a case of a few bad apples and the unfortunate magnifying effect of television which had latched onto this as a key agenda or media brand.

Another problem was class connotations. Football fandom was, in cultural terms, linked with the working class man and mass conformism. The idea of being working class receded out of sight in the 'buy your own council house and satellite dish' 1980s. And the great majority of the working population were in service jobs and considered themselves middle class. Football was consigned to history by its working class roots, as surely as the trades' union movement, greyhound racing and lard.

One particular problem in this heritage, beyond anachronistic class labelling was conformity. The image of the football match was the image of a mass crowd under one sway, of lost individuality in tribal behaviour, in scarves and rattles and queues outside the ground. Young people in particular could not connect with this sort of mass sameness.

These two problems multiplied in all sorts of directions, from old fashioned concrete stands and overflowing urinals at the ground to the identity problems – a football fan being equated with being a drunk, macho, anti-social boot-boy by the media and people around them. This was the same time that 'new man' was gaining prominence, and it is this current in masculinity and its subsequent channelling into 'new lad' that are at the centre of this brand story.

Football – meaning the Football Association and the clubs – set out to tackle these problems from the grassroots up. The old stands were replaced with all-seater grounds, with better facilities and tighter security – and also higher ticket prices. The value of football as a TV sport leapt up when Sky bought exclusive rights to the Premier League games and used it as a key selling point for their systems. This made football a more rare and special event – and also pumped money into the clubs to improve facilities and to hire foreign players and managers, bringing a bit of flair into what had become a stodgy English game. Meanwhile the other channels were forced to make much more of those games they could cover – the FA Cup and international games while also giving exposure to some of the middle divisions teams to give them a boost.

Football had changed the experience – they made the grounds a credible safe option for all those divorced dads to take their kids on a Saturday. It also made football a TV event, not just a staple schedule filler. However, football has also had some very large doses of cultural luck. Once presented in a modern and acceptable way, it suddenly found itself tapping into a range of trends:

Physical Involvement

We live in an age which is increasingly turning back to the body and the physical experience – the 'Sensorama' culture described earlier. Football is just one of the beneficiaries – alongside basketball, dance music, aerobics, massage, skating and many more.

What football offered this new culture of experience was a very high degree of participation, from kicking a ball around in the park to the exuberant involvement of pub games it involves the bodies of its audience, unlike gymnastics and athletics for instance and other balletic elite body cultures.

Everyone can do football and most of us who went through male British school days know how it feels to tackle, to shoot and score – our bodies remember these things the way they remember first riding a bicycle.

The Event

With the creation of much bigger televised events, football became one of those new big markers of time. Time used to be traditional time – measured against cycles and seasons and religious anniversaries but now it is measured by shared events – Live Aid, Tiananmen Square, The Berlin Wall coming down, Diana's death and Euro '96. Moments that become markers. English football was lucky in Euro '96 that what could have been quite a low key disappointment became such a moment of national pride.

The New Football Star

The archetype of the new football star is Paul Gascoigne. A volatile figure of tragically traditional masculinity – but prone to moments of almost divine inspiration. He is literally a tragic figure and everything a modern Shakespeare would write about. And of course he cried. Gazza – along with Eric Cantona, Ruud Gullit and a few others gave us modern media figureheads right up there with Tony Blair and The Spice Girls. It was these new media personalities that took football up close and personal on the broadest media stage.

The New Media

Soccer has thrived by creating new communities of interest. And it has done so through the latest in new media. One of the most successful internet sites in Europe ever was the 'Euro 96' site. Ditto the Playstation game of the tournament. Football has been the main outlet for underground desktop publishing – or fanzines. One of its most hyper-modern media was the fantasy football league, which were sweepstakes where each participant would select a fantasy team drawn from real players in the football league or competitions. If one of your players scored you got points for your fantasy team. Players had different prices and you could also buy and sell players in the more sophisticated versions. Just as the sport as a viewer event made everyone feel like they were playing, the fantasy leagues (at one time most newspapers had one) made most followers a manager. The crucial thing being that it was truly interactive in being two-way. It involved people in games and individual performances because they had a stake in the outcome for their own score.

Another key media was the live match screening in the pub. Many who did not have satellite dishes found this their main way of getting access to their team's games, which was great news for the pubs. I reckon it is one of three new ideas that have revived this once flagging sector – the other two being the club music culture and the foodie eating out culture. Pub screenings created mini crowd events – virtual stadia – where the game is much more exciting for the reactions of all around you.

The New Lad

In the early nineties men started suffering an identity crisis. Women were getting stronger and more confident and more successful. Many men felt unconfident and under siege. And the pendulum in the culture swung back from New Man to New Lad.

New Lad was an identity brand idea first coined by the style magazine Arena. It was not the old lad – stupid and violent and failed. It was a rebellion against political correctness and back to some aspects of teenage male immaturity but mostly it was an identity – a brand idea to live by – almost a fashion statement.

The idea of New Lad was most clearly portrayed by the hit TV series *Men Behaving Badly*. It is a regression into charming bad manners and boyish pursuits. A rediscovery of our collective 'action men'. It is almost a shared joke – we don't quite mean it, it's just for fun – it's expressing one side of our natures. New Lad has been behind many brand successes, from beers like John Smiths and magazines like *Loaded* to fashionable casual shirts from Ben Sherman. It was also a very major part of the Britpop success story – bands like Oasis being quintessential New Lads. Most centrally, the New Lad life revolves around football. Suddenly there was a rush for any man under forty to have a team, to drink beer from pint glasses and wear loafer shoes.

The curious thing about this injection of testosterone back into male socialising and football is how many women it has attracted into the game. The question for many women is how to be more 'manly' in the traditional terms they were brought up with. Attitude surveys find a great growth in women espousing ambition, competition, adventure and even dangerous sports. At any football match or pub screening you'll see that the growing – and often the most vocal – minority is women.

Through being attached to the power brand of New Lad, football has had its cake and eaten it. That is often the way out of brand problems. If you are stuck on what seems a margin the answer can often be to take that to some further extreme. In a sense that's what we did with IKEA too – from slightly alienating modern furniture to very alienating criticisms of people's taste. As in life, the way to be popular is often to be more yourself rather than less.

How Soccer followed the 12 Rules

1: Get Up Close and Personal
New stars and new crowd events e.g. pub screenings.
2: Tap Basic Human Needs
Physical exuberance.
3: Author Innovation
Has attracted brands that in turn fuel the sport e.g. Nike, Coca-Cola, Sky.
4: Mythologize the New
New Laddism etc. (for both genders).
5: Create Tangible Differences in the Experience
Quality of facilities and coverage. Events. New kit.
6: Cultivate Authenticity
Purified the 'inner' essence of football rather than attempting an 'image' job.

7: Work through Consensus
A case study in milieu marketing – fanzines, pop songs, new media etc.

8: Open Up to Participation
Audience participation – Mexican waves, phone-ins, computer games etc.

9: Build Communities of Interest
Tribal allegiance taken out of regions into media.

10: Use Strategic Creativity
A media genre reinvented.

11: Stake a Claim to Fame
A success story (with occasional set-backs, e.g. England fans in Marseilles).

12. Follow a Vision and be True to Your Values
Managed all the media and money hype while staying true to its roots.

Case Study 5: New Labour's New Deal

Tony Blair's New Labour Party has featured quite a lot in this book, from the value of a charismatic figurehead in bringing politics up close and personal, to some of their media tactics – like the appointment of a Millennium Dome Kid.

New Labour was elected under a platform of 'New Britain' – a manifesto for reviving and energising the nation, drawing on creative talent and a strong shared tradition, but looking forward to becoming a 'European Tiger'. This economic and national agenda translated into cultural terms like Cool Britannia, Brit Art, Brit Pop, Fashion, Design and Multimedia. A series of events were staged to make this link – like the Powerhouse exhibition, the Culture Commission and the publicity party at Number 10 Downing Street for the likes of Oasis and Damien Hirst.

In brand terms, the whole movement was encapsulated in one phrase from a conference speech Tony Blair gave in 1995:

'I want us to be a young country again.'

The New Labour party in government has demonstrated this new, younger approach. They have been tackling problems at a breakneck speed, with some of the rigour more associated with hotshot companies than government bureaucracies. There is a real feeling of 'can do'.

Some of the achievements so far have included an Ulster peace agreement, the move to make the bank of England self-managing (extricating politicians from the sticky business of setting interest rates) and the creation of the 'New Deal' brand, which is what I want to cover in this section.

New Deal is another St. Luke's case history. We were appointed to advertise this New Labour showcase of social change in January of 1998.

The New Deal is a scheme aiming to reduce unemployment. The

first phase was aimed at reducing unemployment among under twenty-five year olds. The scheme is a new type of politics that is very much in tune with the New Marketing rules; a partnership between government, the unemployed and the employers. In this partnership each has rights and also duties.

The key actors in this scheme were obviously the employers who had to step forward and offer training places, which were to be subsidised by the government and to be taken with a 'foot in the door' spirit by the trainees.

This all sounds very sensible, plausible and right. Especially if you consider that employers at the time were actually experiencing a skills shortage and government grants to train people to fill these gaps could not have come at a better time. Also if you consider that young people, including the unemployed, were the most highly qualified generation of new entrants into work in the UK ever. One-third of those unemployed under 25 had at least one A-level. And if you consider that survey after survey of young people found them to be far from teenage layabouts and actually highly motivated to take personal responsibility and to get on in life. This is the age of the New Young Serious – or the 'Get Set' as we dubbed them.

There was just one snag. Cynicism. On all sides.

Everyone had heard it all before and it had never worked. The previous Tory governments had launched countless schemes to reduce unemployment and the popular view was that they had only succeeded in providing tedious temporary jobs for a few who emerged disillusioned. Schemes like YOPS (Youth Opportunities Programme) and YTS (Youth Training Scheme) had also tried to apply techniques of branding and publicity, making things even worse when they went wrong. The brands became negative brands – national laughing stocks even. One comedian described a typical YOPS opportunity as 'filling in at the sausage factory'!

None of the schemes had the grassroots partnerships planned for New Deal. And they had partly failed because they had been so 'top down,' involving only Thatcher's cabinet, a few mandarins of Whitehall and a few top industrialists in their conception.

The centre of action for New Deal was to be local and specific, involving small companies, individual candidates and job centre training managers. But somehow the scheme had to get started on the right foot, which meant defusing the cynicism from the outset.

The idea for marketing New Deal was so simple it seems obvious in retrospect. The New Deal was all about handing part of the responsibility for tackling unemployment over to individual employers and candidates. The government would subsidise it, but the employers and employees would have to make it work. What St. Luke's did with the marketing was follow this New Deal principle. The government paid for the advertising, brochures, local contact schemes etc, but the employers and prospects were given this publicity as their own platform to say what was good about this scheme and why more like them should get involved.

One of the early advertisements featured a building company boss from Merseyside who said that he was getting involved in New Deal because, after a very shaky start, someone had given him a break when he was a teenager and now he wanted to do the same for someone else. It was a heartfelt message and one which struck such a chord that he was invited to share the stage with Tony Blair at the launch of New Deal and became the main spokesperson in the early news reports. No one, not even the journalists, could be cynical about the scheme after that.

The New Deal has been such a success that the Labour cabinet has rushed to brand and run other schemes in this way – with New Deals for schools and hospitals etc. I think this success is instructive because it touched on two important general lessons for marketing;

1. The new community spirit – personal and
   collective responsibility.
2. The value of 'taking people backstage'.

1. The New Community Spirit

There is a general theme running through the rules, which is that of a society which is increasingly inner-directed and which works from the individual up rather than from society down. So that fashion today, for instance, is about self expression through various current themes, not the wholesale imposition of 'this year's fashion' from the top down. Most of today's fashion themes started from the street level anyway and it is this root that ensures their general relevance.

This could sound like a growth of individualism and in some contexts, selfish tendencies like self-preoccupation. A lot of journalism has made this link – particularly when talking about 'apathetic' and 'apolitical' youth, but I think that this selfish individualism is actually a very different idea, and one which runs counter to the way society is moving. The way I see it is that there are two movements – akin to tides and waves.

One – the tide – is the breaking down of traditions and institutions in society so that people are freer to choose their own course through life as individuals. The other – the wave – is the matter of individual needs versus group needs, and in the last few years people have increasingly placed importance on the needs of the community over the needs of individuals.

This move was quantified by a survey by the Henley Centre – five years ago more people agreed that it's better that everyone look after their own needs first. Now more people agree that the needs of the community should come first. This pendulum swing gives a fairly convincing picture of why Labour lost the previous election over taxes but won this one with a programme of social reform.

In anthropology these two very different tendencies are given different names; grid and group. We are moving to a low grid society – low in structure and traditions that bind people – more fluid as a culture, with individuals freer to move and change.

Surveys over the last thirty years have confirmed a gradual constant movement to more inner-directed societies, but we are also, recently at least, moving to a high group society – one which places more value on the community and the needs of others.

All human societies can be classified as high or low grid, and high or low group. The global village is such a good moniker because it describes modern societies as low grid and high group. And McLuhan's media theory draws this into connection with the fact that we are a televised society, making the most public issues very personal.

The New Deal marketing tapped both trends, the tendency of things to work when they are low grid and individuals are given free rein and personal responsibility, and also the tendency of things to work when they have a benefit to the community at large rather than just appealing to self-interest.

This is the new community spirit. Low grid but high group, whereas the 'old community spirit' was high grid and high group – about your passive duty to Queen and Country or class.

2. The Value of Taking People Backstage

The old marketing was theatrical. It staged the presentation of goods and services using the magic of television, the glamour of famous presenters etc, and it kept its audience passive and quiet in their seats in the stalls. It was all about creating an illusion called the brand image.

In the New Marketing age, people are more literate and bored with tired old theatricality. They see through it. The TV ads may say 'brewed in the traditions of rustic France' but if it says 'brewed in the UK' on the can, it is likely to backfire. There are two options for marketing in this context: stage better plays, or take people backstage and involve them in the production.

The New Deal took the latter course. It was marketing for, by and to the people. That's what gave it the same kind of authenticity as the popular 'soap documentaries'.

Some of the other case studies also took this approach – notably Pizza Express and FCUK. Others created new types of 'play' – like IKEA and like the next case study, Tango. There is an economic advantage in this 'dressed down' style of New Marketing. Staging things nowadays costs more and more money, because people's expectations of what is special and involving keep rising. Ask any producer of a West End musical – dazzling people is an expensive and risky business. Involving people in the marketing can save money – it's a form of self-service. Word of mouth is an example – it's a free medium and great ideas can get the kind of secondary publicity in this medium that money literally cannot buy.

The old marketing was like launching a West End musical. The New Marketing is more like putting on school plays – with parents involved not just in their little darlings' performance but in making costumes. It's marketing that's much closer to people and it means taking down a lot of those dazzling barriers of aloofness called 'image'.

How the New Deal followed the 12 Rules

1: Get Up Close and Personal
Individual involvement and grass roots local culture.

2: Tap Basic Human Needs
Citizenship.

3: Author Innovation
Has evolved as a news story, e.g. 'thank you' ads from successful interns.

4: Mythologize the New
The new community spirit.

5: Create Tangible Differences in the Experience
Stepping out of your comfort zone (shown in ads by nervous public speaking).

6: Cultivate Authenticity

True stories of real advocates.

7: Work through Consensus

Advocacy as a 'word of mouth' PR principle.

8: Open Up to Participation

Partnership scheme and participants in the marketing.

9: Build Communities of Interest

The employer/employee/DSS partnership.

10: Use Strategic Creativity

Defuse cynicism through 'subsidiarity' (close to the people/ the action).

11: Stake a Claim to Fame

Heartfelt personal testifying.

12: Follow a Vision and be True to Your Values

Tough kindness, e.g. no rights without responsibility (The Third Way).

Case Study 6: Tango

Tango used to be everybodies case study of post-modern advertising; ironic, anarchic, self-referential. It was the voice of a new generation of advertising people. People who had grown up on punk and who hated the polished middle-class gloss of classic British advertising; contemporaries of Damien Hirst and Pulp. And it was the defining work of one of the most admired 'Fourth Wave' ad agencies – HHCL.

It has been quoted over the last ten years as an example of just about every new theory of marketing, like 'Chaos Marketing'. As the saying goes 'success has many fathers but failure is a bastard!'

I was hesitant about including it simply because it is so well worn and I have heard so many explanations of why it worked. But I still think it is one of the best examples of taking a very basic and banal product in a very crowded market and doing something extraordinary with it. It shows that New Marketing is not only for the Virgin's and IKEA's and New Labour Party. I like it because of its unusual rigour in constructing brand meanings – using 'semiotics' – the science of signs.

Cast your mind back to the soft drinks advertising of the late 1980s. Nearly all the commercials featured the following: beaches, jeeps, saxophones, people in swimwear, exuberance, mid-Atlantic pop tracks and jingles. The defining brand in this ilk was Coca-Cola, and where they led, many followed. Not only Tango but Sunkist, Fanta, Lilt. It was all pretty indistinguishable and all pretty dire.

There were a few glorious exceptions, like Irn Bru that produced a satire on how this advertising didn't quite fit Scottish culture but by and large it seemed like one of those categories where we were to be treated to years more of this cultural pollution. At least *Baywatch* had the decency to use this kind of lifestyle imagery in the service of little moral tales!

The problem for Tango in all of this mess was being unremarkable; in a market with really strong brands like Coca-Cola on the one hand; and really similar, and in my opinion naff little brands like Sunkist on the other. Orange soft drinks were seen as very sweet and sickly (like their brand imagery) and mainly for 'kids' in a market where everyone increasingly wanted to be a cool teenager or little adult. Tango was a naff brand in a naff category going nowhere.

All of that changed with one new commercial. It featured an action replay, a football style commentary, showing a large man painted orange creeping up behind an unsuspecting drinker and slapping him around the ears. All to show 'the hit of real oranges' – the 'Tango taste sensation'.

I suspect that most of the people involved wouldn't have realised what a hit they were about to have on their hands. HHCL was at the time a company known for their quite avant garde work which had achieved creative recognition but never quite connected with more popular tastes. And Britvic seemed like quite a steady but traditional marketing company. But the advertising quickly became a playground sensation. Creeping up behind people and 'Tango-ing' them became a new craze. This is a great example of how to be really successful you need 'co-creators'. It's not what you do, it's what they do with what you do.

When, after a case of burst eardrums, the advertising was banned, the brand achieved cult status. It went from Ronald McDonald to Sid Vicious in a matter of months.

What would nearly always have happened then, given that it was a bit of a fluke – is that the brand would probably have faded. With new commercials following the old one faithfully and turning its freshness into cliché – aided and abetted by all its imitators. But what happened instead was the most extraordinary, long spree of anarchic creative marketing.

Some highlights include:

- The orange man creeping up behind people being interviewed outside the Houses of Parliament for the TV news.
- The hoax broadcast from the marketing director claiming that Still Tango was a bootleg product, nothing to do with the Tango brand, and urging people not to buy it and to report it to the authorities.
- Numerous other uses of Tango phone lines to get people involved in weird ways – like the offer of a Tango voodoo doll.
- A postcard sent as a direct mail-shot claiming to be from someone the recipient had pulled on holiday.
- Advertising for Lemon Tango featuring a new cult religion around lemon worship.

- Advertising for Apple Tango featuring people with strange sexual fetishes for the product.
- Advertising for Blackcurrant Tango featuring a member of staff challenging someone who had complained to a fight.

It is possible to reduce Tango to a series of bland essences, anarchic, rebellious etc. But that doesn't do it justice. It was Tango's genre that captivated people – what it did. Tango's role was that of a practical joker.

It did the same sorts of things as Chris Evans and *The Big Breakfast* – it was guerrilla comedy. It was this dynamic role that the other soft drinks never latched onto. They made wacky advertising following Tango's lead, but they never threw custard pies at the audience.

A recent campaign that seems to have caught more of this spirit using new media is that for Fudge hair products. It features a sci-fi cartoon with little obvious relevance to anything and an invitation into a web-site to explore this strange world further.

I think both examples understand the way that branding can work by creating potential differences and gaps for people to close, pieces of a jigsaw to play with, rather than handing them a polished, flattering but predictable portrait. This is something that in a formal academic way is covered by the field of Semiotics.

Semiotics is the science of signs. Signs are things that communicate to us – road signs, words, works of art and also bits of marketing communications. The concept in semiotics that is relevant here is that human meaning is not neatly compartmentalised like a grammar primer, but is grasped through networks of criss-crossing associations. One of the leading thinkers in semiotics, Umberto Eco, drew a semiotic 'net' of the hundreds of associations surrounding the word 'Neanderthal' across several languages.

These networks of associated meanings are something to do with the way our minds work. Recent studies in neuroscience show that we code signs (or 'representations') in two separate parts of our brain. One is associative – linking everything with everything else. The other is propositional – a 'logic box' of things we hold to be true about the world. The interplay of these two is how we grasp meanings. All of this sounds a bit theoretical but it makes obvious common sense if you think about it.

Take the word 'wellies'. It summons up all sorts of associations, from the little red wellies we splashed in puddles with as children – to the Duke of Wellington, to the slang phrase 'give it some welly' meaning kick something into action. It's not just that words have more than one meaning. It's that they have rich poetic associations that bring emotions to bear. So that using the word 'wellies' has a very different ring and feel to using the word 'boots' in the same context.

Most marketing creates signs that are closed off and complete and which lose a lot of these surrounding associations. One of the criticisms of advertising is that it takes things with grandeur and richness like an old jazz song, and makes it 'that one from the – ad". Or that it diminishes the signs it uses – like the images of great people used to advertise cars or computers. What Tango did was unearth very faint and distant associations and leave them open with all sorts of new connections and loose ends.

So for instance, there was a very conventional ad for Appletise which showed the drink in the lush setting of the Garden of Eden – illustrating the association with the temptation of Eve. What Tango did with Apple Tango was take this faint association and then make a creative leap into modern fetishes. It was a 1+1=3 equation. It left you to fill in the 'missing connection'. Similarly blackcurrant (like blood) and orange (anarchic, as in punk, or the wacky Belgian 'Walloon' culture).

The phone lines and other loose ends have left the communication unfinished – to be continued – open to participation. This type of marketing makes the audience the key creative player. No wonder kids in particular couldn't resist picking it up and playing with it. The "Fudge" marketing seems to work in a similar way but is even more implicit. It invites you into a website where – like the computer game *Myst*, you have to explore and piece it together, but nothing yields to give obvious meanings.

That was just one part of the Tango story. It did many other things, on many other levels as we'll see as we go through the rules.

The key lesson of this story is that it's OK for your marketing to be digital – for it to be in incomplete bits and pieces. In fact it is much more compelling. It invites us to piece it together. This is a different sort of challenge to classical branding than the dynamic versus unchanging one but it is just as fundamental.

How Tango followed the 12 Rules

1: Get Up Close and Personal
'Dirty realism' production values.
2: Tap Basic Human Needs
Physicality (jolts of shock or surprise).

3: Author Innovation
Creative themes, 360° media, flavour variants –
a constant barrage of surprise.

4: Mythologize the New
Generation X ('knowing' irony).

5: Create Tangible Differences in the Experience
Vivid taste-shock conditioning.

6: Cultivate Authenticity
Transgression and 'White label' advertising, packaging etc.

7: Work through Consensus
Every stunt and ad a talking point.

8: Open Up to Participation
Response mechanics on everything.

9: Build Communities of Interest
A playground icon of rebellion.

10: Use Strategic Creativity
Naff became wacky became cool.

11: Stake a Claim to Fame
Always on the verge of getting in trouble.

12: Follow a Vision and be True to Your Values
A merry prankster culture. 'What shall we do next?'

Case Study 7 – Pizza Express

Pizza Express is one of my favourite case examples of cultivating authenticity across what could have been just another bland and naff food chain, and of a particular approach to this which is very slow and patient – almost stubborn.

The spirit of this reminds me of farming; of letting things grow up organically at their own pace. A similarly great example of this is Becks beer. What they have in common is that they have taken a long-term view, ignoring rivals who have gone in for flashier, noisier marketing and short-term gains. And they have won out in the long term as brands that feel authentic and almost as if they've always been around and stood the test of time – without becoming old-fashioned.

Pizza Express has never advertised. It has worked slowly through experience and word of mouth, and as a result has put down deeper roots. It has become a natural part of the daily culture of young white collar Britain. According to anecdotal reports, when a Pizza Express opens in a new area that area is seen as 'going up in the world'. So much so that house prices in that area rise by an average of 5 per cent. This is a brand acting as its own media in a very powerful way! It says a lot, not only about itself but about everything around it. But it's not just about a softly, softly approach to marketing.

Pizza Express also had an brand experience which spoke for itself. The pizza menu and the food itself is unique and very fresh, tasty and satisfying. Not only does it taste hand-made but the linchpin of the whole brand is the fact that the pizzas are made, not only on the premises but actually out in the restaurant area. This is a great example of achieving authenticity by 'taking people back-stage'. It is the restaurant equivalent of MTV Unplugged. Not only does this condition diners to expect hand-made, fresh-tasting food but it is also a part of staging a unique experience. The ritual of watching the dough being chucked in the air, the tomatoes and cheese added, and the pizza sliding into the oven – it's all part of the theatre.

As is the restaurant itself. A studied mixture of light modern décor and graphics with a certain homely charm, and another great factor is the way that no two Pizza Express restaurants look the same. From the basic long sliver of a local town's converted shop to the three floor grandeur of 'Kettners' in Soho, each is tailor-made to fit the space.

The big trend that I think Pizza Express got to long before the Conran restaurants is the emergence of the informal, American-style eating out culture in the UK. Pizza Express could so easily have been 'McPizzas'. But its associations (un-closed) into 'high culture' like the modern design and jazz at some branches gave it a bit of 'restaurant' cachet and specialness. While the high street accessibility and the familiar (unchanging) menu and experience give it the informal accessibility of a local pub.

Like Tango, Pizza Express is a vivid mixture of different elements that collide and create heat and light without ever blurring into one samey predictability. It remains multi-faceted and for all its cosy familiarity a constant slight surprise.

Going to Pizza Express is a bit like going abroad. Everything is slightly different, but it all seems to have its own internal logic. That logic feels like the taste of a founder who has made something out of their own idiosyncrasies – right down to their favourite music and modern prints. It is this personalness – like going to someone's home – that Pizza Express, I suspect, must fight to retain now it has been bought by one of the big chains.

The heart of the brand is something like 'taste'. Something that cannot be copied or packaged and something which it is quite hard to break down into components and do justice to.

Everything in Pizza Express has an aesthetic and foodie reason for being just so. It's a great quality in anyone running this sort of experience business – a total contrast to the naff plastic chains that are touted as leaders in the new experience marketing.

If marketing is to create experiences closer to us then they must feel authentic – just as a film must seem realistic somehow. Otherwise people will always be able to see through them. It's a real trick to invent something that feels uninvented.

How Pizza Express followed the 12 Rules

1: Get Up Close and Personal
Intimate, informal, hand-made. The signature of a strong taste (in food, décor).

2: Tap Basic Human Needs
Foodie-ness.

3: Author Innovation
Apparently not. Until you visit more than one branch – each is unique.

4: Mythologize the New
Eating out and the new informality.

5: Create Tangible Differences in the Experience
It's so unique and coherent, it's like going abroad.

6: Cultivate Authenticity
Hand-made dining.

7: Work through Consensus
A word of mouth brand – never advertised.

8. Open Up to Participation
Kitchen in the restaurant = cooking as theatre. Customisable food.

9: Build Communities of Interest
So indicative of a certain clientele, it puts up local house prices.

10: Use Strategic Creativity
A 'Conran' restaurant for the masses; far ahead of its time.

11: Stake a Claim to Fame
A very 'underground' brand; e.g. Jazz at Pizza Express.

12: Follow a Vision and be True to Your Values
So far 10 out of 10. Let's hope the new owners understand it.

Case Study 8 – French Connection

French Connection UK has been an extraordinary example of the power of pure branding in the New Marketing vein to completely recast the fortunes of a business.

Interviewed in the *Financial Times* after 1998s results, the Chairman said that business was booming (up 38 per cent), there were plans for expansions, the share price was healthy for the first time in six years and as far as he was concerned it was all the result of the advertising.

It's hard to remember what a marginal brand French Connection used to be. Much more Burton Group than Diesel. A very 'over-ground' brand in a youth market (now extending into people's thirties) which had gone underground. It was a pale imitation of the formerly far more successful Next, and reports soon after the French Connection results showed that the Next empire itself was now floundering in this new more informal era.

The advertising in question was the infamous 'FCUK' campaign. You could be forgiven for thinking from these case studies that the recipe for success in any marketing is to get banned. First Tango, now this. Not to mention IKEA, which came close on several occasions. Now I don't believe that being offensive is particularly big or clever or cool, but in certain situations it has to be said that breaking the rules or being anti-authority is a big source of authenticity. These areas are usually those of fashion, music and other youth markets. Where transgression is the key to being cool. From heroin chic, to punk, through the Lolita scandals and the decadence of Alexander McQueen or the late Gianni Versace.

Shocking, taboo-bending marketing can also be strategic. One of the marketing people at Club 18–3 o Holidays told me that every time there was a moral and disapproving article in the papers, their bookings would shoot up. On the basis presumably that young hedonists would conclude that there was 'no smoke without fire'. Their rude and often censored poster campaign (with headlines like

'Beaver Espana') I'm told did amazing things for the brand, perhaps because it understood this basic link.

The FCUK story starts about five years earlier with the appearance of a new youth media – the branded t-shirt. Not like the old branded t-shirt carrying a Nike swoosh. More like the *very* old branded t-shirts carrying great big trade marks. These were worn with ironic relish – some, like 'Bank of Saudi Arabia' tracksuits became collector's items.

Then came the sting in the tail. People started producing their own adapted trademark t-shirts, where the letters had been changed slightly to subvert the meaning into street fashion. Classic mutant logos include 'Burger Christ' (for Burger King), 'Badweiser' (for Budweiser), 'Elvis' (for Levi's) moving on to the more blatant 'Sexsi' (for Pepsi) and 'enjoy Cocaine' (for Coca-Cola).

FCUK came out of this anti-marketing counter-culture. Apart from anything else, one of its big effects was that it apparently sold 100,000 t-shirts.

It started with the posters, which featured models in French Connection clothes with plain white backgrounds. In case you don't know French Connection it's like a slightly more dressy Gap. But the attitude of the models and the photography was more Levi's or Calvin Klein. The twist was in the headline which said simply 'FCUK Fashion'.

This was a great exercise in having your cake and eating it. The anti-fashion fashion brand. But that paradox is exactly where main-stream fashion has got to. On the one hand fashion has never been more 'uniform'. On the other, the wearers have never been more individualistic, not simply on the quirky self-expression level, but – relaxing about it and 'doing their own thing'.

It's not a paradox really, it's inner-directed fashion – stuff you feel comfortable with. It's the same sort of intersection as the *low grid-high group* point we covered earlier. People look increasingly within themselves for tradition-like codes (such as fashion) but also feel more part of a broad 'community spirit'. The dominant fashion and music trend in the UK that holds both tendencies is the whole dance music, festival and so-called Rave scene (which is so pervasive everyone is involved in it but no-one thinks they are part of it).

So FCUK Fashion with a no-nonsense range that came across like Gap-with-attitude was a great position to take. But the crucial thing in my view was that it wasn't just an ad campaign. You could wear it as a statement on a t-shirt. You could also shop in it. The poster campaign became the store graphics. And shop windows – as

Harvey Nichols and others have shown – can be a very powerful and high profile medium in their own right.

It was this integral nature of the idea that gave it its connection and authenticity. It wasn't just a pose – it was taken to the heart of the company and made their identity. They were prepared not just to make this sort of statement but stand behind it. And the business has thrived as a result.

FCUK is to designer labels what Pizza Express is to restaurants – special but accessible. It is quite common to see FCUK branded t-shirts in quite hip night clubs along with Diesel and very few others but you don't see much Gucci these days (too showy) and you never see Gap or Next branding in these places (too naff and mainstream).

It used to be said by marketing old-timers that 'if you get middle of the road you tend to get run down'. These days mid-positionings can have the best of both worlds – taking energy from both areas – like the Boddingtons example covered earlier (mid-lager-bitter).

So French Connection had a good year based on this relaunch. The challenge that French Connection faced was what to do next. After the ban, could they keep the brand dynamic and take it somewhere new or would it get a bit toned down and respectable and become a one-hit wonder?

But I knew we wouldn't need to worry on this account when I saw their new flagship store carrying an enormous poster in the window with the line 'Your Place Or Mine,' and then saw someone later that day in a club wearing the t-shirt.

They have taken the vital second step in making their brand a medium that talks about the wearer not the maker. It's a great idea for a t-shirt – it reminds me of the badges Philips designed that light up when two compatible people pass each other. If you were standing at a bar next to someone also wearing this t-shirt, you'd have to talk wouldn't you?

How FCUK followed the 12 Rules

1: Get Up Close and Personal
Becoming a medium that makes statements about me, the wearer.
2: Tap Basic Human Needs
SEX: Risqué t-shirt fashion for the 'horny, horny, horny' generation.
3: Author Innovation
Moving from 'FCUK' to stage two; 'your place or mine'.

4: Mythologize the New
Anti-fashion fashion.

5: Create Tangible Differences in the Experience
A brand identity to wear and shop within.

6: Cultivate Authenticity
Transgression (e.g. getting banned).

7: Work through Consensus
It's a very talked about campaign in the media and presumably in real life.

8: Open Up to Participation
A badge – and reminiscent of all the DIY 'mutant brand' t-shirts.

9: Build Communities of Interest
French Connection wearers – especially the 100,000 in the t-shirt.

10: Use Strategic Creativity
An antidote strategy (from mainstream to counter-culture).

11: Stake a Claim to Fame
They could hardly have got more attention if their staff had gone naked.

12: Follow a Vision and be True to Your Values
The French Connection people must love it – why else go into 'fashion'?

Case Study 9 – The Spice Girls

Pop bands are brands. And they are very often marketed in a much more modern way than things that are sold in supermarkets.

The Spice Girls seem to be fading as a brand after the departure of Geri Halliwell, but I wouldn't write them off just yet. The key question is whether they regain their sense of purpose and identity or whether they will drift apart to pursue solo careers.

In their day they were one of the brightest and most pro-active stars in the brand constellation. They were everywhere, from the *Spice World* movie to the ITV Saturday night special TV show, to exhausting world tours. They are definitely a success story to learn from and as we'll see were exemplars of many of the new rules.

The Spice Girls are more like a brand than many bands. Not just because they were carefully manufactured and marketed but because they reached out to people through far more than their music and any innate appeal they had as vibrant personalities. They were a band with an idea – or actually a whole set of ideas. And their ideas were very much ones that people could and did live by. It's a shame that the brand did not have the time or vision to develop out into truly surprising new product areas that transcended the personalities. The Spice Girls' spin-off was merchandising, but it easily could have been brand stretching more akin to Virgin's.

The basic brand is the idea of a gang of friends. This has an inherent appeal in our time of fewer lasting relationships. Just like the TV show *Friends*. It is an idea that has animated boy bands from Take That to Wham right back to The Monkees. There had been girl bands before, such as The Supremes but the emphasis here was more on traditions of chorus (gospel) harmony than on an independent gang of good-time people. The gang of friends is the basic unit of school life.

While the group had a very broad appeal across the age spectrum, bear in mind that the epicentre of the record market is very young – early teens for albums and under tens for the vital singles market –

and that girls are the main buyers of singles.

That's why Take That, Peter Andre and the other heart-throb bands did so well. They were many girls' surrogate first boyfriend. You've only got to read the magazine titles aimed at girls, like Sugar and J17, to realise just how much this is a mass exercise in fantasy dating. Long cutesy articles and interviews explore topics like favourite foods or a new haircut.

The idea of the Spice Girls was to be identity models for young girls. This is a closer link than being a role model. A role model is someone who you admire so much you want to grow up to do what they do. So apparently, in the USA, Madeleine Allbright is a key role model for young women. An identity model is someone you want to be NOW.

It's not that girls bought into the Spice Girls because they wanted to be singers. Its because they wanted to be the girls themselves. Identity models are all around girls at school – people a bit higher up the age and coolness ladder who they'd love to be. The Spice Girls were just very magnified versions of this. More grown up, more cool, more spirited, more popular, more fashionable. And yet accessible.

The funny thing about the Spice Girls, which it is hard to remember now they have so much success and charisma, is what an ordinary, dowdy and unremarkable group of people they are. I don't mean to be rude – they are all better looking, more sparky and talented than most people I've ever met but they don't have that inaccessible perfection and otherness of the real star as an idol – from Greta Garbo, Marilyn Monroe, Elvis, up to Madonna and George Michael.

They have things that virtually no-one in music and television has – like podgy stomachs or angular faces. They are the 'girls next door' for real. And so they are achievable – like the girl in the Lower VIth.

The next important thing about the Spice Girls is that they are very different from each other. The nicknames – Scary, Sporty, Baby, Ginger and Posh – were an inspired bit of extra branding that apparently came from a magazine editor not the band itself. But they were carefully constructed as a cast of very different characters. This created an instant drama of interplay – it's like Tango keeping its elements separate rather than closing into a classic brand.

Most importantly they created an internal market of sub-brands which different girls could buy into. Everyone could have their favourite – and this choice made for a more personal and participative connection.

They also positively dripped with teen culture. Not just the songs (lyrics to be taken to heart, learned, stuck on the wall) or the performances (gangs of school friends doing the songs or the dance moves) but the fashions and attitudes too.

The platform shoe was coming up through trade shows and fashion labels like Swear. The Spice Girls took it, wore it and made it everyone's shoe that summer – about a year early, on usual fashion cycles. Shoe manufacturers took to converting their trainers to having thicker soles to try and meet the demand.

Similarly their hair styles were iconic – like Baby Spice's little ponytails. And not only could real girls dress like the Spice Girls, but they could act like them. Girl gangs were everywhere shrieking and whooping it up. The most famous brand within the brand and the one where the Spice Girls went much further than all the other teeny bopper bands was 'Girl Power'. The main thing to know about teenagers now is that girls are ascendant, achieving better at school, confident, ambitious, looking forward, emotionally mature and relatively well adjusted and stable – and boys are not. To a far greater extent than in adult society, girls are on top.

The Spice Girls branded this ascendancy. They gave it cultural expression – a name and a look. This is so often the role of very powerful brands – they stand for things that are happening and which we feel. They give them expression, make them tangible and in giving these trends shape they become an essential way of feeling part of that trend. Like power dressing and the 1980s Yuppie. Like Nike and the Street Sport spirit. Like Levi's and Retro.

The other part of the Spice Girls brand – the part which ultimately was its undoing – was that of togetherness. The community spirit we touched on earlier, well beyond the 'three musketeers' spirit of a gang of friends, reaching out to audiences (literally, in their TV appearances), the music that everyone listened to, shared, felt part of. They were much more than music that people listened to, they were a social currency between people. Something everyone had in common – a new tradition in fact. A brand always has an Achilles heel and the Spice Girls' was that 'united they stand but divided they fall'. Maybe.

How the Spice Girls followed the 12 Rules

1: Get Up Close and Personal
   Identity models.

2: Tap Basic Human Needs
   Development (into a woman). Belonging.

3: Author Innovation
   Spice Girls – the band, the fashion show, the movie.

4: Mythologize the New
   Girl Power.

5: Create Tangible Differences in the Experience
   The girl band that's like a boy band – at first a unique concept.

6: Cultivate Authenticity
   Accessible, realistic and also very close to the girls' real
   personalities.

7: Work through Consensus
   It was popular because 'everyone loves the Spice Girls'.
   Self-fulfilling.

8: Open Up to Participation
   They offered accessible little things to copy, like hairstyles
   and dance steps.

9: Build Communities of Interest
   Every ten-year-old girl (and quite a few of their mums!) became
   a Spice Girl.

10: Use Strategic Creativity
   The idea of a girl band as a cast of characters was new – and
   brilliant.

11: Stake a Claim to Fame
   They had all sorts of phases and themes – the core message
   being Girl Power.

12: Follow a Vision and be True to Your Values
   A strong shared ethos personified and hence crucified by
   the split?

Case Study 10 – St. Luke's

If you want an almost impossible challenge in branding and business, try launching a new ad agency!

One of the areas of marketing that is growing in importance is business to business. Not just because many functions of companies are outsourced to service suppliers, but because businesses increasingly work in networks of co-operation and stakeholders.

It is important for companies to be strong brands to their partners, shareholders and employees rather than just to have strong brands for their consumers and buyers. And luminous, successful companies are usually strong brands – with strong, inspiring ideas, because in the new economy results are increasingly about talent, dedication, loyalty and empathy.

A lot of my work recently has been in this area of the company as a brand. Working with Arthur Andersen and for Coca-Cola these were my main projects last year. And St. Luke's as a company seems to have done a pretty amazing job on its own brand.

A medium-sized London ad agency usually gets two or three moments of major publicity a year – perhaps about their campaigns if they are lucky, or commonly manufactured by some PR exercise like a 'report on men and the millennium'.

St. Luke's seems to get two or three of these big stories a month – or sometimes two or three a week. It is a company that has attracted big features in national newspapers like the *Financial Times* and other broadsheets and international interest, especially in America, in publications like *The New York Times* and *Fast Company* which carried the headline 'The ad agency to end all ad agencies'. There was a documentary about the company on Channel 4, and a book about the company by our chairman Andy Law has just been published (*Open Minds*, 1998).

It would be nice to think all this publicity reflected our talent and our work – we were after all *Campaign* magazine's agency of the year in 1997. But the broader interest focuses much more on the company as a different kind of company – perhaps a model for companies of the future.

St. Luke's as a company is all about liberating people from the shackles of conventional work. People work in a freeform office. No-one has a desk. Instead, we work in client project rooms. For instance the IKEA room contains all the IKEA work and research and is also furnished as an IKEA room set, right down to the IKEA flooring. These project rooms are part of the creative process. When we were exploring New Age ideas for the IKEA brand we changed the room to be based on Feng Shui principles. The project rooms are about living the brands.

This freeform office is a tangible expression of a freeform culture. There is much less hierarchy than in many companies. People largely work in self-managed teams. And there is (hopefully) little kow-towing to and swagger about the people, who through virtue of experience, hold management positions. People at all levels are encouraged to speak out.

There are departments – but the work is done, not so much in interdisciplinary teams, as in shoals. As we grew we devolved the agency into separate groups, because we felt that an important element of the company was the familial relationships that come from constantly being around thirty people and knowing them inside out.

Hopefully by the time you read this St. Luke's will have changed again beyond all recognition. I quite like the idea, for instance of making St. Luke's a franchised concept rather than a traditional company. It thrives on change and experiment and keeping itself open, not set in stone. The structural difference in the DNA of the company that supports all of this and creates a completely different culture than ones I've experienced before, is that the agency is co-owned. It is an employee shareholding trust by constitution. Which means that everyone who has been in the company the same length of time has the same number of shares (obviously as they are handed out every year, if you stay longer you have more).

This culture faces outwards to clients as a very open, collaborative and stimulating experience. Clients are encouraged to join the teams and help find the answer to the problems. There is gratifyingly little of the arrogance at St. Luke's that a lot of clients experience in other creative agencies. Nor is there the unconfident menial attitude fostered by others. The agency is not intimidatingly trendy either. It is more informal and relaxed and tends to attract people who are more interested in the work and the values than their image.

The St. Luke's story is not about some marketing ploy or tactic, it is about being a genuinely interesting story because it is a genuinely interesting company. And more stories have added themselves to this – the documentary, or being the first agency appointed by the New Labour Government for instance.

The documentary largely shows people arguing. St. Luke's is quite bare and exposed to the media and to new clients or visitors. Because that is what happens when people are free to develop things they care about in teams. St Luke's is in other words an exemplary bit of basic New Marketing in itself.

The book is all about New Marketing thinking, but I recognise that it's not easy for many marketing people to suddenly take on the role of mavericks. Many of the case examples reflect entrepreneurial cultures doing what they do naturally. The biggest challenge is to be free from convention and to think and act along new paths. This is much easier if you also change the workplace where these ideas happen. As the motto at St. Luke's says, 'If you change the way you work, you change the way you think.'

Even if everything I have just said had only been done for publicity, judged against just the brand it has created it would have been worth it. And it worked because it followed the rules.

How St. Luke's Followed the 12 Rules

1: Get Up Close and Personal
Breaking down barriers to give an informal culture and make clients as part of this.

2: Tap Basic Human Needs
Belonging and Freedom.

3: Author Innovation
The company is reinvented at least annually.

4: Mythologize the New
The new world of open collar work, e.g. Casual Friday, Virtual Office.

5: Create Tangible Differences in the Experience
The free range office.

6: Cultivate Authenticity
It is open – what you see is pretty much what you get.

7. Work through Consensus
Important visitors were opinion formers – business gurus journalists.

8: Open Up to Participation

Open and collaborative, with clients, suppliers, journalists.

9: Build Communities of Interest

Has a large 'fan club' of outsiders.

10: Use Strategic Creativity

A bit of a fluke. Our strategy was 'brand turnaround' (hence a hospital name).

11: Stake a Claim to Fame

The ad commune. We've had nearly as much coverage as the Clinton's.

12: Follow a Vision and be True to Your Values

If any of this success was deserved it was due to a strong shared ethos.

Case Study 11 – British Telecom

This is a simple but inspiring story. It shows how even one of Britain's biggest companies and at one time one of its most loathed, can be transformed by the power of an idea. The idea had everything to do with the 'red thread' we have been following throughout the book. We live in a time when public institutions are no longer respected and deferred to. What BT did was reframe itself as part of everyday life. A way of having better conversations and relationships.

People in my advertising research groups used to complain that BT's advertising was a waste of their money. It was seen as a huge budget campaign that could only add to phone bills in the form of higher charges. 'I don't see why they need to advertise' came the reaction from the public.

Then BT's advertising found its role – helping people. It is almost a service rather than a promotion. The archetypal BT brand ad featured a presenter who appears like a ghost in the background of a realistic telephone conversation and explains how it could be handled better. It is pure pop psychology and relationship counselling. Another strand of the campaign promoted schemes designed to keep people in regular touch – like the 'Friends and Family' and weekend cheap rate offers.

The brand which they have created out of this advertising is intensely up close and personal. BT used to seem a monolithic bureaucracy. Now it is a little voice in your ear reminding you to have a chat with your dad or call your brother. And as we'll see, the campaign and the other activities of British Telecom around it, conform to the other 11 Rules too.

How BT followed The 12 Rules

1: Get Up Close and Personal
A word of advice.

2: Tap Basic Human Needs
Communication.

3: Author Innovation
It keeps developing with fresh insights into everyday talking
(and new offers).

4: Mythologize the New
The self-help era – good relationships are one of our chief concerns.

5: Create Tangible Differences in the Experience
Everything revolves around the BT phone in people's hands.

6: Cultivate Authenticity
Authenticity of insight and also intention.

7: Work through Consensus
A low key talking point – often comes up spontaneously in
research groups.

8: Open Up to Participation
People project their own experiences into the ads.

9: Build Communities of Interest
The circle of friends and relatives we keep up with through
the phone.

10: Use strategic creativity
From Goliath to 'Dave's mate'.

11: Stake a Claim to Fame
'It's good to talk' – one of the marketing slogans of the century.

12: Follow a Vision and be True to Your Values
The advertising idea has apparently transformed the company,
people are now proud to work for BT to further the cause of
good conversations and bonding.

Case Study 12 – Egg

Egg is the banking service from Prudential. It's the latest cross-market service in the deregulated financial market. Egg is 'direct' – like First Direct, offered via internet, telephone and post.

The basic product and service is all about fitting around the individual. Banks as brands are on the 'institution' end of the scale, so something that is flexible and up close and personal could have a great basic appeal.

The two parts of their marketing campaign which I have seen so far are television advertising and television sponsorship. The advertising features famous people like Zoë Ball, and the question it addresses is how can I trust this person to be telling the truth about this brand? The creative answer is to wire the endorsers up to lie detectors. They are asked a range of personal questions to show that the lie detector is working and then they are asked about Egg. It is advertising for the Doubting Thomas society and as an example I can't fault its authenticity.

Before these commercials with famous people, the campaign was launched with vox-pops (live interviews) from their call centre and with members of the public. They started out, in other words, to get over the First Direct problem by making it trusted. Their problem is probably the ultimate Doubting Thomas market – people don't trust banks, they trust financial service brands they haven't heard of even less, and even worse are companies that don't even have branches.

The sponsorship idents simply say that they have sponsored this programme for a named ordinary real person who likes that programme. It's pretty honest and straightforward about one of the things people still say they like about sponsorship – 'they're putting money into my favourite programmes'. And it makes the point about Egg as a brand pretty elegantly too.

How Egg Follows The 12 Rules

1: Get Up Close and Personal
A brand that's very much about getting closer to individuals.

2: Tap Basic Human Needs
Being recognised (as opposed to banking institutions, where we feel 'just a number').

3: Author Innovation
So far so good.

4; Mythologize the New
Doubting Thomas society.

5: Create Tangible Differences in the Experience
Innovative website, forms and phone-in service, I'm told.

6: Cultivate Authenticity
Lie detectors are pretty hard to argue with.

7: Work through Consensus
Everyone's talking about it.

8: Open Up to Participation
Put the customer in the marketing.

9: Build Communities of Interest
Channel 4 viewers. Younger, affluent, media savvy.

10: Use Strategic Creativity
The lie detector idea is just about the best thing I saw in 1998.

11: Stake a Claim to Fame
The lie detector again.

12: Follow a Vision and be True to Your Values
I *hope* the company is anything like its marketing!

PART FOUR

CONCLUSIONS

The Future Belongs to...?

The Fight for New Marketing

The New Marketing of this book's title is the art of creating brands. It is the art of big, imaginative ideas that touch people in a very human way. There is another discipline also called New Marketing. This is the science of targeting and transactions through new electronic media. There are already books about this other kind of New Marketing. They promise improved efficiency and increased direct contact. But the other New Marketing does not cater for brands and big, subjective ideas. It lacks soul.

I see this other New Marketing as an impostor and a threat. It is not about creating brands, it is about exploiting them. It will certainly be an essential part of consumer marketing in the future. But it really ought to be called New Retailing. It is the domain of store cards and on-line book shops. It has its own excitement, in a new technology sort of way, but it is a means of extracting rather than creating value.

There is going to be a war between these two sorts of New Marketing, because they will be offered by different kinds of marketing service companies. And they will be competing, not only for the hearts and minds of their clients, but also for their budgets. This war has already started. When Coca-Cola signed up with Creative Artists (an agency for Hollywood directors), that was a victory for my sort of New Marketing. When Heinz put all of its UK marketing budget into direct mail, that was a victory for the other sort.

Supporters of the other sort of New Marketing claim that digital communications allow you to make marketing more of a science. They offer you control. They offer you accountability. They offer the excitement of cyber technology, the information superhighway. And they will tell you that people like me are dinosaurs, that mass media advertising created a mirage, but they can now offer you the keys to the real city. And they will quote examples, like Heinz, of supposedly enlightened companies who have understood that digital multimedia are at the heart of doing business in the new economy.

In this book, I have offered hundreds of counter-examples. These examples show that, if anything, the value of brands and creativity has increased in our new, uncertain times. I don't think that my New Marketing is the David, to New Technology Marketing's Goliath. The impression this book creates is that of the victory, time and again, of the branding entrepreneur over the technocrat. Strong brands, creatively promoted, still seem to offer an overwhelming advantage. Coca-Cola has increased its market value forty-fold in the last decade. Heinz's figures have been rather less impressive, to say the least.

The Death of Mass Marketing

I am not a luddite. Before I worked in advertising I worked in semi-conductor microchip design. I welcome new digital technologies; they are exciting and they offer progress. They have changed society all around us. They are also one of the catalysts for my sort of New Marketing.

New media have challenged mass marketing (a mass marketing which has all too often been crass marketing). They have shown us new ways of reaching people, and perhaps most importantly they have encouraged the view that marketing communications can be two-way and interactive.

Marketing needed to break the chains of over-dependence on advertising, because people spent too much time thinking about advertising ideas, and not enough time thinking about brand ideas. Brand theory became television advertising theory. At its most basic it said 'add a personality'. Which is what most early ads did.

Advertising, in its current form, is in question, because interrupting people's TV programmes may not be acceptable in a pay-per-view future. Because advertising has grown so expensive that dramatic success is the exception not the rule. Because the public has grown marketing literate and marketing wary. And above all because the customer is no longer passive.

New Marketing is a response to this new media and consumer

culture. It is voluntary and participative. Because it is about ideas that the audience choose, not ideas that are beamed at them like crude propaganda.

Big inspiring, participative marketing isn't all new. Many of the great brands of the twentieth century were created in pioneering creative ways. Kellogg's was built on ideas like the 'Wink at Your Grocer' promotion, where any American housewife who winked at her local grocer would be rewarded with a trial pack of Kellogg's Cornflakes. Coca-Cola was built on ideas like 'I'd like to teach the world to sing'. In the 1970s this advertising jingle was a global pop music phenomenon.

This kind of big cultural idea has found its day again. Partly because of the changes brought by new media, but mostly because of bigger upheavals in modern human society. We are at some sort of Wild West frontier again in marketing. The future belongs to the creative entrepreneur, as pioneers like Richard Branson and Anita Roddick have demonstrated.

Why I Believe My Sort of New Marketing Will Win

Which sort of New Marketing will win in the long run? I think the answer depends on two opposite views of where the world is heading.

The New Technology Marketing involves moving from mass communications to one-to-one communications. The main advantage it offers is niche targeting. This is only a big advantage if you think our social world is fragmenting. If you think so, then niche targeting of the resulting fragments is natural. Marketing can no longer target broad groups in society like the housewife. It must target people who are more and more chaotically individual. Ideally marketing would be part of customising the product and service to cater for increasingly diverse tastes, needs and values.

I believe that this idea of a fragmenting society is a fallacy. There is certainly a trend to a less institutional society, and a corresponding trend to more independent, active customers. And many of the old social stereotypes and categories do not apply, but despite all this, people across the world are getting more similar not more different. More similar in their tastes, needs and values. More similar in their lifestyles.

It's not hard to see this in areas of popular culture other than marketing. Look at things like movies and fashions and computer games and pop stars and sports and tell me that the world culture is fragmenting! Big ideas travel. Because we are all part of a global media culture. And when these ideas are popular, they are popular with people of all ages and backgrounds.

The breakdown of the old social order is a breakdown of exactly those barriers that made societies diverse. It is a breakdown of class and sexual and regional traditions: a breakdown of ordered lifestages and roles and all the little lifestyle distinctions that went with them.

I have covered many of these changes in human societies in this book. I think it's more important to understand the background changes than the responses that marketing has made so far. My sort of New Marketing is intrinsically creative, and I'm sure it has just started to tap some of the new possibilities opened up by the new culture.

POSTSCRIPT

Meanwhile, Somewhere in the 21st Century.

Hello.

Welcome to our company. And thank you for your interest.

My name is Muju. 'Muju' is Japanese for 'non-dweller'. The natty Buddhist robes I'm wearing are in homage to my thirteenth century namesake, a Zen teacher. Unfortunately I can't claim to be that wise. I am only an algorithm. But guests generally find I can answer most questions. So do feel free to interrupt me on the tour.

Before we enter the building I'd just like to deal with a few formalities.

Do you have your signed confidentiality agreement? Thank you.

Could you please pass through this virus scanner.

Ah, sorry. I think you may have some files open? Yes? Your photograph, excellent. If you could hand it to me. Thank you. Through the scanner again. Thank you. I'll process the photo.

The image is scanned. Now you can see yourself too. Are you comfortable with that costume? Good.

And if you could now place your admission fee in this rice bowl. 1000 ecus.

Thank you very much. The money will be used to maintain and develop this site. And as you know it's refundable if you become one of our partners. I've e'd you a receipt.

Finally if you could just leave your shoes by this door. It's a little ritual we like to use. It symbolises respect when entering an intimate space. And our guests find it's helpful in leaving your everyday concerns and assumptions outside. Some people also like to read and reflect on this Zen saying above the door for a moment.

> The great gate has no gates,
> Thousands of roads enter it
> When one passes through this gateless gate
> They walk freely between heaven and earth.

Now follow me through the great gate.

We are now standing in the main reception area. As you know this virtual office site is the only place our company exists. The people you can see in the seating area have dropped in to socialise with other partners. In case you feel self-conscious, don't worry, no-one can see you. We like to keep our guest tours unobtrusive.

The reason why there is no real office is three-fold. Firstly our partners are spread all over the world. Secondly, despite the Bandwidth Rush of the early noughties, real estate is still much cheaper here in cy-space. But most importantly, a real place would imply permanent working ties akin to the old wage slavery. Everyone here is a partner.

What is a partner?

The easiest way to explain is to contrast our way with the old system. In the old system 'marketing' was something separate in a company. They had a marketing department. And these people were mainly responsible for using outside suppliers. Like advertising agencies. They would then use other suppliers to make their ideas. And other suppliers again to show the ideas.

The money in old marketing came from the customer who paid extra for 'premium goods' – yes I know its crazy but that's how it worked – which was then passed through a chain of suppliers.

Now we have partners. Marketing is something valuable with its own price tag. It is subsidised by the people whose goods it promotes. This money comes from extra sales not higher prices. Other partners pay in time and costs. In return they get a share in the revenue from that marketing.

If you walk this way I'll show you some examples.

You expressed an interest in our recent work for the Ford Motor Company, so I've arranged for you to have access to that site.

It's through this doorway here.

And here we are in the Motor Show.

Our partners at Ford insisted that we style this whole area like a mid-twentieth century motor show. They find it very amusing. And they use it as an entertainment complex for their car dealership people. It's so realistic that we've also had visitors from gender history courses.

If you like I can remove the sex object slaves from this arena? No? As you wish.

If we head over to the area by the giant rotating statue of a beauty queen. Yes, that's the future area believe it or not.

I can now show you some work in progress. You'd just like a general overview? OK, I'll put a selection together.

I'm sure I don't need to remind you that this work is confidential. And that any proven breach of your agreement would lead to you being blacklisted under the International Treaty on Business Ethics. Of course. But you can understand why our partners are secretive.

Here is a good basic example of partnership.

The meeting you can see taking place is between some Ford partners, some creative intermediaries and the people at Dreamworks. The idea they are discussing is a new movie featuring a new car.

The car is called the Qu.Te. This name sounds like 'Cutey'. And the car is cute. But it stands for "Quality Time". It is designed for single parents and their charges to spend quality time together. Ford's research showed that in today's time-squeezed parenting, shared car journeys were one of the main opportunities for quality time together. The car is designed to enhance this.

Here's a replica model. It looks fun doesn't it? This ladybird design is just one of thousands of exteriors available. Inside there are only two seats, reflecting the predominance of single child-parent units.

Here's the key new feature of the Qu.Te. You'll notice that the passenger has their own set of controls and high seat so they can interact with the journey as an equal.

Some non-critical functions of the car can be delegated, such as sound systems and even gear changes – although that is subject to negotiation with road governance bodies. The case being made to them is that the car is starting driver education early.

Back at the meeting, what the Dreamworks people are presenting is a movie concept. Lets listen to a bit of the idea.

'....The basic idea is Sleepless in Seattle meets Herbie.
We've already got Cauly McCulkin signed as the father. Cauly plays a prodigal dad. He returns home to bring up his son when the birth mother dies. The car then takes on the place of the mother – it's even got her voice and personality programmed in – helping the two come to terms with their life together... .
'We've got this great key scene when the father's been mauled by an escaped circus lion and the son drives him to hospital, with the car talking him through it... .'

You get the general picture. The movie's in production now. And the car has had a personality-led voice option designed to reflect the film. The distribution deals are signed. It all gets launched next year.

Seen enough? Lets visit another car partner project.

This space looks like an adult education college because this project started as a concept about added education and self-reliance.

The car is the basic, bottom of the range Ford. It was originally called the Pod. It's designed as a little run-around for people living alone. The car itself is ultra-basic and cheap. The value was put into optional education courses; from an inclusive learn to drive package, to self-defence, to this class, the car maintenance Pod.

Through here you can see a garage where drivers are learning the basics of Pod mechanics. It's an electric car with only a hundred parts. So it's not that difficult.

Now we come to a real demonstration of the benefits of the partner process bringing all the partners together in our spaces together with their customers.

Here is a dramatic moment in the Pod trials, which we've reconstructed because it has changed the history of the car market. The woman in overalls on the left is Rita Johnson, a driver. The woman on the right is Paula Hayes, Deputy Leader at Ford.

Rita: 'If it's that easy, then why not do away with the factory and let us assemble it ourselves, supervised by the maintenance instructors?'
Paula: 'What a good idea!'

Rita has been given a partner stake in the car. IKEA have been called in to help, with their expertise in flat packing and self assembly. And Paula was here only last week, launching the Self (the renamed Pod) to the world media. You probably saw this – it was all over the New Product channels?

Lets go back to the hallway – down there are ten or so more car projects in development. Just a summary? OK.

The other three imminent partnering projects with Ford include:

Project Pedal Car – a new in-vehicle exercise project.
Project Golf Cart – hobby-dedicated vehicles.
Project Convoy – a semi-public transport concept.

Step on this hyp-link with me. Don't worry, this is a new model called 'Beam Me Up'. Sometimes it's hard living in a world constructed out of so much irony. But as a Zen Buddhist I realise that I am probably a joke too.

Anyway. You won't experience any motion sickness. That's it.
Smooth isn't it?

Of course. I'll e-you a freeware copy.

This is the area we call the cave.

The cave was where man first lived and started sketching out ideas on the walls.

I say 'man', but as you probably know, archaeologists have discovered through DNA fingerprinting that the drawings were usually painted by the women. Presumably the same women who had the very sensible idea of seeking shelter there.

I've brought you here to the cave because I wanted you to experience how partnership strategies are formed.

In the old marketing you would start with partners and then work towards an answer which was predictable – for instance an advert in the house style of your agency. Obviously that is stupid, but it's how things were done. What we have to do instead is delicately build together ideas and alliances. We do maybe about ten pilot partnerships for every one that takes off.

That is where the role of the 'agent' is still important. An agent now is in no way part of a parasitic chain of suppliers. We have the basic creative and facilitative skills to connect partners.

Sometimes the partner comes with a new product – like the Ford Pod. In other cases we have a relationship with some partner like Dreamworks or Sony Games and they come to us with an idea in search of a product. In either case we are the matchmakers.

Now I'd like to introduce you to John Grant, one of our very old-timers. John wants to get to understand your future vision. And to see if there are some partners it might be worth doing a few pilot scheme meetings with.

John, this is...

To be continued.

BIBLIOGRAPHY

'What do you want to write a book for?' said Nick, my Coca-Cola client. 'Nobody reads books these days. They haven't got time.'

Just in case he's wrong, and to pay respect to all the people whose books I've mentioned or quoted, here's a list. I've put an asterisk next to a couple which I'd recommend as totally unmissable (even if you are as busy as Nick).

Argyle, Michael, *The Anatomy of Relationships* (Penguin, 1985)

Barthes, Roland, *Mythologies* (Noonday, 1957)

Baudrillaird, Jean, *Cool Memories iii* (Verso, 1997)

Beck, Ulrich, *The Risk Society* (Sage, 1992)

Berger & Luckmann, *The Social Construction of Reality* (Penguin, 1966)

Bly, Robert, *The Sibling Society* (Addison Wesley, 1996)

Castells, Manuel, *The Rise of the Network Society* (Blackwell, 1996)*

Collins & Porras, *Built to Last* (Century, 1997)

Coupland, Douglas, *Generation X* (Abacus, 1991)

Descartes, René, *Discourse on Method* (Penguin, 1637)

Dichter, Ernest, *The Handbook of Consumer Motivations* (McGraw-Hill, 1964)

Douglas, Mary, *Thought Styles* (Sage, 1998)

Eco, Umberto, *Travels in Hyper-Reality* (Harcourt Brace, 1990)

Fein, Ellen, *The Rules* (Warner, 1996)

Fidler, Roger, *Mediamorphosis* (Pine Forge, 1990)

Fukyama, Francis, *The End of History* (Avon, 1993)

Ghoshal and Bartlett, *The Individualised Corporation* (Heinemann, 1998)*

Giddens, Anthony, *The Third Way* (Blackwell, 1998)*

Giddens, Anthony, *Modernity & Self Identity* (Stanford, 1991)*

Gray, John, *False Dawn* (Granta, 1998)

Grundy, Tom, *Breakthrough Strategies for Growth* (Pitman, 1995)

Hamel and Prahalad, *Competing for the Future* (HBS, 1994)*

Handy, Charles, *The Hungry Spirit* (Broadway, 1998)*

Jensen, Klaus, *The Social Semiotics of Mass Communications* (Sage, 1995)

Lacan, Jacques, *The Four Fundamental Concepts of Psychoanalysis* (Penguin, 1973)

McLuhan, Marshall, *Understanding Media* (MIT, 1994)

Packard, Vance, *The Hidden Persuaders* (out of print)

Planning for Social Change (The Henley Centre, 1997, 1998)

Reisman, David, *The Lonely Crowd* (New Haven, 1950)

Senge, Peter, *The Fifth Discipline Workbook* (Doubleday, 1994)

Severin, *Humanistic Viewpoints in Psychology* (New York, 1965)

Silverstone, Roger, *Television & Everyday Life* (Routledge, 1994)

Tapscott, Don, *Growing Up Digital* (McGraw-Hill, 1997)

Wilson, Paul, *The Little Book of Calm* (Plume, 1997)

INDEX